T5-CCL-215

African American Women

MSU Series on Children, Youth, and Families
volume 6
Garland Reference Library of Social Science
volume 941

Michigan State University Series on Children, Youth, and Families

Child Maltreatment and Optimal Caregiving in Social Contexts
by Diana Baumrind

Adolescent Parenthood and Education
Exploring Alternative Programs
by Mary Pilat

University–Community Collaborations for the Twenty-first Century
Outreach Scholarship for Youth and Families
edited by Richard M. Lerner and Lou Anna K Simon

Adolescents, Cultures, and Conflicts
Growing Up in Contemporary Europe
edited by Jari-Erik Nurmi

Teaching About Adolescence
An Ecological Approach
edited by John Paul McKinney, Lawrence B. Schiamberg, and Lawrence G. Shelton

African American Women
An Ecological Perspective
edited by Norma J. Burgess and Eurnestine Brown

Making Invisible Latino Adolescents Visible
edited by Francisco A. Villarruel and Martha Montero-Sieburth

African American Woman
An Ecological Perspective

EDITED BY

Norma J. Burgess and Eurnestine Brown

Falmer Press
A member of the Taylor & Francis Group
New York & London / 2000

Published in 2000 by
Falmer Press
A member of the Taylor & Francis Group
19 Union Square West
New York, NY 10003

10 9 8 7 6 5 4 3 2 1

Library of Congress Cataloging-in-Publication Data

African American women : an ecological perspective / edited by Norma J. Burgess and Eurnestine Brown.
p. cm. — (Michigan State University series on children, youth, and families ; v. 6) (Garland reference library of social science ; v. 941)
Includes bibliographical references and index.
ISBN 0-8153-1591-0 (acid-free paper)
1. Afro-American women—Social conditions. 2. Social ecology—United States. I. Burgess, Norma J. II. Brown, Eurnestine. III. Series. IV. Series: Garland reference library of social science ; v. 941.
E185.86.A3343 1999
305.4'8896073—dc21 99-30094
CIP

Printed on acid-free, 250-year-life paper
Manufactured in the United States of America

Contents

Series Editor's Preface
Outreach Scholarship for Children, Youth, and Families
A Foreword to the Michigan State University Series on Children, Youth, and Families

The publication of Norma J. Burgess and Eurnestine Brown's volume, *African American Women: An Ecological Perspective*, signals the continued prominence and success of the Michigan State University Series on Children, Youth, and Families as a resource for scholars, researchers and practitioners whose concern is families and children in communities. The scholarly work of Burgess and Brown in organizing a book which focuses on the ecology of African American women is a prime example of the creative emphasis on cutting-edge scholarship addressing the needs of a diversity of children, youth, families, and communities which the MSU Series represents. In particular, this book promises to be a seminal and landmark volume in providing a framework for understanding the experiences of African American women in context as well as for the development of effective interventions and programs which, in turn, derive from a contextually sensitive approach to human development. The rich and diverse array of chapters on such timely topics as identity issues, career and family, social networks, health care delivery, and the role of the Black Church provide insight into the rich experience and life trajectory of African American women.

Furthermore, this volume is a clear illustration of the goals of the Institute for Children, Youth, and Families (ICYF), as an example of the relationship of outreach scholarship to essential issues of policy and program development which, in turn, has the potential for enhancing the lives of children, youth and families in the diverse communities which the Institute serves. Likewise the publication of this challenging and most impressive volume provides evidence that the MSU Series serves as a compendium of scholarly work reflecting the very best scholarship aimed at enhancing the life experiences of a diversity of children, youth, and families. As such, both this volume and the MSU Series provide evidence for the importance and feasibility of the mission of ICYF in integrating research and outreach.

The mission of the Institute for Children, Youth, and Families at MSU is based on a vision of the nature of a land-grant university as an academic institution with a responsibility for addressing the welfare of children, youth, and families in communities. More specifically, the mission of ICYF is shaped by an ecological perspective to human development which places the life-span development of human beings in the context of the significant settings of human experience, including community, family, work and peer networks (Lerner, et al., 1994; Schiamberg, 1985, 1988). Historically, the ecological perspective has both been associated with, and a guiding frame for, colleges of home economics or, as they are more recently termed, colleges of human development, human ecology, or family and consumer sciences (Miller & Lerner, 1994). Using the ecology of human development as a conceptual framework, the Institute for Children, Youth, and Families continues to develop programs that integrate the critical notion of development in context with the attempt, indeed the necessity, of creating connections between such scholarship and social policy, program design, delivery, and evaluation.

The MSU Series is a unique collection of books, designed to provide a vehicle for the publication and transmission of research/outreach efforts characterized by the collaborative relationship (and potential relationship) between university expertise and the community. The Burgess and Brown book represents the careful thinking of authors who have worked, first hand, within the rich and broad variety of contexts for the support and enhancement of African American women and, as well, with the power and potential of a contextual or ecological perspective for the development of "best practice" efforts for enriching their life prospects. As universities begin to respond to continuing social pressures to apply their resources to address a variety of critical social problems, there is a compelling need for such careful thinking and best practice in helping universities and communities to frame joint programs addressing the needs of the diverse children and families that both serve. The Michigan State University Series on Children, Youth, and Families is, itself, an example of the outreach scholarship which reflects the contextual and practical policy focus of the ICYF research program. The MSU Series publishes reference and professional books, including monographs and edited volumes, which appeal to a wide audience in communities as well as in universities, including such constituencies as scholars, practitioners, service deliverers, child and family advocates, business leaders, and policymakers. The MSU Series has substantial import and appeal to these constituencies primarily because of its focus on the integration of research and outreach and, as well, an emphasis on collaborative relationships between universities and communities.

The unique role and perspective of both ICYF and the MSU Series can be further appreciated in light of the ongoing and persisting trends for both university accountability and social contribution. In particular, the various university stakeholders, including business, government, and community leadership, are increasingly urging universities to use their research and scholarly resources to address problems of social, political, and technological relevance (Boyer, 1990; Votruba, 1992). Thus, communities are seeking a greater involvement in outreach on the part of their universities. Both ICYF and Michigan State University are committed to integrating outreach into the full fabric of university responsibility (Provost's Committee on University Outreach, 1993).

The Burgess and Brown volume represents an outstanding contribution to this emerging outreach/research focus. The MSU Series board of editors, including John Paul McKinney, Vincent J. Hoffman, Lawrence B. Schiamberg, Linda Spence, and Francisco A. Villarruel, as well as the staff editor of the Institute for Children, Youth, and Families at MSU, Linda Chapel Jackson, are proud and grateful to have this path-breaking book on African-American women as part of the MSU Series—a volume which enhances the understanding of the diverse communities of America.

Lawrence B. Schiamberg
Senior Editor, MSU Series

REFERENCES

Boyer, E. L. (1990). *Scholarship reconsidered: Priorities of the professoriate.* Princeton, NJ: The Carnegie Foundation for the Advancement of Teaching.

Lerner, R. M., Miller, J. R., Knott, J. H., Corey, K. E., Bynum, T. S., Hoopfer, L. C., McKinney, M. H., Abrams, L. A., Hula, R. C., & Terry, P. A. (1994). Integrating scholarship and outreach in human development research, policy, and service: A developmental contextual perspective. In D. L. Featherman, R. M. Lerner, & M. Perlmutter (Eds.), *Life-span development and behavior, 12* (pp. 249–273). Hillsdale, NJ: Erlbaum.

Miller, J. R., & Lerner, R. M. (1994). Integrating research and outreach: Developmental contextualism and the human ecological perspective. *Home Economics Forum*, *7*, 21–28.

Provost's Committee on University Outreach. (1993). *University outreach at Michigan State University: Extending knowledge to serve society*. East Lansing: Michigan State University.

Schiamberg, L. B. (1985). *Human development* (2nd ed.). New York: MacMillan.

Schiamberg, L. B. (1988). *Child and adolescent development* (2nd ed.). New York: MacMillan.

Votruba, J. C. (1992). Promoting the extension of knowledge in service to society. *Metropolitan Universities*, *3*(3), 72–80.

African American Women

CHAPTER 1

The Conceptual Framework

NORMA J. BURGESS AND EURNESTINE BROWN

The only thing you have to be that's important in life is just to go on being your own normal, black, beautiful selves as women, as human beings.

—FANNIE LOU HAMER

The impetus for this volume arises from the need for African American women scholars to write and conduct research on ourselves and for ourselves. The limited volume of literature on African American women by African American women scholars has increased over the past several years, but not at the same rate of discovery as research on women in the general population. The meeting of women scholars who attended the 1992 workshop series entitled *Diversity and Context in Studying Children, Youth, and Families: Towards the Integration of Science and Outreach* at the Institute for Children, Youth and Families at Michigan State University, was fruitful for a discussion of this nature. The stimulus provided much-needed awareness about the lives, relationships, families, environments, stresses and strategies involved with the survival of this population in the United States. There were a number of African American women from various disciplines present at the workshop, most of whom are represented in this volume. All of the volume authors hold academic positions at institutions of higher education. Disciplines represented in this book are developmental and general psychology, sociology, psychiatry, social work, political science, business management, ministry and nursing. Rarely do we all meet in one place and are afforded the opportunity to discuss academic issues that are particularly salient for African American women. The general concern that affected all of the contributors is the lack of interdisciplinary approaches to theory development and research methodology on African American women. By design, the academy does not encourage cross-disciplinary approaches to knowing what we know, that is, cross-fertilization of the seeds of knowledge.

The sociohistorical approaches that we have taken and the broad bases upon which we developed the works, author by author, reflects our genuine interest in leaving a legacy of accuracy and introspection for our daughters, our sisters, our mothers and the generations to come when they become scholars and wonder where the materials are that reflect their heritage, lifestyles and conditions in this society. To share with students of life and the academic community such a volume is equally important; what is presented here reflects an ecological perspective steeped in the history of African American people.

This ecological perspective highlights the strengths and challenges faced by African American women as they progress in their developmental trajectories. Our perspective builds upon past ecological frameworks (cf., Brofennbrenner, 1979; Nobles & Goddard, 1984) and gives credence to the powerful effects of culture and context on all aspects of growth and development. Various systems (intra-personal, community, societal) directly mediate self-perceptions and identity, behaviors, beliefs, values and life outcomes for African American girls and women. This ecological perspective builds upon seminal works on the black family by noting that African American women are nested in a Euro-American culture, and that our family system can be characterized as African in "nature" and American in "nurture" (Nobles & Goddard, 1984).

We do not make the claim that this is an all-encompassing work, nor is it exhaustive in any sense of the word. We do, however, claim space in academia to allow our voices to be heard in this manner, to provide a unique environment from which to produce further research, and to grow beyond disciplinary boundaries which for decades have provided narrow perspectives on African American women. When taken in isolation, we tend to know less and less as scholars about our family, dynamics, survival and other issues that make us who we are.

The need to combine the disciplines we represent suggests we understand some of the core issues that directly impact the health, mental well-being and functioning of African American women in this society. In recent years, the diversity within this population has become equally salient in that the migration throughout the diaspora has many representatives from the African continent with many different experiences because of their descent patterns. In years to come, we are certain that even more in-depth analysis will be conducted to discover the richness of Africa which has manifested itself in the lives of our ancestors and in our families.

We take Africa as the starting point. This is in acknowledgment and awareness of the global perspective that one must take in order to understand the far-reaching consequences associated with struggles throughout the world. The struggles are not simply those that we face as women of African descent in this country. We are fortunate to have met at this conference and to have been able to draw on the strengths that we have as colleagues, scholars and sisters in understanding the odds in our quest for success and recognition of the work that we do. We have also rebelled against the feminist literature that has given little voice and direction to our research, as it continues to leave out significant populations who are a force in this society.

As a sociologist, the first editor's work reflects continual thinking about the political implications of a worldview and our role in it. From a developmental perspective, the second editor's work reflects an understanding that the history of Africans in America is essential for the development of roles, employment, family structures, dating, mate selection, parenting, marriage, divorce and kin relationships—basically every facet of life.

The life structures of African American women differ in some forms. We may parent alone, earlier and later in our life cycles, or our marriage patterns will vary; we marry later, may never marry, and work longer and harder and still tend to be disproportionately poor. The global nature of the environment affects not only our own survival, but also the survival of our children and their descendants. We are affected by disproportionate access to economic and health resources. When this book was conceived, we were on much safer ground than we are currently. With the new political agenda of welfare and health reform, we and our families are consistently under attack regarding the hard-fought opportunities that our ancestors died for—the right to vote, access to equal education—and the undoing of both mandatory voting districts that are majority African American and special programs that heretofore have strengthened the presence of African Americans in higher education; and we are seeing challenges to affirmative action. As the debates rage, many opponents share vividly an ahistorical notion of life in America. One must become aware of how these attacks permeate society, as the problems net similar consequences here and abroad, be they class-based or race-based.

We approach a new era where we write about what affects us from our perspective and with a positive light. We are committed to providing the very best picture of how survival occurs in our communities. What is generally known about African American women and their families is usually so negative that we rarely recognize ourselves in the data analysis. Can we always reduce what we know to data interpretation and a sociological analysis? We think not. The underlying quality of the research process sheds far more light on how what we believe contributes to what we know. Women academics face considerable scrutiny in the workplace, particularly when we write about ourselves. At some point, the realization then becomes, who better to say it and discuss the findings in a different light than us?

The sociohistorical perspective that we use reflects the desire for us to focus on our history and how that history affects our writing and thought processes about our communities and the work that we do. Without this approach it would be impossible for us to formulate thinking about the old conclusions that were drawn about women. The very nature of women's work is reexamined in light of the woman's place as we see it (Burgess & Horton, 1993; Burgess, 1994). For example, unless we first understand that the woman's place for African American women was not in the home, we cannot understand the role of women as culture bearers into the next century. Our role is similar, but double the recipe and stir! This should provide a level of understanding about the complexity of what we do. In addition to the womanly things we do, the additional barrier of bearing and raising children in a racist society provides a layer of challenges and stresses for our physical and mental health. To survive and see that our families survive is imperative to our well-being. The many community resources we have built reflect these needs. We are responsible not only for ourselves but for our families, our community and our race. Suffice it to say that African American women do not have to ask for these roles. They are ours for the taking.

Black women are the regenerative
force to uplift the race.
—LUCY CRAFT LANG, C.1880

REFERENCES

Bronfenbrenner, U. (1979). *The ecology of human development.* Cambridge, MA: Harvard University Press.

Burgess, N. J. (1994). Gender roles revisited: The development of the "woman's place" among African American women in the United States. *Journal of Black Studies, 24,* 391–401.

Burgess, N. J., & Horton, H. D. (1993). African American women and work: A sociohistorical perspective. *Journal of Family History*, 18, 53–63.

Nobles, W. W., & Goddard, L. L. (1984). *Understanding the black family: A guide for scholarship and research.* Oakland, CA: Black Family Institute Publications.

CHAPTER 2

Sociohistorical Perspectives

NORMA J. BURGESS

History reminds us that our life traditions were wholly encompassed by our kinships and tribes.

—DOROTHY HEIGHT

Increased attention to women's familial and work roles in the United States necessitates further development and refinement of conceptual frameworks used to explain adjustments. The incorporation of an Africa-centered perspective reflective of the historical status of women of African descent in the United States is discussed as a basis for contemporary roles. This approach incorporates the enslavement experience, refines the generic concept of gender role development commonly used for non-African-origin women in the United States, and provides more accurate inferences about gender role development for women of African heritage than in past literature.

SOCIOHISTORICAL PERSPECTIVES

While feminist scholars have effectively confronted male analyses of their own experiences as mothers, the controlling stereotypical image of women in African American families has yet to be challenged (King, 1988). Feminist theories, as a result of different points of departure for women of color, have had limited utility in the explanation of role development for African American women. Collins (1990) prompts scholars to examine the experiences of African American women with more microlevel phenomena such as kin networks (fictive and nonfictive), support strategies, self-definition and activism. These survival techniques were used by enslaved Africans to adjust to their surroundings in the new world (Holloway, 1990). Collins effectively demonstrates the need for theory development about African American women from an Africa-centered perspective.

Early in the development of the United States, the effects of subjugation and subsequent oppression and discrimination in employment policies invariably impacted African American women both individually and collectively. Works by Collins (1986, 1990) and Dill (1983) document life experiences from an African American woman's perspective, noting the presence of a community of women as compared to the woman's perspective. The development of a theoretical explanation regarding African American women and their roles is necessary for a clearer understanding of the relationship between contemporary and historical African American women.

The perspectives from which studies on African Americans are derived suffer from ahistoricism in that they do not take into account experiences prior to the emancipation (Oyebade, 1990). Ladner (1986) suggests that most of the analyses concerned with African Americans (largely the poor) were ahistorical because they did not attempt to place them in the context of their African background through slavery and into the modern era. Little systematic progress has been made to integrate African American women's unique experiences into a theoretical perspective which systematically explains their development as women in the United States. It is virtually impossible to understand the African American woman today without a perspective on her forebears, especially as it relates to the roles, functions and responsibilities she has traditionally held within the family unit. The "neat" paradigmatic categories developed to capture white women's experiences are blatantly absent (Higginbotham, 1984). More often, emphases on the historical role of African American women depict the continuance of African traditions wherein women were farmers, craftswomen and entrepreneurs as well as mothers and wives (Sudarkasa, 1987). Such an acknowledgement indicates the present and continuing conflict of accepting variations in the roles of white women as appropriate for women of African descent.[1]

The enslaved African woman's place was not in the home. Gutman (1976) discusses the strong reaction by former slave owners when freed African American women, with the support of their husbands, chose work that allowed them to remain in their homes following emancipation. Some landowners attempted to charge rent for nonworking women who "played the lady." Studies on post-Civil War occupations showed that many women washed and ironed clothes in their homes, which allowed them to perform their individual household chores and to rear their children (Harris, 1982; Wertheimer, 1977).

The lack of initial consensus between slaves and slave owners existed early in the forced migration process. Enslaved Africans did not contribute to the situational definition of their well-being and social position. The roles set were of necessity accepted by the slave publicly; severe structural constraints and established procedural mechanisms reinforced them (i.e., physical punishment or separation from family members). However, reviews of the experiences of exslaves (White, 1985) and contemporary domestic workers (Dill, 1988) suggest that the women's private behavior differed. The slaves' habit of hiding beliefs from whites was a long-established custom, transferred from generation to generation.

For African American women, then, the initial role of worker was predetermined, developed, reinforced and supported by a significant segment of society (Mintz & Price, 1992; White, 1985). As an alternative to embracing the structurally restrictive roles, enslaved African women adapted and altered roles as necessary. The adaptation undoubtedly included either: (1) the development of multiple roles for males and females; (2) the blurring of what appears to have been socially distinct roles in African society; (3) a variation of roles parallel to mainstream society for assimilative purposes; or (4) effective, continued use of real and adoptive kin networks to survive if one or both parents were sold. Studies on societies in West Africa showed distinction in the tasks assigned to men and women but not the hierarchy structure (Sudarkasa, 1987). The major concern and threat to an African American family during slavery was the fear that one of its members would be sold away (Jones, 1985), not the characterization of the family's basic task or role structure. This issue is most compelling; it highlights the fact that some scholars defined for the slave the problems encountered by the slave, complete with labels, interpretations and substantive meanings (Jones, 1985).

This emphasis on the roles performed by enslaved African American women raises several issues for consideration. First, the responsibilities they were expected to fulfill revolved around their status as enslaved African workers but not as women. Adjustments to the initial slave owner's role expectation occurred as the owner became aware that his wealth could be increased through reproduction without additional costs (Davis, 1971; Degler, 1980). Enslaved men and women were often paired with the expectation that offspring would be produced. These pairings were sometimes recognized as marriages. However, the infrastructure did not provide support for slave marriages and associated longevity. As a result, many marriages ended with the sale of one of the partners.[2] The legacy of survival in an alien environment, then, characterized enslaved African women's experiences rather than traditionally conceived gendered roles.

The role of the spouse and the development of kin relations for the enslaved Africans were viewed as considerably less significant by the property owner and therefore received less reinforcement than occupational roles outside the home, with the exception of childbearing, once slave owners discovered the value of African offspring as an investment (Collins, 1990; Davis, 1983; Jones, 1985; White, 1985). Family roles were redefined both publicly and privately (Degler, 1980; Jones, 1985). The private roles may not have resembled the traditional, established nuclear family roles. Contrary to popular literature, families exhibited continuity, even when their members were sold away (see Davis, 1983).

Role differentiation for African American women and men during the late 1800s to early 1900s was more traditionally defined than it had been during slavery. Davis (1983) notes that males and females performed gender-specific roles at home, but it is not clear what type of work was actually performed by males.

Africa Centeredness and Gender Role Development

The incorporation of an Africa-centered (Afrocentric) perspective on gender role development for African American women would provide consistently more insight into understanding their life experiences and motivation. In its broadest sense, an Africa-centered perspective represents a counter paradigm to the Eurocentric domination of knowledge and social thought (Asante, 1987, 1988). Proponents see the African American experience as a dimension of African history and culture. Afrocentrism provides the opportunity and an additional dimension for scholars to rethink past approaches to the study of African Americans and their families.

The importance of the historical background of African women in the United States makes Africa basic to the study of contemporary diasporic women (Collins, 1990; Rodgers-Rose, 1980; Sudarkasa, 1987). The legacy of struggle and oppression representing the definition of "place" or role within society is equaled only by the vigor with which early family scholars and social psychologists (both psychological and sociological) pursued and cast definitions of role, primary/secondary groups' instrumental and expressive behaviors, and specific descriptions for the "woman's place." The multiple roles of African American women did not illustrate the traditional woman's place (Collins, 1990; Steady, 1981). Because the arena of Afrocentric feminism has emerged within the past 20 years, the issue of inclusiveness may not be a major barrier to understanding African American and white women's issues as it has in the past (Dill, 1983). What is currently known about African American women is reflected in research and theoretical formulation—traditional in character, method, generalization and conclusion on a nontraditional population. Collins discussed the importance of allowing the experiences of African American women to become a part of the role they play in society. The value of integrating a historical approach to a sociological discussion adds much, mainly because of the unique history of slavery in the United States and its effects on African American communities over long periods of time.

For most of the seventeenth century, and at least the first third of the eighteenth, the system of slavery relied upon African males. A sample of slaves taken from inventories in 1730 and 1731 revealed that on large plantations throughout the colonies, slave men outnumbered slave women 180 to 100. This uneven sex ratio clearly made colonial slavery different for African men and women. It was much harder for a man to find a wife than for a woman to find a husband (Nichols, 1963).

The majority of women, whether willingly or by force, immigrated to the United States via indentured servitude, marriage, slavery or as free women. The social positions assigned to the various categories of female immigrants carried different expectations for marital, familial and work roles. Each woman's culture encompassed different behavioral expectations (Rodgers-Rose, 1980). Slavers transported African women as an afterthought (Nichols, 1963); this ingredient in the history of African American women separated them from other categories of immigrant women. In this context, establishing traditional husband–wife and familial relationships among the enslaved became a challenge.

The role of women in West Africa had primarily been motherhood; according to Nichols (1963), in the early years of settlement they played a prominent role in plantation building as a means of keeping male slaves "regular" (i.e., contented). Other research, however, has suggested that African women were purchased primarily as workers; familial and spousal roles for these women were altered from ones most well known to them in Africa to accommodate the slave owner (Davis, 1971).

Along with values and belief systems from their culture, enslaved Africans were forced outwardly to embrace new rules, values and roles in the New World. The first African women in the New World began childbearing earlier than their mothers, and thus had more children, including more females, than their mothers. The second generation also had more children than the first. This was perhaps due to the enormous expectations of increased parity under pressure from slavers. West African women had previously adhered to certain childbearing practices, particularly the timing of pregnancy, nursing and childrearing.[3] With few mechanisms in place to accommodate cultural practices, a different perspective on family life evolved (Menard, 1975).

West African women usually did not raise small children with the help of their husbands, but raised them alone or with the assistance of other women in their compounds. While West African men lived with their spouses in the same compound, and couples were free to come together at will, they did not share the same hut or area of the compound. Since a husband and wife did not compose a family alone, there was no reason for them to reside alone together (Sudarkasa, 1980). In colonial North America, the African woman was separated from the cultural foundations and environment that had lent meaning to sex-segregated living and independent child rearing in Africa, but the demographics of slave settlements indirectly allowed such living and rearing patterns to continue in a similar form (Nichols, 1963). Though Gutman (1976) intensively examined plantation records to determine the presence of two-parent households, family structures may have been a solely Western phenomenon because of cultural practices present in pre-colonial Africa (White, 1985).

Traces of the African heritage continue to exist in the daily lives of African Americans, including the links for understanding current women's roles (Gutman, 1976; Holloway, 1990; Ladner, 1986; Levine, 1977; McAdoo, 1988; Sudarkasa, 1987). Over the course of history, family roles for both African American and white women were generally accepted as similar (Staples, 1987). An increase in single parenthood, changes in support networks, racial discrimination and social policies which do not accommodate African American families, merely highlight differences in strategies used by families since the 1940s (Jewell, 1988).

The African Link

The majority of slaves who labored in the development of what is now the United States were of African descent. Inadequate information exists on the role of Africa in the development of African American women.

Women's roles in Africa and the diaspora may have important implications for the roles in which African American and African women are currently involved (Mintz & Price, 1976/1992; White, 1985). The reprinting of earlier classic works of DuBois (1903/1990) and Levine (1977), the theoretical perspectives of Asante (1987, 1988), as well as a direct focus on Africanisms (Holloway, 1990) have prompted scholars to examine contemporary African American family life within a sociohistorical framework, rather than discounting the place of Africanisms in the lives of African Americans.

The essence and richness of a pluriversal history in the United States suggests that additional avenues of research must reflect existing diversity, which is consistently as much a factor in the lives of individuals as the roles that were developed and set aside for them during slavery (Keto, 1989). Continued change in social and economic conditions, along with the employment of women outside the home, have broadened society's attitudes toward the multiple roles that women perform in the United States. Changes have been most significant following World War II and the shortage of male labor. There were standard, rigid expectations regarding a "woman's place." Primary duties for women were oriented toward homemaking and child-rearing responsibilities. White women entering the labor market during the 1940s had fewer role models to follow; additionally, they lacked peers with whom to share common experiences in the workplace, especially in the South. If the women were married, employment outside the home somehow reflected negatively on the husband's ability to provide adequately for the family (Degler, 1980).

Barriers to successful women's employment continue to prevent full absorption through economic development, including difficulties in establishing effective parental leave policies in industry, and a lack of general support for nondomestic/nonfamilial roles of women (Higginbotham & Burgess, 1992).

A better understanding of the history of Africans who came to America enslaved acknowledges the presence and practice of beliefs; values; varying degrees of knowledge of their political, economic, technological, religious, artistic, recreational and familial organization; and codes governing interpersonal behavior between such societal groupings as chiefs and citizenry, old and young, and female and male (Holloway, 1990; Lebeuf, 1963).

Though the context of slavery did not permit the exact replication of African patterns, the survival instinct that emerged appears to have had its roots in these patterns.[4] Outside this context, the inadequate explanations of African American women's roles as variations of white women's roles provide little information for understanding African American women and their place in future development.

Rethinking approaches used in discussions of African American families is critical for scholars of family and gender. Traditional views of defining what an individual is expected to do should include activities that have helped individuals become who they are. For African American women and their families, lack of opportunities, underemployment and unemployment have dictated the adjustments necessary in contemporary society. Circumstances that enable individuals to define situations and react to them must be incorporated into a general theoretical framework, if it is to be useful for explanation.

NOTES

[1] Women, according to the prevailing Victorian image, were supremely virtuous, pious, tender and understanding as wives, charity workers, teachers and sentimental writers. These professions were, in large part, culturally defined as extensions of motherhood—all similarly regarded as nurturing, empathetic and morally directive (Bloch, 1978).

[2] Gutman (1976) discussed the compromises enslaved persons made to remain together, including forced sexual contact to prevent the selling of family members.

[3] West African women usually nursed their children for two or three years and abstained from sexual intercourse until the infant was weaned. Such practice produced an interval between live births of three to four years, much longer than that usually found among European women in the colonies. If this practice had been widely followed, it would have severely depressed the birthrate among African-born women (Menard, 1975, as cited in Gutman, 1976).

[4] Examples of support networks, public and private behaviors, feigning illnesses and ignorance and other similar activities have been noted as examples of survival strategies that were not learned from slavers due to limited contact.

REFERENCES

Asante, M. K. (1987). *The Afrocentric idea.* Philadelphia: Temple University Press.

Asante, M. K. (1988). *Afrocentricity.* Trenton, NJ: Africa World Press.

Bloch, R. H. (1978). American feminine ideals in transitions: The rise of the moral mother, 1785–1815. *Feminist Studies, 4,* 101–109.

Collins, P. H. (1986). Learning from the outsider within: The sociological significance of black feminist thought. *Social Problems, 33,* 14–30.

Collins, P. H. (1990). *Black feminist thought: Knowledge, consciousness, and the politics of empowerment.* Boston: Unwin Hyman.

Davis, A. (1971). Reflections on the black woman's role in the community of slaves. *Black Scholar,* 3–15.

Davis, A. (1983). *Women, race and class.* New York: Vintage Books.

Degler, C. N. (1980). *At odds: Women and the family in America from the revolution to the present.* New York: Oxford University Press.

Dill, B. T. (1983). Race, class, and gender: Prospects for an all-inclusive sisterhood. *Feminist Studies, 9,* 131–148.

Dill, B. T. (1988). Our mother's grief: Racial ethnic women and the maintenance of families. *Journal of Family History, 13,* 415–431.

DuBois, W.E.B. (1990). *The souls of black folk.* New York: Vintage Books. (Original work published by Forethought, 1903.)

Gutman, H. (1976). *The black family in slavery and freedom: 1750–1925.* New York: Pantheon.

Harris, W. H. (1982). *The harder we run: Black workers since the Civil War.* New York: Oxford University Press.

Higginbotham, E. (1984). *Work and survival for black women* (PS 11/88–868). Memphis, TN: Memphis State University, Center for Research on Women.

Higginbotham, E., & Burgess, N. (1992). *Work and family life: Public policy strategies for women of color.* Washington, DC: Center for Women Policy Studies.

Holloway, J. E. (1990). *Africanisms in American culture.* Bloomington: Indiana University Press.

Jewell, K. S. (1988). *Survival of the black family: The institutional impact of U. S. social policy.* New York: Praeger Publishers.

Jones, J. (1985). *Labor of love, labor of sorrow: Black women, work, and the family from slavery to the present.* New York: Basic.

Keto, T. (1989). *The Africa-centered perspective of history.* NJ: K. A. Publications.

King, D. (1988). Multiple jeopardy, multiple consciousness: The context of black feminist ideology. *Signs, 14,* 42–72.

Ladner, J. (1986). Black women face the 21st century: Major issues and problems. *Black Scholar, 17(5),* 12–19.

Lebeuf, A. (1963). The role of women in the political organization of African societies. In D. Paulme (Ed.), *Women of tropical Africa.* Berkeley: University of California Press.

Levine, L. (1977). *Black culture and black consciousness.* New York: Oxford University Press.

McAdoo, H. P. (1988). *Black families.* Beverly Hills, CA: Sage Publications.

Menard, R. (1975). The Maryland slave population, 1658–1730: A demographic profile of blacks in four counties. *William and Mary Quarterly, 32,* 29–54.

Mintz, S., & Price, R. (1992). *The birth of African American culture.* Boston: Beacon Press. (Original work published in 1976.)

Nichols, C. H. (1963). *Many thousand gone: The ex-slaves' account of their bondage and their freedom.* Bloomington: Indiana University Press.

Oyebade, B. (1990). African studies and the Afrocentric paradigm: A critique. *Journal of Black Studies, 21,* 233–238.

Rodgers-Rose, L. (1980). *The black woman.* Beverly Hills, CA: Sage Publications.

Staples, R. (1987). Social structure and black family life: An analysis of current trends. *Journal of Black Studies, 17,* 267–286.

Steady, F. C. (1981). *The black woman cross-culturally.* Cambridge, MA: Schenkman Publishing.

Sudarkasa, N. (1980, November/December). African and Afro-American family structure: A comparison. *Black Scholar,* 37–60.

Sudarkasa, N. (1987). The status of women in indigenous African societies. In R. Terborg-Penn & A. B. Rushing (Eds.), *Women in Africa and the African diaspora: A reader* (pp. 25–42). Washington, DC: Howard University Press.

Wertheimer, B. M. (1977). *We were there: The story of working women in America.* New York: Pantheon.

White, D. G. (1985). *Ain't I a woman?: Female slaves in the plantation south.* New York: W. W. Norton.

CHAPTER 3

Identity Issues

CHERYL S. AL-MATEEN, CARMEN T. WEBB, FRANCES M. CHRISTIAN, AND LUCIA S. DONATELLI

She knows who she is because she knows who she isn't.

—NIKKI GIOVANNI

Our understanding of human development comes from models based on, for the most part, an andro- and Eurocentric view of human beings (Berzoff, 1989). Anna Freud (1965) noted that assessing isolated developmental scales was not sufficient for understanding a child's total personality. Freud (1965) discussed the concept of developmental lines, noting that an individual does not progress at the same rate along each line.

Brown-Collins and Susswell (1986) described a tripartite model of self-concept formation for African American women. The self-concept is a composite of the psycho-physiological, the African American and the "myself." The psycho-physiological refers to the knowledge of herself as a woman. The African American self-conceptualization extends from her African American tribal heritage. The "myself" referent alludes to those aspects of self that pertain only to the individual, such as eye color, family history, health, etc.

An African American woman progresses through the well-known lines of human development: psychosexual, cognitive, psychosocial, object relations, interpersonal and moral. She must also understand herself as a member of a particular racial/ethnic group: African American. The interaction of each of these three "developmental lines" (human, ethnic and gender) contributes to her identity development as woman. The mature African American woman combines all three lines of her identity. This may be quite challenging against the backdrop of an androcentric- and Eurocentric-focused society.

To discuss the identity development of the African American

woman, we explore several "developmental lines" in her maturation, - focusing on three areas: (1) basic human development, (2) ethnic identity development, and (3) womanist development (see Table 3.1). We describe various models of development which occur within these developmental lines as they progress for girls, adolescents and women.

As seen in all developmental models, tasks that occur in childhood are somewhat more concrete, occurring within specific age ranges, related to the rapid physical and neurologic development known to occur during that time. Once adolescence is underway and physical maturity is reached, the time span required varies for each individual's developmental line, as the task is no longer directly related to the physical ability to accomplish it, but to the incorporation and consolidation of internal factors and experiences.

DEVELOPMENTAL MODELS

Human Development

Models that specifically relate to basic human development include those proposed by Jean Piaget (1951, 1952), Erik Erikson (1950) and Margaret Mahler (Mahler, Pine, & Bergman, 1975). Piaget (1951, 1952) described cognitive development in children. Through his four stages, the child adapts by assimilation (understanding new information in relation to current schemas, or information that one already knows) and accommodation (reorganizing schemas based on the new information). Erikson's (1950) "eight stages of man" described how individuals (i.e., heterosexual white males) developed psychosocially. Erikson also focused on the roles of society, culture and the historical milieu in the development of self-identity. As such, this model is central to understanding the development of identity in African American women (Roland, 1994). Mahler et al. (1975) described the formation of object relations—how an individual comes to relate to those around her.

Ethnic Identity Development

Ethnic identity encompasses that part of the self-concept which comes from the consciousness of membership in an ethnic group. This includes the language, behavior, values and knowledge of relevant history, including society's attitudes toward the group (Phinney, 1990; Spencer &

Markstrom-Adams, 1990). It is separate from one's identity as an individual (Rotheram & Phinney, 1987). For African American women, that knowledge of history must include the legacies of slavery, bondage, sexual exploitation and compulsory labor (Bell, 1990).

The formation of ethnic identity involves stages of exploration and commitment. A review of several authors shows that Cross's (1978) model seems to serve as a foundation. Cross (1978) delineated four stages of ethnic identity. In *pre-encounter*, ethnicity appears to have little consequence. The individual may or may not prefer the dominant culture. This stage is followed by *encounter*, in which there is realization that ethnicity affects one's experiences in society. In the third stage, there is an emotionally intense *immersion-emersion* into one's culture. There may be a rejection of the dominant culture. Finally, in *internalization*, there is a consolidation of group and personal identity. This does not require a choice of involvement in ethnic group customs. There is, however, a respect for and acceptance of one's own ethnicity. Ethnic identity development continues throughout the life span with further reexploration/rethinking of one's ethnic identity.

Womanist Identity Development

Ossana, Helms and Leonard (1992) describe the development of womanist identity. This model states that healthy identity development for women means overcoming "the tendency to use male (or female) or societal stereotypes of womanhood and define for themselves what being a woman means" (p. 403). The stages complement Cross's (1978) model on ethnic identity. During pre-encounter, there is conformity to societal gender views with a limited view of the roles of women. In the encounter stage, there is a questioning of societal values. In immersion-emersion, there is an intense association with women. Finally, with internalization, there is an incorporation of a definition of womanhood which is not limited by others' definitions. The authors contrast models of feminist and womanist identity. Feminist identity requires a specific political ideology with an emphasis on the alteration of the perception of women as they relate to men. Womanist identity, however, emphasizes an "ideological flexibility" that may include the feminist identity, perhaps starting with immersion-emersion. The feminist identity is, therefore, a subcategory of womanist identity.

Table 3.1. Developmental Lines: Identity Development in African American Women

Age	Human Development			Ethnic Identity	Womanist Development		
	Piaget	Erikson	Mahler		Female Identity	Lesbian Identity	
0-1 years	Sensorimotor	Trust v. Mistrust	Autistic Symbiotic Separation-Individuation			Sensitization	
1-2		Autonomy v. Shame and Self-Doubt			Solidifies gender identity (female)		
2-3	Pre-Operational	Initiative v. Guilt					
3-4				Awareness of ethnicity	Chooses models of sex role stereotype consistent with mother		
4-5							
5-6							
6-7	Concrete Operations	Industry v. Inferiority					
7-8					Learns further acceptable gender role behaviors		
8-9				Awareness of permanence of ethnicity			
9-10							
10-11							
Adolescent	Formal Operations	Identity v. Identity Diffusion				**Lesbian**	**African American Lesbian**
Young Adult		Intimacy v. Isolation				Identity: Confusion Comparison Tolerance Acceptance Pride Synthesis (coming out process)	Denial of conflicts Bisexual v. lesbian Conflict in allegiances Priority in allegiances Integrating the various communities
Adult		Generativity v. Self-Absorption or Stagnation					
Mature Age		Integrity v. Disgust and Despair					

CHRONOLOGICAL OVERVIEW OF DEVELOPMENTAL ISSUES FOR AFRICAN AMERICAN WOMEN

Childhood

Human Development. Mahler et al. (1975) show that the infant cannot recognize that she is a separate being from the mother. In the *autistic* phase, an equilibrium is achieved outside of the womb with a lack of awareness of others. Subsequently, in *symbiosis*, the infant becomes aware of the mother, but only as a part of herself. After about 6 months of age, the *separation-individuation* process begins. The child becomes increasingly independent, exploring physical separation from the mother, and starts to recognize her own individuality.

In Piaget' s *sensorimotor* stage (ages 0 through 2), the child is developing schemas and can appreciate only what is learned directly through the senses (sight, taste, touch, smell, hearing) and her own movements. She does learn that there is cause and effect. In *pre-operations* (ages 2 through 6), the child begins to process what she has learned. The child will learn that objects exist even if hidden several times (object permanence) and uses herself as a measure for what exists for others (egocentrism). In *concrete operations* (ages 6 through 11), the child learns to classify, to arrange things in order (seriate) and to recognize that the volume of liquid does not change between two containers of differing shapes (conservation). Rules are developed and more clearly understood. There remains a certain egocentrism; the child understands the difference between truth and fiction, but must learn that her truth is not always the truth for all (Yates, 1991).

Erikson's first stage, *trust versus mistrust*, occurs in the first year of life. If cared for adequately, the child will grow to trust herself, others, and the world around her. With inadequate or inconsistent care, the child may be fearful and mistrustful. In the second and third years of life, *autonomy versus doubt* occurs. The child, during the time of toilet training, learns to control her own body in a socially acceptable manner. With this, she will ultimately feel that she is able to affect the world around her. Without this ability, if she receives inconsistent, overprotective or overcritical care, she will not recognize that she can control herself or the environment around her. In *initiative versus guilt*, during the fourth and fifth years of life, the child becomes more independent and creative. If she is not supported in this, she will feel guilt about activities that she initiates. *Industry versus inferiority*, the next stage, occurs from about the sixth year through the onset of adolescence. The child learns to reason, and wants to understand how everything works. She learns to follow rules. As she is encouraged and rewarded for her accomplishments, she wants to achieve more. If she is not encouraged, a sense of inferiority will result.

Ethnic Identity Development. Awareness of ethnic identity can be present as early as age 3 or 4, with further consolidation developing by age 7. At that age, children accurately categorize others as belonging to their own or another ethnic group, recognizing the permanence of another's ethnicity. The constancy of one's own ethnicity may not be recognized until 8 to 10 years of age (Aboud, 1987).

Cross (1987) discusses the process of ethnic identity development in children as an extension of nigrescence in adults, involving the combination of the constructs "personal identity" (PI) and "reference group orientation" (RGO). PI is a measure of individual self-esteem separate from race or color while RGO measures those aspects of self-esteem that are gender-, race-, or culture-specific. Although earlier scientific research lumped these two constructs together and made them predictive of one another, current theory suggests that they are not correlated. Race can, however, affect the PI sector of self-esteem. While being a member of a minority group does not automatically result in an inferiority complex, "the stigma of racism, ethnocentrism, and poverty may negatively affect the ability of underclass, underrepresented children to refine their global self-concept through incorporation of a 'self-as-student' or 'self-as-learner' component that facilitates successful performance in traditional middle-class academic contexts" (Cross, 1987, p. 130). Thus, global PI measures may not be predictive of context-specific PI measures, and vice versa.

RGO studies with African American children yield inconsistent results. Cross (1987) emphasizes the need to interpret these findings with caution. He states (p. 130):

> When black children show preferences for white, it does not follow that they "hate" black, or that they "want to be white," unless being white is taken in the following way. In young (normal) children the liquidity of their ego allows for some very interesting transformational fantasies which, if found operative in adults, might define psychosis. When children like something, they often play at being it. Thus in their own minds they can "become" a lion, a tiger, or an airplane. Why should we become alarmed when a black child expresses an attraction to the white world by playing white?

Cross (1987) also suggested that black families instill a dual cultural perspective in their children. Thus, in studies assuming a monodactic pattern of responses to indicate positive racial identification, African American children are bound to score lower than white children because they are attracted to both choices.

Such findings in the scientific literature, of African American children demonstrating positive self-images despite exhibiting white preferences and attitudes, led Spencer (1987) to suggest a model for identity formation in African American children that naturally leads to "identity imbalance" (racial dissonance). Spencer (1987) noted that African Americans are a caste-like minority group, in that the group is marginal in society with an accompanying inequality of empowerment, and a resulting at-risk status for children. Noting that American society is Eurocentric, she predicts that all children raised in this society will be Europeanized, or white-biased, unless there are specific influences that divert this outcome.

Spencer (1987) likens this process to the differentiation of sex in a human embryo (which is naturally female until the introduction of testosterone). The only way to avoid this identity imbalance is to intervene with a "compensatory cultural emphasis on the strengths of the caste-like minority group" (p. 108). This is the responsibility of parents, who are the first conveyors of ethnic and racial information. With regard to the educational system, Spencer and Markstrom-Adams (1990) write that African American youth are often presented with primarily negative images of their ethnic group. The history of African Americans generally taught in school usually includes slavery, for the most part. However, if African Americans are taught about their heritage of great inventors, researchers or royalty, their view of themselves and their reference group may be quite different.

One example of an African American girl's challenge in reconciling her "ethnic" characteristics with society's values lies in the politics of hair texture and skin color. These politics are introduced to the African American girl from an early age by her own community. She learns that these characteristics differentiate her not only from mainstream society, but from other ethnic minorities as well. Color consciousness frequently begins within the family unit. In African American families, parents may use skin color as a reference to gauge expectations from children and to create favorites among siblings. The favoritism of a lighter-skinned child versus a darker-skinned child is arbitrary. In some families, lighter skin is valued in accordance with history. In others, dark skin and traditionally

African features are considered badges of honor. The issue of skin color, hair texture, and facial features among African Americans becomes even more complex as the girl child ventures into the African American community, and then into mainstream culture, encountering either reinforcing or opposing social attitudes in comparison with what occurs at home. Skin color itself is completely relative. The same shade of color may be considered dark in one environment and light in another. Derogatory and preferential treatment may occur simultaneously within the same setting. For example, a girl may receive privileges from parents because she has light skin, yet be ostracized by other members of the family for the same reason.

Social scientists have documented the concerns of young African Americans regarding hair and skin color for many years. In their review, Hughes and Hertel (1990) point to the lack of consensus among researchers regarding favoritism of light over dark skin. They attribute the discrepancy either to methodological flaws or evolving racial attitudes. In addition, past assumptions that choosing lighter skin over darker skin translates into negative racial identification in African American children (Clark & Clark, 1940) are being challenged (Porter & Washington, 1979). Spencer (1992) studied a group of African American preschoolers and found that although these children adopted Eurocentric ideals, this did not adversely affect their own self-images. Rather, it is the health and security of the family, in addition to its relationship to the immediate community, that shapes an African American child's self-image (Spurlock, 1986).

Womanist Development. Socialization as a female begins at the time of birth (Lipman-Blumen, 1984). Parents (fathers more so than mothers) treat an infant girl more gently than an infant boy. This gentle handling continues throughout childhood and adolescence, encouraging dependence on others. During the preschool years, starting by 18 months, the young girl begins to develop an appreciation of being female as opposed to male. The gender identity is solidified during the next 18 months; by age 3, the girl knows that she is female, and identifies with her mother's appearance and behaviors. By age 5, she can tell the difference between males and females by their external appearance; she is aware of acceptable "girl" activities, such as what toys are acceptable, that she should be a girl in fantasy role play, and that perhaps she should play with other girls instead of boys. The concern about her well-being continues, and little girls are kept closer to home than their male counterparts. Historically, girls are not encouraged to engage in rough-and-tumble play.

These young ladies learn household and child-care tasks early as well—activities that are carried over into the classroom, where girls are more likely to assist the teacher, as well as to help the boys follow instructions (Lipman-Blumen, 1984). In general, girls are taught that overtly competitive behaviors are unacceptable, and that relationships take precedence over winning. Collaboration is fostered. Achievement is acceptable, however, and is most appropriately sought by attaining it through association with a successful man ("the football captain's girlfriend"). Competition in this arena, therefore, is acceptable.

Many of these preferred feminine characteristics, however, are only accurate when looked at from a Eurocentric view. African American women encompass a different perspective, and may pass a different viewpoint on to their daughters. For example, historically delicacy was a highly valued "feminine" characteristic for the woman by Eurocentric standards; however, strength has been a far more adaptive characteristic for an African American woman. Further, the majority of African American women are descended from women who were slaves, and who, later, more frequently worked outside the home than not. Indeed, the concept of gender roles is different in many African societies. Women were leaders in the home and community and respected in the workforce. There was an equality between the genders, and more neutrality in gender roles. Further, women of privilege continued to work outside the home (Burgess, 1994). The gender role expectations passed on to African American girls are affected by the history of African American women as well as by the current socioeconomic status and values held by those who influence them.

Adolescence

Human Development. Piaget described formal operations as beginning about age 11 and progressing through adulthood. The child develops the ability to draw hypothetical deductions from facts, and to appreciate and use the thought processes of others in testing hypotheses. This may be done through the use of symbols, which she did not heretofore appreciate fully.

Through adolescence, Erikson delineated the *identity versus identity diffusion/role confusion* conflict. During this time, the adolescent develops a sense of self and family in relation to the rest of society. Thus, identity development is the major task of adolescence (Erikson, 1950). Streitmatter (1988) reviewed the literature, and found four statuses that an adolescent could progress through in this stage: *foreclosure*, in which the teen simply accepts the values passed on by parents; *diffusion*, in which the adolescent is not particularly interested in establishing an identity; *moratorium*, in which there is information gathering in order to make an appropriate decision; and *identity achievement*, the final stage in which beliefs, values, and behaviors have been explored and some have been accepted.

Ethnic Identity. Aries and Moorehead (1989) found that for African American adolescents, ethnicity was more important than religion, politics or sexual interpersonal attitudes and behavior in predicting overall identity status. Most of what is known about the ethnic identity development of African American adolescent girls has been gleaned from the literature on all African American adolescents. There is very little research that addresses gender differences in adolescent ethnic identity development. Studies of adolescents and adults have shown that African American females endorse attitudes from later stages than males (Phinney, 1989, 1990).

A girl's self-identification is the first component of her ethnic identity. The American environment places great importance on one's race, so it is an integral piece of the development of self-identity. One indication of her ethnic identity development is her sense of belonging to her ethnic or racial group. As adolescents primarily identify themselves in terms of a peer group, this is particularly significant at this age level. A girl may identify which group she feels excluded from the least, depending on her level of identification with any group. Another component of ethnic identity involves positive and negative attitudes toward the group. If the teenager cannot identify any positive attitudes, or can only identify negative ones, it is likely that identification with African Americans is weak. A further indicator of ethnic identity development is involvement in African American social and cultural practices. This is manifested in the ethnicity of her friends and significant others, whether she participates in any primarily African American social groups, and her involvement in political activities that pertain to the African American community. Her style of clothing, preferred music, periodicals read, and types of movies, television and plays enjoyed are all indicative of identity (Phinney, 1990).

Both societal factors and personal/demographic factors affect ethnic identity development in adolescents. Spencer (1987) listed parents and mainstream society as important socializing agents to the identity formation of African American youth. However, these youths also face numerous risks that may impede optimal development: poverty, poor health, family status, racism, prejudice and lack of political power. Spencer (1992) stated that race consciousness is crucial to the resilience and development of appropriate coping strategies of African American youth. Societal development includes the impact of the media, toys, societal stereotypes, changes and cultural group expectations. Personal/demographic factors include family, peers, role models, school and neighborhood.

In American society, the media has a tremendous influence on public and personal ideas, beliefs and opinions. Children are bombarded by images on television and in movies. Adolescents, who have greater mobility and financial resources, have even greater access to TV, movies, magazines and newspapers (Spencer & Dornbusch, 1990). Both are very open to the voice of the wider society. Spencer and Markstrom-Adams (1990) note that television programming has a strong psychological impact on our youth. There are very few African American heroes portrayed on television outside the sports arena. Most regular series portray African Americans as victims, villains or one-dimensional comedians.

The adolescent, with greater cognitive skills than the child, has challenges as cognitive maturity makes one painfully aware of others' negative feelings about one's ethnicity. Studies examining the relationship between self-esteem, self-concept and psychological adjustment in African American adolescents are limited. One study of African Americans, aged 13 to 14 and of low socioeconomic status (SES), found that acceptance of one's racial identity was significantly correlated with self-concept. A study of the stages of ethnic development of 10th-grade African American, Asian American, and Mexican American adolescents found that those at higher stages of ethnic identity had a better psychological adjustment (Phinney, 1989).

An African American adolescent who lives in a predominantly white suburb has to negotiate two cultures. Banks (1989) studied this issue with 98 African American suburban adolescents in one geographic region. Six stages of ethnic identity development were outlined. The earlier stages involve negative feelings about one's own group first, and then the dominant group. The third stage culminates in genuine positive feelings toward one's own culture. The later stages (four to six) involve growing acceptance of other cultures, while not devaluing one's own (bi-ethnicity, multiethnicity and finally, globalism).

Banks (1989) found that adolescents retain the characteristics of earlier stages as they move to the next higher stage. Some suburban African American adolescents had biracial attitudes (positive toward both African Americans and whites). Yet, as attitudinal assimilation increased, the students became more positive toward their schools and neighborhoods, more positive toward whites and less positive toward African Americans and ethnocentrism. Adolescents had significantly more negative attitudes toward their neighborhoods and toward African Americans than younger children. The effect was greatest for African American girls. They liked their neighborhoods less and had more negative attitudes toward African Americans than did African American boys.

Womanist Development. In her historical review of womanist theories, Berzoff (1989) noted the masculine assumptions and values inherent in them; autonomy, independence and individuation represented healthy mature adult development. Within these assumptions, women's connections and relationships with one another were characterized as deficiencies because they were variations from the norm of male development. In her conclusion, Berzoff (1989) espoused a need for a female paradigm which does not assume pathology but difference from males.

By adolescence, the African American girl has developed the cognitive ability to understand others' feelings about her ethnic and gender group. Many of these ethnic and gender attitudes (stereotypes) are negative. For example, growing up in a society that devalues all women becomes a recognizable phenomenon. More specifically, in this society the dominant culture idealizes white women as having sexual purity and virtue but devalues African American women as sexually evil and lustful (Greene, 1990a). This discovery of the society's negative perceptions of African Americans is difficult (Spencer & Dornbusch, 1990). If the dominant group's attitude is internalized, the adolescent may reject her own group and she may choose to have less ethnic involvement; or if she can "pass" (present herself to others as belonging to the dominant culture), she may choose to do so. In addition, in order to maintain self-esteem, she may find ways to separate herself from her ethnic group and feel less of a sense of belonging to her own culture.

As noted previously, a girl's relationship with her mother influences the psycho-physiological aspect of her identity. In the African American community this relationship is also the setting for the transmission of racial socialization. As in other ethnic groups, mothers are usually charged with this task. The factors that impact upon the racial socialization process and ultimately, on the development of ethnic identity, are myriad. A mother communicates, directly and indirectly, to her daughter about the relative attractiveness of her physical characteristics. If she makes great efforts to alter them (hair-straightening, bleaching creams, etc.), a daughter learns that she is not acceptable (Greene, 1990b). A mother's early and direct discussion of racism may be very helpful and may offset a disproportionate influence of society's stereotypes on the daughter's perceptions. Unfortunately, if a mother has significantly different racial challenges from her daughter, she may be limited in her understanding and in her ability to help.

Clark (1989) reviewed the peer group as another factor in ethnic identity development. African American females are more likely than white females or white males to select peers of their gender-race group as work partners or desired classmates (Clark, 1989). Studies find that girls are more similar to their friends than are males in values, attitudes and behaviors. Girls expect more intimacy and emotional support, and intentionally keep their number of intimate friends small. They are less likely than boys to accept the friendship advances from another same-sex peer.

From these results, one might speculate that the African American adolescent female, who values highly close relationships with her peers, would be very vulnerable in a predominantly white environment. Not only may she find fewer friends with whom to bond, but she may find herself in a peer group that has antipathy toward her ethnic group. Because adolescents tend to compare themselves to others (especially to their peers), she may constantly find herself "not measuring up."

In urban neighborhoods, one's peer group may be characterized by ethnic similarity; thus, while at home, one may not have to negotiate the ethnic differences. If the neighborhood is poor, one must struggle with the message that being black means living with poverty and violence. It is important to note, however, that racial identity attitudes cannot be predicted by SES. Carter and Helms (1988) studied college students and compared racial identity attitudes with socioeconomic status. They found that "researchers cannot assume automatically that if one is black one identifies with blacks or black culture, or that if one is middle class or upper class one does not identify with blacks or black culture . . . It may be possible for a black person to feel good about . . . herself and have mixed or negative feelings toward his or her racial group" (pp. 29–30). Identity is also developed through identification with role models (Taylor, 1989). Adolescents identify with those whom they believe will assist them in attaining their goals. Few studies are available for African American female adolescents and role models. Taylor (1989) studied African American males from a private university and the inner city. He found that they chose features of role models based on preferences shaped by the environment in which they grew up as well as their own successes, failures and assessments of their opportunities. Early belief systems, values and aspirations shaped the function and attraction of an individual to a role model. Youth are attracted to role models based on how well the models can meet their present needs. As they move through the life cycle, their perspective of the role model changes and the nature of the role model's function changes. Thus, early identification influences and limits the range of present objects of identification (Taylor, 1989).

Literature and the media have exerted much influence on public opinion of what constitutes African American beauty. Originally, African American literature portrayed its female characters with Caucasian features. African American adolescents see the white standard of beauty portrayed in magazines, movies, TV and even billboards: long, straight flowing hair (that "swings and bounces"); thin, small noses; and fair skin. Even the models who are African American women frequently have many of these features (Neal & Wilson, 1989; Love, 1990). The cosmetic industry has lines produced exclusively for African American consumption; however, many of these beauty enhancers are skin-bleaching creams and permanent hair relaxers, to remove the natural curl (kink). Concurrently, however, an increasing number of authors, actors, and directors are attempting to cut across these color barriers within the African American community, to redefine the perception of beauty and its accompanying assumptions.

Spurlock (1986) further stated that the existence of racial tensions may augment the stress of adolescence, and the African American child may find self-esteem on the streets if she cannot find it within the at-large community.

Adulthood

Human Development. During adulthood, Erikson (1950) described three stages: *intimacy versus isolation*, *generativity versus self-absorption/stagnation*, and *integrity versus disgust/despair*. These occur in young, middle, and mature adulthood, respectively. In the first, the person learns to become emotionally intimate with others without losing the sense of self, otherwise feeling isolated and alone. Next, the individual is concerned with the future of the society at large; the opposite is a preoccupation with his own needs to the exclusion of others. Finally, the individual may review and reflect on his life with a sense of satisfaction, unless there have been numerous missed opportunities and irreversible mistakes that result in a sense of despair over the lack of life accomplishments (Erikson, 1950). Erikson also noted that men complete their identity formation at the end of adolescence, although it continues to develop. Women, however, could complete their formation only through a relationship with a man (Erikson, 1968). This results in a woman being defined by whom she marries or mothers (Berzoff, 1989).

Ethnic Development and Womanist Development. As an African American female matures, she finds herself stereotyped according to either her race or her gender (Copeland, 1977). This pertains especially to the myth of the matriarch and the effect of this stereotype on an African American woman's relationship with African American men. Copeland (1977, p. 398) stated:

> Black women in general have suffered tremendously by internalizing the belief that they are matriarchs . . . They experience continuous conflict between, on the one hand, having a need to be assertive and independent, but at the same time feeling that to do so may "strip" black men of their dignity and manhood and may be in total opposition to the "black cause." Dispelling the myth may not be an easy task since some black men, who also believe the myth, resent the inner strivings of black women and may feel threatened by their assertiveness.

While society as a whole may have gauged African American women by the norms expected of white women, and adolescents find role models in various places, Myers (1975) found that this is not true of the women themselves. The study examined the development of self-esteem among African American women, and found that African American women selected other African American women as their normative and comparative groups in the pursuit and the maintenance of self-esteem. Robbie Steward (1991) wrote an essay detailing progression from a black person to a black female to an African American woman. The development of her anger, assertiveness and aggression in challenging her surroundings and feeling empowered are reviewed. The literature clearly specifies that an African American woman is seen as an African American person first, and a woman second. This has affected the involvement of African American women in feminist movements. Sojourner Truth's comments at the Women's Rights Convention in 1862 are particularly relevant; she stated:

That man over there say
a woman needs to be helped into carriages
and lifted over ditches
and to have the best place everywhere.
Nobody ever helped me into carriages
or over mud puddles
or gives me a best place. . . .
Ain't I a woman?
Look at me
Look at my arm!
I have plowed and planted
and gathered into barns
and no man could head me . . . .
And ain't I a woman?
I could work as much
and eat as much as a man—
when I could get it—
and bear the lash as well
and ain't I a woman?
I have borne 13 children
and seen most all sold into slavery
and when I cried out a mother's grief
none but Jesus heard me. . . .
and ain't I a woman?

Hemmons (1980) reported a study of African American women's attitudes toward the women's liberation movement. The subjects included working-class and middle-class African American and white women. There was no significant difference in the amount of anomie (feeling of alienation from society) experienced by the women based on race or socioeconomic status. There was a trend toward African American women showing a slightly higher level of anomie. African American women were found to endorse acceptance of traditional feminine characteristics more than white women. This was measured by response to such statements as, "A wife should do everything she can to help her husband further his career, even if it means sacrificing her own," and, "One of the most important duties of a woman is to act like a lady at all times." There was a difference in the acceptance of feminine norms based on socioeconomic status, with the working class having higher levels of acceptance. As might be expected, Hemmons (1980) found that a high endorsement of traditional feminine characteristics did not correspond with interest in the women's movement. However, African American women were found more likely to score highly on both the feminine and female liberalism scales. The author pointed out that African American women have historically performed nontraditional feminine roles, such as working outside the home, while simultaneously being required to "act feminine," which would support this dichotomy. Steady (1981) noted that African American women are burdened not only by their gender and race, but also very frequently by socioeconomic class. Feminism is generally seen as a middle-class white female cause, and socioeconomic issues are not a priority. Both conclude that African American women may not have joined the women's movement because of differing priorities. The women's movement has focused on separation-identification issues (regarding the woman as an individual separate from her husband and children), while African American women have been geared more toward preoccupation with underemployment and the undereducation of African Americans and equality between the races, not just the genders.

Hemmons (1980) also found that African American women were willing to "return home and take care of the home and children if the economic system were not so oppressive on African American men . . . a return to the home did not change their independent nature" (Hemmons, 1980, p. 297).

Neal and Wilson (1989) published a review regarding the "significant albeit quiet" effect that skin and hair color has had in the lives of African American women. Through the scientific literature, they found attractiveness studies indicating that physical beauty is associated with goodness, financial success, and, ultimately, self-esteem. They assert that while these characteristics are tagged onto both men and women, the psychological consequences are more severe for women. Neal and Wilson (1989) attribute this to a sexist society. Likewise, Lakoff and Scherr (1984) suggest perhaps this is because beauty represents power for the majority of women, and therefore it is a more important characteristic to possess.

Lesbian Development. African American lesbians live within three separate communities: the African American, the gay/lesbian and American society at large (Morales, 1990). These women are a minority within a minority, and are "relatively invisible" (Mays & Cochran, 1988). They are subject to discrimination because of their ethnicity, as well as because of their sexual orientation. Minority communities as a whole are less accepting of homosexuality, saying "that only happens with white people." Consequently, a woman may be forced to make a choice between her ethnicity (and remain "in the closet") or her homosexuality (and be shunned by her family or ethnic group). Mays and Cochran (1988, p. 55) report that:

> Black lesbians, in contrast to white lesbians, may be more likely to remain a part of the heterosexual community, maintaining relationships outside of the lesbian population . . . black community values emphasize ethnic commitment and participation by all members of the community. Second, the relatively smaller population of black lesbians (a minority within a minority) puts more pressure . . . to maintain their contracts with a black heterosexual community in order to satisfy some of their ethnically related social support needs. Third, black lesbians may contribute much needed financial and informational resources to their families of origin. This assistance may be critical for the maintenance of a reasonable standard of living.

Mays and Cochran (1988) surveyed African American lesbians from around the United States. They found that the mean age at which these women first reported attraction to a woman was 15.8 years. Their first lesbian sexual encounter was at about 19 years of age. There was a low rate of involvement with other women of color. They found that women who were isolated from other African American lesbians (i.e., spent more time in the mainstream white lesbian community for support as well as for access to partners and lovers) were more likely to suffer from depression. They also found that those women who were more involved with the African American lesbian community were more likely to have substance abuse problems.

There are models of gay/lesbian identity development that are similar to those outlined above for ethnic identity development. Several authors have described stages of such models. Troiden (1989) describes an initial stage that occurs from infancy to puberty—sensitization—in which the child assumes she is heterosexual but does experience some feelings of being different from her female peers. Cass's model (1979) has been quoted most widely, and has six stages:

1. Identity confusion, in which there is an awareness that homosexuality has some relevance to one's feelings and/or behavior;
2. Identity comparison, in which there is a sense of alienation related to the possibility of being homosexual;
3. Identity tolerance, in which the individual concludes that she is most likely homosexual and seeks out others as a support;
4. Identity acceptance, in which she fully accepts a homosexual identity but is selectively open about her sexual orientation;
5. Identity pride, in which she becomes immersed in gay subculture; and
6. Identity synthesis, in which she is able to integrate a homosexual identity with other aspects of her self-concept.

Morales (1990) described additional states that *combine* ethnic minority and homosexual identity development:

State 1: Denial of conflicts—The individual denies any discrimination because of ethnic minority or sexual preference status;

State 2: Bisexual versus gay/lesbian—the individual may choose the "less stigmatizing" self-description of bisexual, but remains dysphoric and hopeless.

State 3: Conflict in allegiances—the individual is anxious over which "status" takes precedence: being gay, or being African American (or other minority).

State 4: Establishing priorities in allegiance—the individual identifies primarily with the ethnic group, and has some anger with the gay community for rejection because of her race.

State 5: Integrating the various communities—a multicultural perspective predominates, recognizing effects of ethnicity and sexual preference.

Morales's model focuses on states because an individual may be at more than one stage of development at a time (between ethnic and sexual identity development).

While a woman may discover that she is lesbian at any stage in life, there are different effects at different times. This realization may come during adolescence. The girl may feel "intense self-doubt, alienation, wounded self-esteem, fear, and guilt. On the other hand, changing identity after adolescence can be disruptive and painful, sometimes leading to a replay of an earlier developmental stage . . . that must be worked through in a new way" (Falco, 1991, p. 90). She reports that as in any individuation process, it is necessary that the "young" lesbian be able to approach and retreat from the lesbian subculture as needed in order to resolve any of her anxiety and conflicts in development until she feels comfortable.

CONCLUSION

The development of an African American woman takes place along several lines: as a human being, as an African American, and as a woman. All contribute significantly to identity and self-concept. An African American woman's identity is a confluence of the several cultures in which she lives, and the development of her identity may involve the resolution of conflicting views from each aspect of her life. Lesbian African American women have the additional gay subculture with which to identify, resulting in more conflict.

The existence of these multiple developmental lines and cultures has policy implications. Many social programs address only one aspect of African American identity development. Often programs that attempt to assist African Americans do not take into account the differences between African American men and women in experiences, needs or perspectives. Similarly, programs designed for women are often based on the experiences of European women and do not consider the ethnicity or historical experience of the participants. Policies directed specifically toward African American women are primarily focused on encouraging teenagers not to become pregnant. These efforts are critical, but rarely address the identity issues that may lead to teen pregnancy. Even programs designed specifically to increase the self-esteem of African Americans are often limited to acquainting participants with African American role models or with mastery of academic skills. Again, these efforts are needed, but true improvement in self-esteem results from identity development in all areas. Social programs based more solidly upon these developmental lines may have greater impact and longevity.

There are separate developmental stages for African American women's female, ethnic and sexual identities. The literature indicates that more study is needed in each of these areas.

REFERENCES

Aboud, F. E. (1987). The development of ethnic self-identification and attitudes. In J. S. Phinney & M. J. Rotheram (Eds.), *Children's ethnic socialization: Pluralism and development* (pp. 32–55). Newbury Park, CA: Sage Publications.

Aries, E., & Moorehead, K. (1989). The importance of ethnicity in the development of identity of black adolescents. *Psychological Reports, 65,* 75–82.

Banks, J. A. (1989). Black youth in predominantly white suburbs. In R. L. Jones (Ed.), *Black adolescents* (pp. 65–79). Berkeley, CA: Cobb & Henry.

Bell, E. L. (1990). The bicultural life experience of career-oriented black women. *Journal of Organizational Behavior, 11,* 459–477.

Berzoff, J. (1989). From separation to connection: Shifts in understanding women's development. *AFFILIA, 4,* 45–58.

Brown-Collins, A. R., & Susswell, D. R. (1986). The Afro-American woman's emerging selves. *Journal of Black Psychology, 13,* 1–11.

Burgess, N. J. (1994). Gender roles revisited: The development of the "woman's place" among African American women in the United States. *Journal of Black Studies, 24,* 391–401.

Carter, R. T., & Helms, J. E. (1988). The relationship between racial identity attitudes and social class. *Journal of Negro Education, 57,* 22–30.

Cass, V. C. (1979). Homosexual identity formation: A theoretical model. *Journal of Homosexuality, 4,* 219–235.

Clark, K., & Clark, M. K. (1940). Skin color as a factor in racial identification of Negro pre-school children. *Journal of Social Psychology, 11,* 159–169.

Clark, M. L. (1989). Friendships and peer relations of black adolescents. In R.L. Jones (Ed.), *Black adolescents* (pp. 155–174). Berkeley: Cobb & Henry.

Copeland, E. J. (1977). Counseling black women with negative self-concept. *Personnel and Guidance Journal, 55,* 397–400.

Cross, W. (1978). The Thomas and Cross models of psychological nigrescence: A literature review. *Journal of Black Psychology, 4,* 13–31.

Cross, W. (1987). The two-factor theory of black identity: Implications for the study of identity development in minority children. In J. S. Phinney & M. J. Rotheram (Eds.), *Children's ethnic socialization: Pluralism and development* (pp. 117–133). Newbury Park, CA: Sage Publications.

Erikson, E. (1950). *Childhood and society.* New York: W.W. Norton.

Erikson, E. (1968). *Identity: Youth and crisis.* New York: W.W. Norton.

Falco, K. L. (1991). *Psychotherapy with lesbian clients: Theory into practice.* New York: Brunner/Mazel.

Freud, A. (1965). *Normality and pathology in childhood.* Madison, WI: International Universities Press, Inc.

Greene, B. A. (1990a). What has gone before: The legacy of racism and sexism in the lives of black mothers and daughters. *Women & Therapy (Special Issue: Diversity and complexity in feminist therapy), 9,* 207–230.

Greene, B. (1990b). Sturdy bridges: The role of African American mothers in the socialization of African American children. *Women & Therapy (Special Issue: Motherhood, a Feminist Perspective), 10*(1–2), 205–225.

Hemmons, W. M. (1980). The women's liberation movement: Understanding black women's attitudes. In L. F. Rodgers-Rose (Ed.), *The black woman* (pp. 285–299). Beverly Hills, CA: Sage Publications.

Hughes, M., & Hertel, B. R. (1990). The significance of color remains: A study of life chances, mate selection, and ethnic consciousness among black Americans. *Social Forces, 68,* 1105–1120.

Lakoff, R. T., & Scherr, R. L. (1984). *Face value: The politics of beauty.* Boston, MA: Routledge & Kegan Paul.

Lipman-Blumen, J. (1984). *Gender roles and power.* Englewood Cliffs, NJ: Prentice Hall.

Love, B. (1990, January-February). Negative self-image. *African Commentary, 2,* 25–26.

Mahler, M. S., Pine, F., & Bergman, A. (1975). *The psychological birth of the human infant.* New York: Basic Books.

Mays, V. M. (1986). Identity development of black Americans: The role of history and the importance of ethnicity. *American Journal of Psychotherapy, 60,* 582–593.

Mays, V. M. (1996). Mental health symptoms and service utilization patterns of help seeking among African-American women. In H. W. Neighbors & J. S. Jackson (Eds.), *Mental health in black America* (pp. 161–176). Thousand Oaks, CA: Sage Publications.

Mays, V. M., & Cochran, S. D. (1988). The Black Women's Relationships Project: A national survey of black lesbians. In M. Shernoff & W. A. Scott

(Eds.), *The sourcebook on lesbian/gay healthcare* (pp. 54–62). Washington, DC: National Lesbian and Gay Health Foundation, Inc.

Morales, E. S. (1990). Ethnic minority families and minority gays and lesbians. *Marriage and Family Review, 14,* 217–239.

Myers, L. W. (1975). Black women: Selectivity among roles and reference groups in the maintenance of self-esteem. *Journal of Social and Behavioral Sciences 21,* 39–46.

Neal, A.M., & Wilson, M. L. (1989). The role of skin color and features in the black community: Implications for black women and therapy. *Clinical Psychology Review, 9,* 323–333.

Neal-Barnett, A. M., & Smith, J. S. (1997). African-Americans. In S. Friedman (Ed.), *Cultural issues in the treatment of anxiety* (pp. 154–174). New York: Guilford Press.

Nickerson, K. J., Helms, J. E., & Terrell, F. (1994). Cultural mistrust, opinions about mental illness and black students' attitudes toward seeking professional help from white counselors. *Journal of Counseling Psychology, 41,* 378–385.

Ossana, S. M., Helms, J. E., & Leonard, M. (1992). Do "womanist" identity attitudes influence college woman's self-esteem and perceptions of environmental bias? *Journal of Counseling and Development, 70,* 402–408.

Piaget, J. (1951). *Play: Dreams and imitation in childhood.* London: Routledge & Kegan Paul.

Piaget, J. (1952). *The origins of intelligence in children.* New York: International Universities Press.

Phinney, J. (1989). Stages of ethnicity in minority group adolescents. *Journal of Early Adolescence, 9,* 34–49.

Phinney, J. S. (1990). Ethnic identity in adolescents and adults: Review of research. *Psychological Bulletin, 108,* 499–514.

Porter, J. R., & Washington, R. E. (1979). Black identity and self-esteem: A review of studies of black self-concept, 1968–1978. *Annual Review of Sociology, 5,* 53–74.

Randall, J. (1994). Cultural relativism in cognitive therapy with disadvantaged African American women. *Journal of Cognitive Psychotherapy,* 195–207.

Rix, S. (1987). *The American women, 1987–1988.* New York: W. W. Norton.

Roland, A. (1994). Identity, self, and individualism in a multicultural perspective. In E. P. Salett & D. R. Koslow (Eds.), *Race, ethnicity and self* (pp. 11–23). Washington, DC: National Multicultural Institute.

Root, M. P. P. (1990). Disordered eating in women of color. *Sex Roles, 22,* 525–536.

Rotheram, M. J., & Phinney, J. (1987). Introduction: Definitions and perspectives in the study of children's ethnic socialization. In J. S. Phinney & M. J. Rotheram (Eds.), *Children' s ethnic socialization: Pluralism and development* (pp. 103–116). Newbury Park, CA: Sage Publications.

Satterfield, J. M. (1998). Cognitive behavioral group therapy for depressed low-income minority clients: Retention and treatment enhancement. *Cognitive and Behavioral Practice, 5,* 65–80.

Spencer, M. B. (1987). Black children's ethnic identity formation: Risk and resilience of castelike minorities. In J. S. Phinney & M. J. Rotheram (Eds.), *Children's ethnic socialization: Pluralism and development* (pp. 103–116). Newbury Park, CA: Sage Publications.

Spencer, M. B. (1992, June). *Black males and context: Identity processes and behavioral outcomes.* Paper presented at the Workshop Series on Diversity and Context—Studying Children, Youth and Families: Toward the Integration of Science and Outreach. East Lansing: Michigan State University, Institute for Children, Youth and Families.

Spencer, M. B., & Dornbusch, S. M. (1990). Challenges in studying minority youth. In S. S. Feldman & G. R. Elliott (Eds.), *At the threshold: the developing adolescent* (pp. 123–146). Cambridge MA: Harvard University Press.

Spencer, M. B., & Markstrom-Adams, C. (1990). Identity processes among racial and ethnic minority children in America. *Child Development, 61,* 290–310.

Spurlock, J. (1986). Development of self-concept in Afro-American children. *Hospital and Community Psychiatry, 37,* 66–70.

Steady, F. C. (1981). The black woman cross-culturally: An overview. In F. C. Steady (Ed.), *The black woman cross-culturally* (pp. 7–41). Cambridge, MA: Schenkman Publishing Company.

Steward, R. J. (1991). From black person to black female to African American woman: A critical developmental transition for a feminist therapist. *Women & Therapy, 11,* 71–78.

Streitmatter, J. L. (1988). Ethnicity as a mediating variable for early adolescent identity development. *Journal of Adolescence, 11,* 335–346.

Taylor, R. L. (1989). Black youth, role models and the social construction of identity. In R. Jones (Ed.), *Black adolescents* (pp. 155–174). Berkeley: Cobb & Henry.

Troiden, R. R. (1989). The formation of homosexual identities. *Journal of Homosexuality, 17,* 43–73.

U.S. Department of Health and Human Services. (1992). *Statistical abstracts of the United States.* Washington, DC.

Yates, T. (1991). Theories of cognitive development. In M. Lewis (Ed.), *Child and adolescent psychiatry: A comprehensive textbook.* Baltimore, MD: Williams & Wilkins.

Zambrana, R. (1987). A research agenda and issues affecting poor minority women: A model for understanding their health needs. *Women and Health*, 12, 137–160.

CHAPTER 4

Dating and Mating Patterns

KATHLEEN H. SPARROW

To understand how any society functions you must understand the relationships between the men and the women.

—ANGELA DAVIS

Most men and women search and strive for meaningful human interaction. Emotions and the relating of emotions play an important part in the establishment and maintenance of meaningful relationships. The status of African American male-female relationships emerged as a controversial topic in the 1980s; today, social scientists continue to examine it from various perspectives.[1] Negative societal and economic factors that affect African American men disproportionately, such as high rates of unemployment, mortality, incarceration and drug addiction, to name a few, influence the development of relationship patterns experienced by African American women and men. This chapter examines African American male-female relationships, including dating and mate selection, sexual behavior and love.

REVIEW OF THE LITERATURE

Research by Heiss (1988) addressed values about marriage and family in African American and American white women. African American women and American white women were not different in terms of values and attitudes toward divorce, in spite of the higher divorce rates experienced by African American women. Moreover, little difference between groups was found in terms of accepting nontraditional forms of family life. African American women were more concerned about such matters as family responsibility, income and the quality of life.

Eight percent of African American women and 7 percent of African American men were still single or never married at the marriageable ages of 35 to 44 years (Staples, 1981). Between 1975 and 1985, the proportion of African American women who had ever married declined sharply from nearly 80 percent to 65 percent (Norton & Moorman, 1987). The African American male-to-female sex ratio has been steadily decreasing since the 1920s, and some have suggested that this prolonged shortage of men has led to a broadening of mate selection standards among African American women. Spanier and Glick (1980) found that African American women compared to white women were more likely to marry men who were previously married, less educated and older.

DATING AND MATE SELECTION

Mate selection through dating is a Western invention and is relatively new, having accelerated after World War I (Cox, 1980). Dating is viewed by some as the most significant mechanism of mate selection. However, not every date leads to marriage and individuals date for many reasons in addition to mate-seeking. Dating can be a form of recreation or fun, a form of socialization or a means of status grading (Winch, 1971). For example, innovative means of meeting African American men include attending happy hour at bars frequented by African American professional men and women, and church-sponsored events (Staples, 1978).

The major factor that determines how a woman evaluates her dating experience is how well she can cope with the dating game. Realistic as well as unrealistic expectations can have detrimental effects on relationships and dating experiences. In a study of single African American professional women (Sparrow, 1987), the women reported that their dating experiences were not very positive. This correlated with their attitude that "love is a prerequisite for sex." Dating was exclusive to one person and dinner was the main activity on the date. Most of the women did not share in any of the expenses on a date. Communication problems and lack of honesty were the most significant problems cited by the African American women in the study. Man-sharing was also an issue. Whether as a choice or a dilemma, it is a traumatic situation. A small group of women who have opted for shared relationships create their own terms.

Factors that influence mate selection are varied and complex. Most singles have a "shopping list" of characteristics that they seek in a date or mate, including physical traits; most are psychological traits. African American women look for qualities such as compatibility, sincerity, love, physical attractiveness, sensitivity, money, religious affiliation, occupation, sense of humor, sex appeal, companionship and family size (Sparrow, 1991). They also seek honesty, intelligence and personality in a mate. On a personal level, the African American woman seeks a mate/partner who affirms her strength, capabilities and potential; least important qualities are fashion/taste, political affiliation and family size (Sparrow, 1991).

The role and function of education in the lives of African American women is very important in regard to their dating and mating patterns. In all contemporary societies that have been studied, women tend to marry men who are more educated, slightly richer, and older than themselves (Buss, 1990). Sociologists report the tendencies of women to marry up and men to marry down slightly, on the average, and usually within the same class. Bell (1971) suggested that African American college graduates had generally more favorable responses toward marriage than lower-status and middle-status African American women. African American women search for African American men with comparable education, but they also face competition from other professional women as well as competition from less educated African American women. Professional African American women are also challenged by professional African American men's perceptions of their being very assertive or domineering. Some believe that this perception may lead some African American men to marry less educated women or women outside of their racial group. This perception is not generalized and may not necessarily be applicable across African American men from all educational backgrounds. Cazenave (1983) reported that the majority of a sample of middle-class African American men preferred traditional gender roles for women and men. Many African American men have internalized the matriarchy argument (although successfully challenged), which in turn creates tensions between the sexes.

For many years the proportion of African American women graduating from college was greater than that of African American men. African American women who have graduated from college are the least likely of all African Americans to have married by the age of 30 (Staples, 1981). Professional college-educated African American women prefer to "marry up" when there are simply not enough college-educated African American men to go around (Campbell, 1996). Some African American women have dealt with this issue by a willingness to marry outside their ethnic group, or to marry men with less status (Campbell, 1996; Spanier & Glick, 1980). Using this criteria, the rate of intermarriage among African American women and males outside the group continues to be comparatively small.

Benjamin (1982) addressed the marginality of upwardly mobile African American women and the sociological consequences of their status. The report examined two "ideal" types of African American women achievers, Type A and Type B. Benjamin (1982) defined the "ideal" Type A woman as one who identifies with the traditional goal of marriage and motherhood. Characteristics typical of Type A women are materialism, a political social climber, greater dependency on men for identity, and self-actualization through marriage and motherhood. In contrast, the "ideal" Type B woman is idealistic, politically and socially conscious, less dependent on men for identity, and self-actualized through a service-oriented career (Benjamin, 1982). It should be noted that contemporary professional and nonprofessional African American women tend not to fit in such restricted "ideal" types, but rather have continued to evolve and redefine their roles and ideas of marriage and motherhood.

In some instances both single men and women appear to accept the generalization that for those marriages where the wife experiences higher occupational prestige than the husband, less satisfaction is noted than for those in which the spouses are equal or the husband's occupational prestige is higher. However, having the same, higher, or lower educational attainment or occupational prestige as their spouses has no impact on either the marital or global happiness of African Americans (Zollar & Williams, 1992).

In summary, single professional women continue to find innovative ways to meet men and deal with the issues of love, commitment, marriage, rejection and man-sharing.[2] Like most women, African American women hold the strong belief that love is a prerequisite for sex. In selecting a mate, the single African American professional woman seeks honesty, intelligence and personality, despite the skewed sex ratio. Superior educational levels of African American women do not necessarily lead to lower levels of marital happiness and overall life satisfaction (Sparrow, 1991).

SEXUAL BEHAVIORS

Studies about African American sexuality are limited in the social science literature. Studies about sexual attitudes and behavior are also limited. When these factors are included in the studies of the 1960s, 1970s, and 1980s, the biases in the research, the orientation of the times and the problems with the reporting of sexual activities tend to be major issues. Thus, there are limitations to the generalizations that can be made about

African American sexuality from the available literature. The practice of African American sexual behavior varies by region, age, religiosity, social class and gender.

Historically, African American sexuality has differed from its white counterpart in a number of areas. Economic, demographic and historical factors have accounted for reported racial differences between African Americans and whites in sexual behavior. African Americans generally experience their first sexual intercourse when they are younger than their white counterparts (African American women at 15.5 years compared to white women at 16.4 years, according to Zelnick and Shah, 1983). Prevailing attitudes in the 1980s also supported some notion of acceptance of sexual activity, in that 69 percent of African Americans approved of sexual relations between a man and a woman before marrying but 41 percent did not approve of such relations (Singh, 1980). McBride-Murry (1990) concluded that the social and economic environment of African American adolescent females over four decades influenced timing of first coitus. McBride-Murry (1990) analyzed data from two nationwide surveys in 1982 and 1988. Specific life experiences (such as racial/ethnic pride and religion) appeared to have insulated the adolescents from either engaging in sexual activity or delaying the onset of coitus. Some studies only reflect small samples of this population, however, and may therefore not be generalizable.

In their study of African American sexuality, Weinberg and Williams (1988) reported that in general, African Americans are more likely than whites to engage in premarital sex earlier and more frequently (men and women) and with more partners (men only). They are more likely to engage in extramarital sex (men and women), and with a greater number of partners (men only). In addition, African Americans are more open about it, and report fewer problems with premarital sexual relations. In this case, it is unclear how valid such conclusions may be.

More recently, Anderson's (1990) study of life in an inner-city neighborhood showed how poverty may create its own sex code. Exploitative sexual relations are common among middle-class as well as lower-class African American teenagers. But for most middle-class teenagers, having a strong interest in future goals and plans influences their recognition of the negative impact of pregnancy on those future goals. Thus, the behavior pattern of early sexual encounters among African American teens is changing.

Various classical studies have found religion to be a factor that influences premarital sexual values and behavior (Bell & Blumberg, 1959;

Dedman, 1959; Kinsey, Pomeroy, & Martin, 1953). Individuals who are very religious tend to be less permissive in their sexual attitudes and behavior. Those less religious—as measured by devoutness, belief in God, church attendance and church activities—are more likely to have premarital sex. Degree of religiosity as measured by church attendance is a strong predictor in determining whether love is a prerequisite for sex. A majority of single African American professional women who attended church on a frequent basis responded that love is a prerequisite for sex (Sparrow, 1987).

Middle-class African Americans have never approved of and strongly condemn premarital or extramarital sex (Staples, 1981). This has in part been due to the negative stigma attached to African Americans as being highly permissive. The middle-class response to this has been to assume an exceptionally rigid moral code. The socialization of African American females begins early and as Robert Staples (1978) suggested, the training of African American middle-class females has been closely supervised by mothers. The fear of pregnancy was instilled early in the minds of these females. Chastity was always the key to catching men and to upward mobility, so great care was taken in rearing girls to be respectable (Noble, 1978). African American middle-class and professional women have generally been sexually conservative (Staples, 1981).

The fear of AIDS and other sexually transmitted diseases has had a direct effect on sexual attitudes and behaviors. These concerns force individuals to seek monogamous relationships. Educated African American women who have remained unmarried past the age of 30 continue to date and interact with men. As noted by Sparrow (1987), few have chosen total abstinence. Sparrow (1987) found that single African American professional women were currently engaging in sexual intercourse with only one partner (66 percent) and only seven percent of the sample had two sexual partners, in comparison to 28 percent having no sexual partner.

To summarize sexual behaviors, early research (Reiss, 1971; Staples, 1978; Weinberg & Williams, 1988) revealed that African Americans engaged in premarital sex earlier and more frequently than whites. However, more recent studies by McBride (1990) and Anderson (1990) revealed trends that are moving in the opposite direction of the early research. Two important factors in analyzing the sexual behaviors of African American women are religion and social class. Religion is a major factor that influences the sexual behavior of African Americans. Single African American professional women who are very religious hold strongly to the belief that love is a prerequisite for sex (Sparrow, 1987). Sexual attitudes and behaviors of African American males and females have been affected by the increasing incidences of sexually transmitted diseases. Single African American professional women are either seeking monogamous relationships and engaging in sexual intercourse with only one partner or abstaining from sexual relationships. Class differences among single African American professional women play a role in the socialization process in terms of sexuality. In the past, the middle-status single African American professional woman has been more conservative in her sexual behaviors and attitudes compared to her lower-status sister.

LOVE

In comparison to research on sexuality among African Americans, there is very little scientific information on attitudes or beliefs about love. Most individuals experience at least one love relationship in the course of their lives. Romantic love is a complex social and psychological state involving thoughts and feelings that provide humans with a powerful sense of intimacy and self-worth (Zinn & Eitzen, 1987). Women are more strongly socialized than men to fall in love. As relationships are established, women invest more love. A longitudinal study of nonmarried couples found that women give more of themselves to love relations and they have a greater stake in the success of these relationships (Rubin, 1970).

The limited research on the attitudes African Americans have toward love is primarily confined to those under the age of 25 and shows African American males to be more oriented toward romance and love than their white counterparts (Broderick, 1965). The research also claims that women tend to be more careful about who they fall in love with than men. The factor that most decisively motivates women to engage in sexual intercourse and intimacy is the belief that they are in love (Reiss, 1971). Therefore, for most women love and sex go together; however, there are some women who can separate the two.

The conditions under which sexuality and love are related also vary with social class. Kinsey et al. (1953) found an inverse relationship between socioeconomic status and premarital sexual relations. For African American women, the stigma of being morally loose carries with it a special historical and social meaning (Staples, 1981). Most single professional African American women are socialized into conservative sexual values. For them, sex is tied to romantic love. More research is needed in this area.

DISCUSSION AND FUTURE DIRECTIONS

Defining, describing, and examining what it means to be an African American woman in America is a vast and fertile area for scientific research. Although the literature on the study of women has increased in recent years, the dearth of firsthand materials addressing the needs of females by race in the United States still remains. This chapter has focused on the dating and mating patterns of single African American professional women in the areas of love, sexual behavior, mate selection and satisfaction. The professional, occupational and educational status of African American women assures them of a unique experience in dating and finding a mate.

There is an imbalance in the sex ratio in the African American community. An estimated excess of one million women in the African American population results in a ratio of 90 males per 100 females. The ratio of marriageable men to women is even lower in some large cities. A number of sociological and economic factors explain the imbalance in the sex ratio for African Americans. Young African American men have a comparatively high mortality rate and many are in the military or confined to prisons or mental hospitals. Male homosexuality and interracial marriages also deduct from the pool of eligibles. The two latter factors are perhaps even more relevant for middle-class African Americans (Staples, 1981). This shortage of marriageable African American men made it necessary for many African American women to forego marriage or to rethink their marriage options (Burgess & Horton, 1992; Wilson, 1987).

Over the past few decades, researchers have found that a high percentage of educated African American women are single. Class and cultural factors seem to play an important role in the marital options of educated African American women. Middle-class African American women are socialized to marry, yet they also internalize values that emphasize employment and careers. The parents of lower-middle-class African American women emphasize higher education to prepare their daughters for social mobility (Higginbotham, 1981).

Fear of not finding a mate pervades the life of some single, professional African American women (who are more likely to identify with the traditional goal of marriage and to be interested in a "career" as a means of economic reward rather than traditional labor). Some single, professional African American women also fear that additional success will further limit their potential in finding a mate (Benjamin, 1982). The frustrations of being an unmarried woman sometimes outweigh the value of education, leading some women to regret seeking further training as they feel their educational efforts may decrease their chances of marriage. Marriage is by no means a certainty for African American women, and for those who do marry, being a wife may not offer the security of a career. The marginal position of African Americans in society brings about difficulties encountered in conforming to traditional obligations of financial support of the family, a factor that results in the educated African American woman's tentative marital status (Epstein, 1973). African American women are prepared in both subtle and direct ways to adapt if the good-life-through-marriage dream does not happen or fails to take place. They may invest less time in the dream. There is some evidence that quite a few feel they can do without it (Bell, 1971). For the African American woman achiever, this situation has many implications. First, she has difficulties in finding a mate, and then even more difficulties in finding one with comparable educational status. This is largely a result of the fact that African American females have traditionally acquired higher education levels than their male counterparts. These circumstances are particularly problematic because, for most African American women, getting married and becoming a mother are still the most salient decisions in the setting of a life course (Bell, 1971).

Factors in mate selection for African American professional women are varied and complex. The women may redefine their life goals for marriage and careers. They may continue to concentrate intensely on their educational/occupational advances and adjust to singlehood as a stable state of life. In redefining their goals, they may continue to search for a mate and include men from socioeconomic levels other than their own.

Dating and finding a mate for African American women is complicated by a number of sociopsychological factors as well as structural restraints. Some positive aspects include networking and meeting individuals in a variety of settings. The dating process enables African American women to develop interpersonal skills for communicating with African American men.

Some African American women have reacted to the African American male shortage by parenting outside of marriage (Jackson, 1971). Some are sharing partners (Chapman, 1986). Some are dating and marrying outside of their race (Staples, 1992; Tucker & Mitchell-Kernan, 1990), and still others are choosing to remain single (Karenga, 1982).

Future research in this area should continue to explore the dating experience of single African American professional women. Emphasis could be placed on examining the reasons and expectations surrounding dating. Moreover, it would be important to investigate whether these reasons and expectations are similar to or different from those held by African American men, more specifically their reasons for dating and whether those reasons differ from those of African American men. Further studies on the changing expectations of marriage and family for African Americans could provide insight into how the decision to remain single becomes a part of one's life choice. Research that focuses on communal living, gay and lesbian relationships and interracial dating and mating among single African American professional women would add tremendously to the present literature.

NOTES

[1] Popular literature (*Ebony,* 1986, 1987, 1989; *Essence,* 1994, 1995) continues to focus on African American male–female relationships. Main areas of concern or interest include: the shortage of African American males in general, and the shortage of eligible African American men who are college-educated; the needs and desires of African American women and men in the dating game; the new sexual morality and the question of equality of African American males and females.

[2] In addition, there are singles newsletters and magazines such as Chicago's *Black Gold* and *Chocolate Singles* in New York that help African Americans find mates and serve as support groups.

SUGGESTED READING

Aldrige, D. (1991). *Focusing: Black male/female relationships.* Chicago, IL: Third World Press.

Chapman, A. (1986). *Man sharing—dilemma or choice: A radical new way of relating to the men in your life.* New York: William-Morrow.

Staples, R. (1981). *The world of black singles.* Westport, Connecticut: Greenwood Press.

Whyte, M. K. (1990). *Dating, mating and marriage.* Hawthorne, NY: Aldin de Gruyter.

REFERENCES

Anderson, E. (1990). *Streetwise: Race, class and change in an urban community.* Chicago: University of Chicago Press.

Bell, R. (1971). The related importance of mother-wife roles among black lower-class women. *Journal of Marriage and the Family, 48,* 389–394.

Bell, R., & Blumberg, L. (1959). Courtship intimacy and religious background. *Marriage and Family Living, 21,* 356–360.

Benjamin, L. (1982). Black women achievers: An isolated elite. *Sociological Inquiry, 52,* 140–151.

Broderick, C. (1965). Social heterosexual development among urban negroes and whites. *Journal of Marriage and the Family, 27,* 200–203.

Burgess, N. J., & Horton, H. P. (1992). Where are the black men? Regional differences in the pool of marriageable black males in the United States. *National Journal of Sociology, 6,* 3–19.

Buss, D. M. (1990). International preferences in selecting mates: A study of thirty-seven cultures. *Journal of Cross-Cultural Psychology, 21,* 5–47.

Campbell, B. M. (1996, April). Love across the class line. *Essence, 16,* 83–84.

Cazenave, N. A. (1983). Black male-black female relationships: The perceptions of 155 middle class black men. *Family Relations, 32,* 341–350.

Chapman, A. (1986). *Man sharing—dilemma or choice: A radical new way of relating to the men in your life.* New York: William-Morrow.

Cox, F. (1980). *Human intimacy: Marriage, the family and its meaning.* New York: West Publishing.

Dedman, J. (1959). The relationship between religious attitudes and attitudes toward premarital sex relations. *Marriage and Family Living, 21,* 171–176.

Epstein, C. (1973). Positive effects of the multiple negative explaining the success of black professional women. *American Journal of Sociology, 78,* 912–935.

Heiss, J. (1988). Women's values regarding marriage and the family. In H. P. McAdoo (Ed.), *Black families* (2nd ed.). Beverly Hills, CA: Sage Publications.

Higginbotham, E. (1981). Is marriage a priority? Class differences in marital options of educated black women. In P. Stein (Ed.), *Single life.* New York: St. Martin's Press.

Jackson, Jacquelyn S. (1971). But where are the men? *Black Scholars, 3*(4), 30–40.

Karenga, M. (1982). *Introduction to black studies.* Inglewood, CA: Kawaida Publications.

Kinsey, A., Pomeroy, W., & Martin, C. (1953). *Sexual behavior in the human female.* Philadelphia: W. B. Saunders.

McBride-Murry, V. (1990). Socio-historical study of black female sexuality: Transition to first coitus. In R. Staples (Ed.), *The black family: Essays and studies* (pp. 73–87). Belmont, CA: Wadsworth Publishing Company.

Noble, J. (1978). *Beautiful, also, are the souls of my black sisters.* Englewood Cliffs, NJ: Prentice Hall.

Norton, A. J., & Moorman, J. E. (1987). Current trends in marriage and divorce among American women. *Journal of Marriage and the Family, 49,* 3–14.

Reiss, I. (1971). Premarital sexual permissiveness among negroes and whites. In R. Staples (Ed.), *The black family* (pp. 127–130). Belmont, CA: Wadsworth.

Rubin, Z. (1970). Measurement of romantic love. *Journal of Personality and Social Psychology, 6,* 265–273.

Singh, B. K. (1980). Trends in attitudes toward premarital sexual relations. *Journal of Marriage and the Family, 42,* 387–393.

Spanier, G., & Glick, P. (1980). Mate selection differentials between whites and blacks in the United States. *Social Forces, 58,* 726–738.

Sparrow, K. H. (1987). *Dating and mating partners among single black professional women.* Paper presented at annual meeting of the Mid-South Sociological Association, Memphis, TN.

Sparrow, K. H. (1991). Factors in mate selection for single black professional women. *Free Inquiry in Creative Sociology, 19,* 103–109.

Staples, R. (1978). Race, liberalism, conservatism, and premarital sexual permissiveness: A biracial comparison. *Journal of Marriage and the Family, 40,* 733–742.

Staples, R. (1981). *The world of black singles.* Westport, CT: Greenwood Press.

Staples, R. (1992). Black and white: Love and marriage interracial relationships: A convergence of desire and opportunity. In E. F. Borgatta & M. L. Borgatta (Eds.), *Encyclopedia of Sociology* (pp. 968–974). New York: Macmillan.

Tucker, M. B., & Mitchell-Kerran, C. (1990). New trends in black American interracial marriage: The social structural context. *Journal of Marriage and the Family, 52,* 209–218.

Weinberg, M., & Williams, C. (1988). Black sexuality: A test of two theories. *The Journal of Sex Research, 25,* 197–218.

Wilson, W. J. (1987). *The truly disadvantaged: The inner city, the underclass and public policy.* Chicago: University of Chicago Press.

Winch, R. F. (1971). *The modern family.* New York: Holt Press.

Zelnick, M., & Shah, F. K. (1983). First intercourse among young Americans. *Family Planning Perspectives, 15,* 64–70.

Zinn, M., & Eitzen, D. (1987). *Diversity in American families.* New York: Harper & Row.

Zollar, A., & Williams, J. S. (1992). The relative educational attainment and occupational prestige of black spouses and life satisfaction. *The Western Journal of Black Studies, 16,* 57–63.

CHAPTER 5

Mothering and Parenting Styles

EURNESTINE BROWN

When I have extended myself beyond my reach and come toppling humpty-dumpty down on my face in full view of a scornful world, I have returned to my mother to be liberated by her one more time. To be reminded by her that although I had to compromise with Life, even Life had no right to beat me to the ground, to batter my teeth into my throat, to make me knuckle down and call it Uncle. My mother raised me, and then freed me.

—MAYA ANGELOU

The socialization of children by African American mothers has often been explored. One of the primary goals of parenting is to rear competent children who thrive in the society within which they live. Thus, the question of how African American mothers socialize their children to become competent members of their ethnic group and of society continues to be both timely and fundamental. African American mothers use a variety of developmental, contextual and culturally specific methods to parent and socialize their children. Their parenting style is not unidimensional but rather multidimensional, characterized by a dynamic and evolving approach to child rearing. These child-rearing and parenting styles range from, but are not limited to, the "no nonsense" (discipline), the "grandma hands" (healing), the "mother love" (nurturant), the "omnipotent" (savior) and finally the "sisterly" (teacher) style. Historically, African American women have been surrogate mothers, nannies, "aunties" and grandmothers to generations of all of America's children. African American mothers have reared, nurtured and disciplined their children and the children of others. Their parenting style has helped to shape and polish the foundation of family life in the United States. African American mothers of the twenty-first century are different from but very similar to African American mothers of the past.[1]

Phoenix and Woollett (1991) describe mothering as the "daily management of children's lives and the daily care provided for them . . . the intensity and emotional closeness of the idealized mother-child relationship as well as the notions of mothers being responsible for the fostering of good child development" (p. 6). Darling and Steinberg (1993) have defined parenting styles as "a constellation of attitudes toward the child that are communicated to the child that, taken together, create an emotional climate in which the parent's behaviors are expressed" (p. 488). This emotional climate has often been researched and measured through the domains of warmth and control. Warmth and control are expressed through parameters of affection, emotional display and availability, tone of voice, verbal and nonverbal gestures, sensitivity and responsivity, proximity, flexibility, and limit setting, to name a few. African American mothers demonstrate a variety of mothering and parenting styles to help guide their children toward optimal development in all arenas of life.

In a study of relations between parenting styles and early childhood social competence, Brown (1992) asked 80 urban African American mothers of preschoolers between 3 and 5 years of age the following open-ended questions: "How have you learned how to become a parent?" and "What do you feel children need most from their parents?" All of the mothers were between 19 and 45 years of age ($M = 26.4$ years); the majority were single and most had attained a high school education or attended community college. Mothers listed other African American women, that is, their mothers, sisters or grandmothers as the primary sources for learning how to become a parent (47 percent). This response was followed by learning: (1) day by day and from experience (40 percent); (2) naturally ("it comes naturally") (8 percent); (3) books and other printed materials (3 percent); and (4) prayer (2 percent). Love (81 percent), support and comfort (13 percent) and attention (7 percent) were the top three responses reported by the mothers concerning what children need most from their parents.

This chapter examines some of the determinants and functions of maternal parenting practices in African American families. An ecological and cultural perspective is presented. One of the primary objectives of this chapter is to discuss individual variations in maternal parenting style demonstrated by African American women. Maternal parenting styles may be influenced by a variety of factors and contexts including maternal age, education, parity, family structure and socioeconomic status, as well as by both cultural and societal goals and values. Emphasis is placed on presenting general patterns of parental style and competence as well as those aspects of parental competence that previous research has found to be influenced by culture and context. The premise for this chapter is that African American women do not engage in "singular" parenting styles and practices, but rather multiple styles and practices that reflect both a sociocultural and a personal perspective (McAdoo, 1988).

HISTORICAL AND CULTURAL OVERVIEW OF PARENTING BY AFRICAN AMERICAN WOMEN

Historically, research on mothering and parenting by African American women has operated within a deficit or comparative framework. However, ethnic researchers have long recognized the importance of examining African American families within culturally sensitive–based research paradigms (Allen, 1978; Hill, 1971; Staples, 1986; Young, 1974). More current research continues to recognize the existence of diversity within and across African American families (Allen, Spencer, & Brookins, 1985; Harrison, Wilson, Pine, Chan, & Burriel, 1990; Hunter, 1992; McAdoo, 1988; McLoyd, 1990; McLoyd & Wilson, 1991; Willie, 1991). This updated research operates within a cultural-ecological framework that highlights the role of context in development. It contrasts the majority of past research on African American mothers and their families, especially research on low-income families, that has erroneously assumed homogeneity. This more recent research on parenting among African American women also recognizes that past studies have often confounded race and social class. Socioeconomic status is a marker variable that relates to the resources and environmental context in which the mother and child exist, but does not offer explanatory power itself (Franklin & Franklin, 1985; Garcia-Coll, 1990; McLoyd, 1990; Sudarkasa, 1988). In addition, these categories do not have the same meaning across minority and majority cultures (Dodson, 1988; Harrison, Serafica, & McAdoo, 1984). Individual variations exist within and across African American families, and are not limited to socioeconomic strata.

Further, this more recent research recognizes the importance and uniqueness of the sociostructural context in which African American parents in the United States live (Harrison et al., 1984; McLoyd, 1990; McLoyd & Wilson, 1991; Ogbu, 1981, 1985; Scott-Jones & LeGall-Nelson, 1986). The sociocultural history of African Americans in America has a unique effect on establishing the context of parenting. The parenting styles demonstrated by African American mothers as well as fathers are as much a function of the social milieus in which they exist as a function of their personal beliefs and goals. African American women have often been prevented or only allowed limited access to partaking either economically or institutionally in all of the roles of the American society (Burgess, 1994; Peters, 1988; Scott-Jones & LeGall-Nelson, 1986).

As can be expected, there are multiple pathways to the development of "optimal" parenting skills that relate to "optimal" child competence (McAdoo, 1988; McLoyd, 1990; Ogbu, 1985). Context and culture play very important roles in defining "optimal" and/or "successful" development for all families, especially for African American women and their families. An important goal of parenting is to help children develop competencies that complement those in their culture (Allen et al., 1985; Hale-Benson, 1986; Laosa, 1981; Ogbu, 1985; Peters, 1988; Powell, 1983). It is through the parenting process that culturally appropriate and inappropriate ways of thinking and behaving are transmitted.

For most African American families the transference of traditions, values and beliefs, that is, socialization, includes an emphasis on collective responsibility and cooperativeness, unity and spirituality (Allen, 1978; Franklin & Boyd-Franklin, 1985; Hill, 1993; Nobles, 1974). More importantly, most African Americans tend to be *bicultural* (Allen, 1978; Laosa, 1981; McAdoo-Pipes, 1988; Valentine, 1971, as cited in Powell, 1983; Young, 1974). They have the "ability to function optimally in two cultural contexts, and to switch their repertoire of behavior appropriately and adaptatively as called forth by the situation" (Laosa, 1977, p. 29). This biculturalism has a unique effect on parenting.

For African American mothers, parenting practices and styles are often defined by context and culture. Context takes on an all-encompassing quality and includes, but is not limited to, physical, financial, emotional, psychological, community and societal resources. Bronfenbrenner's (1979) ecological model of development emphasizes understanding development in context. This ecological perspective focuses on interrelations among the individual and his or her various environmental systems (e.g., family, church, peers, community, school, and legal and social services). Four layers of context are delineated in Bronfenbrenner's (1979) ecological model. The *microsystem* is the child and his or her immediate environment, which includes the family, peer, church, health and community/neighborhood systems. For African American mothers and children this inner layer helps to set the structure (protective/fostering or inhibitive/restrictive) for parenting competence. The *mesosystem* includes the interrelations among the child and his or her immediate environmental systems. For example, support systems from family, friends and coworkers influence child development and parental competence. The *exosystem* consists of social systems such as the workplace, education structure, neighborhood conditions, extended family and friends, social welfare services and legal services. All of these systems impinge upon the structure and competence of parenting. Historically, African American women have had to work to help support and provide resources for their families. Again, it is not uncommon for African American women of today to parent and/or socialize the children of others along with their own (i.e., African American women continue to work as domestic workers or nannies). Negative conditions in the work environment (relations with supervisors, coworkers, institutionalized racism, etc.), stress; fatigue; lack of resources; and inferior food, housing; and education systems may impinge on the African American woman's ability to parent in an effective and sensitive manner. Finally, the *macrosystem* refers to the attitudes, values, customs, beliefs and ideologies of the culture and society. African American individuals tend to be bicultural. Our parenting styles tend to reflect this biculturality. For African American parents, the values of both cultures (African and Euro-American) influence the attitudes, beliefs, customs and behaviors that are transmitted to our children. Borrowing from the Afrocentric perspective of Nobles and Goddard (1984), for African American families, parenting reflects being "African in 'nature' and American in 'nurture'" (p. 39). For both the parent and child, development is active and ever-changing. Context and culture texturize the ecology in which African American mothers, children and families are embedded. Research presented herein reflects some of the complex interactions among parenting styles and behaviors by African American women and gender, culture, ethnicity, economic status and society.

TRANSITION TO MOTHERHOOD

The transition to parenthood can be a challenge for most women. This transition brings increased demands on individual and family resources (economic and emotional). Social networks, including family, friends and the larger community, can serve as a mechanism to guide, support and help navigate its members through major life transitions, including parenthood. Furthermore, because African Americans are more likely to bear children outside the confines of marriage in low-income environments, and across incomes African Americans are more likely to live in nonnuclear households, the transition to parenthood tends to involve negotiations and the redefining of roles within complex household and kinship structures, across varied generational lines as well as within marital/partner relationships (Brown, Hunter, & Brownell, 1996). This extension and intensity of involvement of kin, friends and community in a woman's transition to parenthood likely varies as a function of economic status, maternal age and marital status. Unfortunately, research on the transition to parenthood has typically been conducted within the confounds of conventional nuclear family structures and marital/childbearing patterns, with an emphasis on changes in the marital dyad (see Cowan, Cowan, Hemming, & Miller, 1991). One exception has been the work on adolescent parenthood; however, this work is focused on examining the impact of an early transition to parenthood on developmental outcomes for adolescent mothers (education, work, poverty) and their offspring (Burton, 1990; Furstenberg, Brooks-Gunn, & Morgan, 1987; Stevens, 1988). Two critical contextual categories that influence the African American woman's transition to motherhood and the parenting role are presented below. The first, *economic resources*, encompasses poverty, single-headed households and wealth. The second, *maternal age*, encompasses early or adolescent parenting and parenting in the later years, that is, 30-plus years of age.

Economic Resources: Poverty, Single Parent–Headed Household and Wealth

Poverty. Poverty has a unique and challenging effect on parenting. Numerous aspects of mothering and parenting style are affected by poverty, including warmth and nurturance, disciplinary practices and harshness, irritability and consistency (Brown et al., 1996). Most findings point to the disruptive, debilitating effects of poverty on parenting (Garcia-Coll, 1990; Longfellow, Zelkowitz, & Saunders, 1982; McLoyd, 1990; McLoyd & Wilson, 1991). The mechanism hypothesized to mediate this relationship is parental psychological distress engendered by chronic stress, frequent negative life events, and other frustrations attending poverty (McLoyd, 1990). African American women are disproportionately likely to begin parenthood and rear their children in poverty or near poverty (Duncan & Rodgers, 1988; Farley & Allen, 1987; Huston, 1991). During the 1980s and 1990s the proportion of families with children living in poverty increased; this pattern has been most pronounced for African Americans (Farley & Allen, 1987; U.S. Bureau of the Census, 1991). In 1979, 40 percent of African American children lived below the poverty line; by the mid-eighties, 44 percent were poor (U.S. Bureau of the Census, 1990). Currently, 45 percent of African American children are poor, over half of whom are at least 125 percent below poverty level (United States Bureau of the Census, 1992). In addition to the increased risk of poverty, African American children stay poor longer than non-African American children (Duncan & Rodgers, 1988).

Single Parent–Headed Households. Single parenthood can be an outcome of many different types of circumstances. African American women may be single parents due to nonmarriage, divorce or widowhood. Single parenthood may also be the result of personal choice. That is, an increased number of African American women have made a proactive choice to parent a child without a male partner. African American women may choose to become biological or adoptive parents. Although African American women have often "adopted" children, both kin and nonkin, adoption by single African American women (and men) has increased over the past few years. Moreover, the decision to become a single parent is not dictated solely by socioeconomic status. African American women of all socioeconomic status brackets enter single parenthood due to a variety of factors, some by choice and others by circumstance. Unfortunately for all concerned, the transition to single parenthood often results in educational and income losses that may push African American women and children into poverty (Duncan & Rodgers, 1988).

Far too often for African American children, African American mothers serve as both mother and father. Fifty-nine and a half percent of African American children under the age of 6 are raised in female-headed households, and 54.1 percent under the age of 18 years are raised under the same circumstances. This is in comparison to 32.5 percent of African American children under 6 and 36 percent under the age of 18 years being raised in two-parent households (U.S. Bureau of the Census, 1991). However, even when African American children live in two-parent households throughout their childhood, they are at greater risk for poverty than white children who spend their entire childhood in single-parent households (Duncan & Rodgers, 1988). The majority of young African American children (under 5 years of age) are in low-to-moderate-income African American families. In addition, the rate of nonmarital childbearing, divorce and separation, and the comparatively low rate of remarriage among African American parents, have increased the likelihood that African American children will spend some part of their childhood years in a single-parent household headed primarily by women (Bumpass, 1984; Farley & Allen, 1987; Hofferth, 1985). The majority of children in female-headed households are poor.

It is also important to remember that, although not reported, primarily because of the existing Aid to Dependent Families (AFDC) requirements in most states, biological as well as nonbiological males often function as father figures for African American children. Research that explores the role and influence of child rearing by nonbiological or noncustodial African American males is needed.

Wealth. The proportion of African American women acquiring professional and advanced education and having careers continues to rise. This increase has contributed to a greater proportion of African American families achieving middle- and upper-income status (U.S. Bureau of the Census, 1991). Approximately 7.4 percent of African American families earn more than $50,000 a year (U.S. Bureau of the Census, 1992). This group of upper-middle-income African American women consists of both single and married women.

Conner-Edwards and Edwards (1988) described three types of families that have emerged as the African American middle class. The first type, the nouveau middle class, acknowledges the existence of racial discrimination and its consequences. However, individuals within this group redirect their energies toward the development of a psychologically healthy and positive racial and ethnic identity (Helm, 1987, as cited in Conner-Edwards & Edwards, 1988). Individuals in the second and third types of middle-class families, both untitled, harbor negative feelings about racial issues. Individuals in the second family type are able to use those feelings in a positive manner for further advancement and success. Individuals in the third middle-class family type maintain hostile feelings toward the dominant society but are determined to become successful despite racial discrimination. African American women play important roles in all three family types. Each family type has developed an acceptance of the dominant culture as well as a strong belief in the sense of self, empowerment and the importance of one's culture or "blackness."

The psychological complexity of being an African American woman and well-to-do (e.g., upper-middle class and/or upper-income economic status) creates added opportunities and challenges for African American mothers. For example, being of an upper-income status affords access to quality health care, day care and schools, but may also limit access to a culturally validating environment (e.g., a loss of connection from other African Americans mainly because of residential locations). These African American mothers may also experience an increase in psychological problems (guilt, and a sense of insecurity and anxiety in having to maintain their status at home, in the community and at work). Both poverty and wealth create unique socialization and parenting challenges for African American mothers.

Although a few historical examinations of the African American middle-class family have been conducted, most operated from a pro-assimilation or cultural-deficit perspective (see Frazier, 1957). However, McAdoo (1992) examined cultural patterns of economically secure African American families from within an ecological and culturally sensitive framework. Two major hypotheses were examined and supported: (1) the socialization of children in African American families differs from that of other families because of their nonsupportive wider environment; and (2) the extended kin network facilitates upward mobility. Demographics for her sample were as follows: solid middle class (31 percent), upper-middle class (42 percent), and lower-middle class (9 percent, N = 305). Sixty-six percent of the families reported receiving a great deal of help from their extended family in their upward mobility. In fact, the extended family was seen as the most important source of help with child care, financial aid and emotional support. In addition, these families did not separate themselves from their extended kin to be upwardly mobile, nor from their community once they achieved a higher status. Although family mobility was based primarily on the father's income and education level, mobility could not have been maintained without the mother's additional income. In most cases, the mother's employment was due to low family income, otherwise they were more inclined to stay at home with their children. Thus, for a majority of African American mothers, providing financial support to their families continues to be a fundamental role in acquiring and maintaining economic stability.

Maternal Age

Given that an African American woman tends to begin the mothering process earlier and continue this process for longer periods than an Anglo American woman, maternal age and parity, that is the number of children she has borne, are primary in understanding motherhood and parenting.

Early Parenting. Adolescent pregnancy and parenting now exist in almost all racial, geographic and socioeconomic spheres (Children's Defense Fund, 1993; National Center for Health Statistics, 1991; Rosenheim & Testa, 1992). However, adolescent parenting continues to affect disproportionately African American girls and low-income children of color (Children's Defense Fund, 1993). Further, a high proportion of adolescents who become pregnant are unmarried and tend to remain so thereafter. Findings by Furstenberg, Brooks-Gunn, and Morgan (1987) suggest that African American adolescent mothers who marry into financially unstable unions fare less well than those who remain unmarried. More important, adolescent mothers who remain single generally fare less well than their single counterparts who remain childless until adulthood.

When discussing adolescent parents, it is also important to note the statistical composition of adolescent mothers. Although the overall birth rate to African American adolescents is double that of white adolescents, births to white and Latino adolescents have shown a steady increase (7 percent and 6 percent, respectively) while rates for African American adolescents have remained unchanged (Children's Defense Fund, 1993). For example, in 1989, white teens accounted for nearly two-thirds of the total births to adolescents; African American adolescents accounted for less than one-third of the births. However, African American teens accounted for more than half of the births to girls younger than 15 years of age (Children's Defense Fund, 1993). Thus, the rates for "younger" African American adolescents continue to be of primary concern and alarm for African American families.

In contrast to adult mothers, the adolescent mother is undergoing a dual developmental transition, first from adolescence to adulthood, and second to parenthood (Sadler, 1987). The first process is often difficult for most adolescents. The demands of parenthood may present a situation in which the adolescent doesn't successfully complete either process, successfully completes both processes or only successfully completes one process (Osofsky, Peebles, & Hann, 1993).

Although the early research on adolescent parenthood suffered from major methodological problems which increased the difficulty of teasing out effects due to maternal age and/or maternal sensitivity, responsivity and skill (Phipps-Yonas, 1980), more methodologically sound studies have arrived at similar results. Most of this literature seems to suggest that if the mother receives early and comprehensive care during her pregnancy, the medical risks for neonatal outcomes are reduced (Baldwin &

Cain, 1980; Broman, 1981; Phipps-Yonas, 1980; Wise & Grossman, 1980). However, rates of early prenatal care for African American adolescent and adult mothers are less than optimal. Only 3 out of every 5 African American babies born to African American mothers receive early prenatal care, compared to 4 out of every 5 white babies (Children's Defense Fund, 1993). Thus, for African American women, regardless of maternal age, inadequate or lack of prenatal care remains a significant neonatal and parenting risk factor.

Current research suggests that, on average, adolescent mothers do not exhibit the same quality of parenting with their infants as do adult mothers (Garcia-Coll, Hoffman, & Oh, 1987; Landy, Clark, Schubert, & Jillings, 1983; Osofsky & Osofsky, 1971). However, it is also clear that not all adolescent mothers are at risk for parenting failure (Brown, 1992; Buccholz, Ester, & Gol, 1986; Burton, 1990; Furstenberg et al., 1987; Geronimus, 1992; Sadler, 1987; Wassermann, Rauh, Brunelli, & Garcia-Castro, 1990). Some adolescents make successful transitions to adulthood and to the parenting role—that is, they continue to develop self-autonomy as individuals and are able to provide their children with an optimal socioemotional environment (Buccholz et al., 1986; Burton, 1990; Furstenberg et al., 1987; Phipps-Yonas, 1980; Sadler, 1987). Current research has begun to focus on identifying means by which adolescent parents can best adapt and cope with the demands of parenthood. This perspective is in drastic contrast to the initial view of adolescent mothers being ill-equipped to support themselves or to nurture a new generation of children (Furstenberg, 1976).

In particular, research by Burton and her colleagues (Burton, 1990; Burton & Dilworth-Anderson, 1991; Burton, Dilworth-Anderson, & Merriwether-de Vries, 1995; Hagestad & Burton, 1986) presents an alternative view of adolescent parenting for African American girls and their mothers. Burton's (1990) longitudinal work highlighted the sociocultural context of early parenting. For particular communities, early childbearing may be perceived as a viable option that fosters individual growth, family continuity and cultural survival in an environment that offers few other avenues for developmental enhancement. Burton (1990) notes that early parenting is not condoned in African American families. However, for some economically disadvantaged, multigenerational African American families, early childbearing reflects an alternative life-course strategy rather than a nonnormative life event. Becoming a parent helps to project one's worth and esteem, both individually and in the community. Moreover, grandmothers and other female kin play essential roles in the socialization of children born to adolescent mothers. Grandmothers are the primary socializing agents or caregivers. Social support (emotional and financial) is more often received from other females than from males. Thus, for her sample of impoverished African American girls and their families, early parenting plays an important role in establishing the context of their life trajectories.

Nevertheless, despite this refocus, existing research also shows adolescent or early parenthood to be correlated with decreased education and employment opportunities, welfare dependency, increased parity and higher divorce rates (Alan Guttmacher Institute, 1989; Baldwin & Cain, 1980; Furstenberg et al., 1987; Goddard & Cavil, 1989; Phipps-Yonas, 1980; Scott-Jones, Roland, & White, 1989). In addition, adolescent parenthood has been tied to strengthening the cycle of poverty and the intergenerational cycle of adolescent pregnancy for low-income families (Scott-Jones et al., 1989). Further, this research has shown adolescent parenting to be correlated with low achievement in their children (Baldwin & Cain, 1980; Brooks-Gunn & Furstenberg, 1986; Furstenberg et al., 1987). It is important for future research to clarify individual differences in adolescent parenting, and in particular how adolescents may promote social competence in their offspring.

Parenting in Later Life. The prevalence of first-time mothers who are 30-plus years of age has continued to rise (U.S. Bureau of the Census, 1991). Although this trend has been found for both single and married women, few studies have explored the dynamics of parenting for African American women and their families. An increased number of single and married African American women are beginning the parenting process for the first time after age 30. Many single, professional African American women have chosen to have a child without a male partner, either biologically or through adoption.

Although recent studies have begun to focus on the psychological implications of parenthood in later life, the majority of the initial studies focused on delineating the medical risks associated with pregnancy after age 30. Pregnancy for women after age 35 introduces increased risk of pregnancy and delivery complications and birth defects. For example, children born to women 35 years of age or older have increased likelihood of being born with a chromosomal anomaly such as Down's syndrome. However, conclusions similar to those generated concerning medical and health complications for adolescent mothers have also been stated for older mothers. That is, maternal age per se may not be the culprit that leads to risk, but rather maternal health factors such as nutrition, stress, rate of disease and emerging health risks such as hypertension, diabetes and alcoholism; environmental pollutants may also contribute to difficulties in pregnancy and birth.

Research that examines popular perceptions of when it is appropriate to start a family (i.e., for a woman to bear her first child) has also begun to be conducted. Coleman and Brown (1994) found that in a southeastern sample of young adults (undergraduates at a state college), most held the perception that 24 years of age was ideal for a woman to bear her first child. More specifically, 53 percent felt that the 20 to 25 age range was ideal for first-time childbirth; 42 percent reported that 26 to 30 years of age was ideal; and only 5 percent perceived the 31 to 35 age range as being ideal. However, respondents indicated that women who have children after 35 years of age tend to be more sensitive, nurturing, and tolerant as compared to mothers younger than 35 years of age. Thirty-two and 39 percent, respectively, felt that the main effect on children born to parents after age 35 would be better parenting for the child, and generally a good experience because these children would be wanted. New research has begun to highlight the importance of "wantedness" and the quality of the mother-child relationship during the early years (Weller, Eberstein, & Bailey, 1987).

Finally, fertility plays an important role in defining motherhood and parenthood for professional and older women. Although equivocal results have been generated, it appears that African American families are experiencing an increase in infertility rates, especially for older (30-plus) and more financially secure African American women (Burns, 1995). For example, the National Center for Health Statistics (1991) reported a lack of difference in infertility rates between African American and Anglo American women in the 25 to 44 year old age group. However, other sources, such as RESOLVE, report higher infertility problems among African American women; 1.5 times higher, according to Burns (1995). Infertility may be one of a number of problems that are faced by African American couples but often not discussed. Further, for African American women, links between infertility, chronic infections and fibroid tumors have been generated. African American women are at an increased risk of developing fibroid tumors compared to their Anglo American peers (50 to 75 percent for African American women, 38 percent for Anglo American women). Again, maternal health factors play an important role in understanding the African American woman's transition to motherhood and the parenting role.

In summary, multiple contextual, psychological, economic, cultural and health factors influence the parenting process for African American women. The following sections discuss variations in parenting style and attitudes exhibited by African American women.

MATERNAL PARENTING STYLE IN AFRICAN AMERICAN FAMILIES

The domain of parental styles and attitudes is an area that has waxed and waned over the past 20 years. However, it is a domain that continues to generate much discussion and research. Questions concerning how parents parent, what is parenting, and what are the optimal and suboptimum styles and attitudes mothers engage in to socialize their children have dominated much of the literature. Current exploration of parenting style and attitudes has been expanded to include parental beliefs and behaviors as well as aspects of positive and negative parenting (Darling & Steinberg, 1993; MacDonald & Parke, 1984; Petit & Bates, 1989).

However, it is apparent that much is yet to be known in our understanding of the familial context of parenting and mothering styles demonstrated by African American women. One of the primary contributors to this gap in knowledge stems from the paradigm of exploration, that is, the exploration of African American mothers, parenting and children from a deficit or cultural comparative framework versus an ecological or culturally sensitive framework (see McLoyd & Randolph, 1986). Most of the literature on African American families has focused on what African American mothers were *not* doing in comparison to Anglo American mothers or on the negative implications of their behaviors with their children. Little research has focused on identifying the positive or proactive attributes African American mothers and fathers demonstrate with their children during the socialization process. (Note: classic works by African American authors [Hill, 1971; Stack, 1974; Staples, 1986; Willie, 1991] that highlighted family strengths and competencies existed, but were not well known in the psychology arena.)

Another contributing factor is that African American women and families are ever-changing; thus the parenting styles and attitudes demonstrated by African American women in the 1960s may contrast with those demonstrated by mothers in the 1980s, and in the twenty-first century. Regardless of style changes, we do know definitively that individual variations in parenting style and attitudes can have long-term consequences for a child's social, emotional and cognitive development (see McAdoo &

McAdoo, 1985; Maccoby & Martin, 1983). For example, parental warmth and control have been linked consistently to young children's security of attachment, peer social competence, prosocial behavior, self-esteem and moral orientation (Baumrind, 1971; Baumrind & Black, 1967; Radke-Yarrow, Zahn-Waxler, & Chapman, 1983). Thus, for all parents, regardless of ethnicity, understanding parental styles and attitudes is paramount to understanding growth and development in families.

Dimensions of warmth such as affiliation or affection and dimensions of control such as restrictiveness or hostility have often been explored to index parental style and practices both generally and in African American families specifically. Warmth has been described in many ways, such as emotional affection and tenderness (e.g., hugs, kisses, positive tactile stimulation); parental concern, love and compassion; contingent responsivity and sensitivity (e.g., anticipating children's feelings, concern for their welfare, comforting, helping); acceptance, approval and reinforcement (e.g., physical or verbal); and positive regard and involvement. Maternal control has been used to refer to parental structuring or limit setting, restrictiveness/flexibility, disciplinary practices, punishment style, consistency, demandedness, hostility and intrusiveness, to name a few. The issue of parental control continues to be addressed in the literature. Too much or too little control seems to have unfavorable outcomes in most children.

As previously stated, research on the parenting styles of African American mothers has frequently been flawed as well as mixed. For example, some authors have found African American parents to be warm, controlling but nonrejecting, and supportive (Bartz & Levine, 1978; Baumrind, 1972; Taylor, in press), while others have found them to be punitive, harsh and using power assertion (Blau, 1981). At first glance these results may seem contradictory; however, these results demonstrate the heterogeneity in parental style among African American parents. These results also highlight the need for further exploration of individual differences in African American parental style and its relationship to the development of childhood social competence (McLoyd & Wilson, 1991). Research that examines parenting style variations within as well as across socioeconomic brackets for African American parents continues to be lacking.

Further, in spite of these flaws, a few ecologically based studies have identified several patterns of competent parenting styles that relate to childhood socioemotional development. Dimensions of parental style that consistently have been found to characterize socialization by African

American mothers include: (1) nurturance/warmth; (2) control and discipline, which may include inconsistency and physical punishment; (3) respect for authority and obedience; (4) the encouragement of independence, early maturity, achievement, self-confidence and noncompetitiveness; (5) value for interpersonal relations in both genders (Allen, 1978; Bartz & Levine, 1978; Hale-Benson, 1986; Holliday & Curbeam, 1981; Kelley, Power, & Wimbush, 1990; McAdoo, 1988; Ogbu, 1985; Silverstein & Krate, 1975; Washington, 1988; Young, 1974). As might be expected, the socialization patterns emphasized by African American mothers complement those fostered in the culture, which include a focus on collective responsibility, cooperation, interdependence and spirituality (Franklin & Boyd-Franklin, 1985; Nobles, 1974).

The following section provides an overview of a few dimensions of parenting and mothering styles found to characterize African American women during the socialization of their children. (Note: this overview is not exhaustive and is meant to provide a beginning base for understanding socialization patterns among African American women. See also Allen et al., 1985; McAdoo-Pipes, 1988.) Warmth, control (including consistency in control), the encouragement of independence, and gender relations are discussed below.

Warmth/Nurturance

Although African American mothers demonstrate a fair amount of nurturance, parental nurturance has often been overlooked (Ogbu, 1985; Silverstein & Krate, 1975; Taylor & Macmillan, 1988). Warmth has been found to be important, especially during the infancy period when great amounts of nurturance and affection are expressed by African American mothers (Taylor, in press). Taylor (in press) and his colleagues have consistently found maternal affiliation to be an important indicator of parental competence in African American parents. Maternal warmth and nurturance have also been found to be significant factors in the promotion of childhood social competence. For example, strong positive relations were found between maternal affiliation and security of attachment in African American infants (McKeithen, 1976, as cited in Taylor & Macmillan, 1988). Brown (1992) also found similar results for slightly older African American children. That is, mothers who demonstrated high levels of warmth with their preschoolers were more likely to have preschoolers who were more socially competent with their peers. Research that further explores as well as highlights the roles of nurturance, warmth and affiliation in African American families is needed.

Control and Disciplinary Practices

In contrast to parental nurturance, the disciplinary practices of African American mothers have been studied repeatedly. Although past research on African American parent-child socialization has found African American parents to be restrictive and to employ physical punishment, multiple confounds have often existed between socioeconomic status and parenting style. For example, low-income African Americans have been compared to middle-income whites (Allen, 1978). Furthermore, the often-cited strict discipline style or "no-nonsense" style of African American parents has been shown to be functional and adaptive (Peters, 1988; Young, 1974). Silverstein and Krate (1975), Kelley and her colleagues (1990) and McLoyd (1990) have noted that this strict discipline style, including threats and punishment, is meant to protect the child from dangerous external forces such as drugs, fights or racial encounters. The use of physical punishment is meant to discourage emotional dependency while encouraging independence and self-reliance (Ogbu, 1985; Silverstein & Krate, 1975). Moreover, although low-income parents have been found to be more likely to use punishment as a form of control, punishment is not associated with rejection of the child or with love withdrawal (Silverstein & Krate, 1975).

In addition, Peters (1988), in her classic, ecologically oriented descriptive study, examined relations between parental discipline and early childhood socioemotional development in two-parent, working and middle-income African American families. Most of the mothers in the study emphasized control through obedience; however, these mothers did not view obedience negatively. Mothers reported that obedience serves different functions. Thus, although low-income African American parents may emphasize obedience, they do not socialize blind obedience.

Similarly, Kelley (1989; Kelley et al., 1990) found that single versus married African American mothers were more likely to have a parent-orientation versus child-orientation attitude toward child rearing. That is, rule-setting, obedience, manners and politeness were emphasized. Single parents also reported restrictive child-rearing attitudes. Kelley (1989) suggested that this orientation might be a function of (1) economic pressures, (2) low social support, or (3) psychological stress. More importantly, she found that 68 percent of the mothers showed a combination orientation. Thus, a high degree of diversity in maternal parenting style was found in a low-income population.

Consistency in Control

Research on parental control has also examined whether parents are consistent in their reactions to their children's transgressions. Environmental and emotional stresses, as well as poverty, have been linked to inconsistency in disciplinary practices and to the use of physical punishment (McLoyd, 1990; Silverstein & Krate, 1975). For example, Silverstein & Krate (1975) found that on some occasions low-income African American mothers were harsh and inflexible but on other occasions they paid little attention to disciplining their children. This inconsistency in parental discipline was also found in Young's (1974) sample of low-income mothers. In addition, Longfellow and his colleagues (1982) found that mothers who were highly stressed and depressed were less likely to respond to their children's needs and more likely to be hostile and domineering with their children. Moreover, these mothers were more likely to yell and hit their children, and less likely to use reasoning with them. Further, these mothers were more likely to place high demands and household responsibilities on their children.

An interesting finding from both Silverstein and Krate (1975) and Longfellow et al. (1982) was that mothers in both samples were aware of and regretted the times when they were impatient, nonnurturing and uninvolved with their children. Mothers who are faced with the immediate demands of their family and of survival may have less energy to cope with the ever-present demands of parenting. It may be that the correlations of socioeconomic status (e.g., high stress, few resources) exert a stronger hold on parenting style, which may in turn lead to differences in childhood developmental outcomes (Garcia-Coll, 1990; McLoyd & Wilson, 1991). Thus, it seems important to examine further relations between consistency in discipline, parental style and childhood competence.

Finally, as previously mentioned, relations have been found between parental inconsistency and child gender, especially in low-income and ethnic families (McLoyd, 1990; McLoyd & Wilson, 1991; Patterson, Kupersmidt, & Vaden, 1990). Male ethnic children with parents who tend to be inconsistent are more likely to demonstrate conduct problems, including antisocial behaviors. Thus, inconsistency in parental control seems to have a powerful and salient effect on male children. These relationships warrant further exploration.

Independence Fostering

A relationship between parental style and early maturity demands and independence has been found in African American families. For example, both Ladner (1971) and Ogbu (1985) note that the encouragement of independence and self-reliance starts early in the African American child's life. They also noted that this early focus on independence encourages affiliation with the street culture.

In a classic study, Young (1974) examined parenting style in African American, low-income, urban and rural mother-child pairs. Fostering adaptive and early socioemotional and cognitive development was especially important to these mothers. Mothers in this study were highly invested in training their children to be goal-persistent while maintaining a sense of self-autonomy; to develop strategies for dealing with institutional and personal discrimination; to develop mechanisms for dealing with their membership in embedded contexts—that is, being bicultural. For ethnic children, especially African American children, being able to alternate between assertiveness and acquiescence fosters success and survival (Allen et al., 1985; Ladner, 1971; Washington, 1988; Young, 1974). Ladner (1971) noted that parental fostering of mechanisms of self-defense helps to protect low-income African American children against external as well as internal forces that might impede their survival. It also teaches children that fair play may not always be reciprocated. This emphasis on standing up for oneself can be seen as adaptive in particular sociocultural contexts, especially when it is expressed within the limits established for those contexts (Ogbu, 1985; Silverstein & Krate, 1975).

GENDER RELATIONS

African American parents tend to be egalitarian in their child-rearing practices. Peters (1988) asserted that African American parental socialization is more a function of age and competency than gender. However, Bartz & Levine (1978) found that among African American parents with only children, parents with a female child were less controlling than parents of a male child. Likewise, Blau (1981) found that low-income African American mothers expressed more discipline with their sons. She also found that working-class and middle-class African American mothers expressed significantly higher ambitions for their daughters than for their sons. Silverstein and Krate (1975) also noted that African American mothers were more controlling and assertive with their sons. It is likely that these differences in control, based on gender, have a culturally adaptive function such as preventing negative encounters with others. Although the literature on differences in parenting style as a function of gender is inconclusive (Allen et al., 1985; McLoyd, 1990), continued examination of gender differences as a function of parental style and attitudes in African American families is warranted.

MEASURING PARENTAL COMPETENCE ACROSS CULTURES

While there are unique dimensions of socialization associated with African American parenting, most of the parenting literature seems to suggest that differences in parenting style are a matter of degree or function rather than of type. For example, most parents, regardless of age or culture, demonstrate some degree of warmth and control during interactions with children. The levels displayed vary across individuals and cultural goals, for a variety of reasons, but the fundamental behaviors remain the same.

It is inappropriate to assume that a particular parenting style that produces optimal outcomes in one cultural or economic context is the optimal parenting style for all children in other cultures and subcultures (Laosa, 1981; McAdoo-Pipes, 1988; Ogbu, 1981). However, much can be learned from examining the patterns of parenting style that have been found to lead to childhood social competence. This can be accomplished without one pattern being labeled as superior to others, regardless of context. Child-rearing practices need to be evaluated with the knowledge of the environment in which the parents and children exist (Belsky, 1984; Bronfenbrenner, 1979; Maccoby & Martin, 1983; Ogbu, 1981; Peters, 1988).

Baumrind's (1967, 1970, 1971, 1972) well-established work provides a classic case for understanding parenting styles and attitudes in context. She and her colleagues (e.g., Baumrind & Black, 1967) described molar social interactions between mothers and their children. Her definitive work has found consistently that for Anglo Americans, high parental warmth and high parental control lead to social competence in children and young adolescents. Baumrind identified three parenting styles: authoritarian (low warmth/responsiveness and high control/demandedness), authoritative (high warmth and high control [maturity demands, consistent in discipline demands]) and permissive (high warmth and low control). These three classifications were based on her observations of young children during nursery school, and observations of the same children when they were 8 and 9 years of age. (Note: she has continued to observe these children as adolescents and young adults; see Baumrind, 1991a,b.)

Baumrind's work can be used to illustrate how patterns in parenting style that have been found to lead to childhood social competence in one culture (Anglo American) can be applied to understand the development of social competence in another culture (African American). Again, this can be accomplished without one pattern being labeled as superior and the other as inferior. For example, the parenting style labeled "authoritarian" by Baumrind (1972) related to negative outcomes in Anglo, educated middle-income families. But, in African American educated, lower-middle-income families this style had a beneficial effect. Girls were observed to be self-assertive, dominant and independent, even though the labeling of the parents as "authoritarian" denoted a negative parenting style in the original classification system. African American families also scored higher on discouraging infantile dependence and lower on paternal rejection. These families were authoritarian in their expectations of behavior but they were spontaneous and warm with their daughters. Thus, African American parents were not so much rejecting their daughters as training them to take care of themselves from an early age (McAdoo-Pipes, 1988; Silverstein & Krate, 1975). African American boys were expected to behave in a mature fashion, and their fathers were more likely to encourage independent behavior.

Similarly, Bartz and Levine (1978) investigated the relations between child rearing and ethnicity in African American, Chicano and Anglo families. Seven qualities of child rearing were indexed. These were: control, strictness, acceleration of development, authoritarianism, support, permissiveness and time pressure. African American parents were found to: (1) encourage autonomy and the wise use of time; (2) believe in control (expect a child to do his or her best, being strict about behaviors); (3) support egalitarianism (emphasize and respect child input); and (4) believe in providing support to their children (saying nice things, offering help when needed). Thus, African American parents did not differ from other parents in their basic orientation toward child rearing, but in the strength of their advocacy for certain practices. More importantly, African American parents were found to accomplish these goals in the context of strong emotional support. Lastly, the authors noted that the parenting style demonstrated by these African American parents (high support, high control, open communications and demands for maturity) was consistent with Baumrind's (1967) authoritative parental style.

In sum, past research has shown that further exploration of parental style and competence in African American parents is warranted. Continued research that seeks to extend our understanding of African American parenting styles by examining individual differences in maternal style is warranted.

RESEARCH AND POLICY: IMPLICATIONS AND CHALLENGES

This chapter has reviewed some of the psychological literature on parenting and mothering in African American families by African American women. The framework for this chapter has been one of highlighting the strengths as well as the challenges encountered during the parenting process. It is clear that African American women continue to redefine their roles as mothers and parents. This chapter closes with a brief review of critical issues and questions that continue to affect the African American woman's ability to mother and parent her children.

First, we live in a time of heightened poverty for all, especially for women and children. Increases in homelessness, domestic violence, child abuse, the placement of children in foster care, violence against women and children, juvenile delinquency and school dropout rates abound. The debilitating effects of poverty as well as its negative consequences (e.g., poor housing, inadequate health care, chronic stress) continue to affect African American mothers and their children disproportionately, regardless of age. These families face increases in the numbers of very young mothers with children and early grandmothers raising their grandchildren and/or great-grandchildren on limited incomes. The developmental outlook for all involved continues to be bleak. We are in need of a critical overhaul in our thinking and actions, including the value and priority we place on women and children. It is no longer acceptable to think that the optimal rearing of children will progress naturally or that it is someone else's work. National statistics on the state of children indicate otherwise. We are truly facing a crisis. Although this crisis is great, it can be turned into opportunities for positive change. One strategy to facilitate this change is for all individuals to become proactive child advocates. Helping a mother or child in need at every opportunity, or volunteering or joining organizations that support mothers and children are both viable means to proactivity. Keeping abreast of and making one's opinions known on legislation that has a positive or negative effect on the quality of life for mothers and children is another.

Second, welfare and health-reform policies continue to affect overall outcomes for women and children. An important question whose answer looms in the air is how these changes will influence the long-term welfare of African American mothers, especially adolescent mothers and their children—the future mothers and fathers of tomorrow. At one point in time, we were moving toward the recognition of individual variations in outcomes for adolescent mothers and their children, and were focusing on strategies to reduce the occurrence of a second pregnancy. However, the pendulum seems to be swinging away from this direction and back to penalizing young mothers for having children (e.g., reduced financial support and medical coverage). Although early parenting is not condoned for any young woman, in reality children continue to be born to young mothers. It is also time to reemphasize father education and responsibility, especially since statistics indicate that the majority of children born to very young mothers are fathered by adult men. Parenting is a developmental process, and all members need to be active participants. It is up to each of us to facilitate a healthy process.

Further, all women continue to struggle with the challenges of "having it all." In the nineties we have seen an increase in the number of chronic and severe health conditions associated with trying to do it all. Unfortunately, African American women tend not to have the choice of dropping out of the work environment temporarily to raise our children, or the luxury of being able to stay home as full-time caretakers and homemakers. Economics dictate their having to work to support themselves and their family, with or without a mate. The question of how African American mothers socialize their children to become competent members within their ethnic group and society continues to be both timely and fundamental.

There continues to be a strong need for information about African American mothers as defined by African American women. This volume serves as one means to this end. It is only through this process that we will reach a true understanding of the multifaceted mothering and parenting styles exhibited by African American women during the socialization of our children.

NOTES

[1] Mothers/motherhood includes all female caregivers of children and is not limited to biology.

REFERENCES

Alan Guttmacher Institute. (1989). *Teenage pregnancy in the United States: The scope of the problem and state responses.* New York: Author.

Allen, W. R. (1978). Black family research in the United States: A review, assessment and extension. *Journal of Comparative Family Studies 2,* 167–189.

Allen, W. R., Spencer, M., & Brookins, G. K. (1985). Synthesis: Black children keep on growing. In *Beginnings: The social and affective development of black children* (pp. 301–314). Hillsdale, NJ: Lawrence Erlbaum Association.

Angelou, M. (1993). In P. Bell-Scott, B. Guy-Sheftall, J.J. Royster, J. Sims-Wood, M. DeCosta-Willis, & L. P. Fultz (Eds.), *Double stitch: Black women write about mothers and daughters*. New York: Harper Perennial.

Baldwin, W., & Cain, R. (1980). The children of teenage parents. *Family Planning Perspectives, 12,* 34–43.

Bartz, K., & Levine, E. (1978). Child-rearing by black parents: A description and comparison to Anglo and Chicano parents. *Journal of Marriage and Family, 40,* 709–719.

Baumrind, D. (1967). Child care practices anteceding three patterns of preschool behavior. *Genetic Psychology Monographs, 75,* 43–88.

Baumrind, D. (1970). Socialization and instrumental competence in young children. *Young Children, 26,* 104–119.

Baumrind, D. (1971). Current patterns of parental authority. *Developmental Psychology Monograph, 4,* (1, Pt. 2).

Baumrind, D. (1972). An exploratory study of socialization effects on black children: Some black-white comparisons. *Child Development, 43,* 261–267.

Baumrind, D. (1991a). Parenting styles and adolescent development. In R. M. Lerner, A. C. Petersen, & J. Brooks-Gunn (Eds.), *Encyclopedia of adolescence* (pp. 746–758). New York: Garland Publishing.

Baumrind, D. (1991b). The influence of parenting styles on adolescent competence and substance use. *Journal of Early Adolescence, 11,* 25–95.

Baumrind, D., & Black, A. E. (1967). Socialization practices associated with dimensions of competence in preschool boys and girls. *Child Development, 38,* 291–327.

Belsky, J. (1984). The determinants of parenting: A process model. *Child Development, 55,* 83–96.

Blau, Z. (1981). *Black children/white children: Competence, socialization, and social structure.* New York: Free Press.

Broman, S. H. (1981). Long-term development of children born to teenagers. In K. Scott, T. Field, & E.G. Robertson (Eds.), *Teenage parents and their offspring*. New York: Grune & Stratton.

Bronfenbrenner, U. (1979). *The ecology of human development.* Cambridge, MA: Harvard University Press.

Brooks-Gunn, J., & Furstenberg, F. F., Jr. (1986). The children of adolescent mothers: Physical, academic, and psychological outcomes. *Developmental Review, 3,* 224–251.

Brown, E. (1992). *Black mothers and their children: Competent parenting and the promotion of childhood social skills.* Ph.D. dissertation, University of Pittsburgh.

Brown, E., Hunter, A., & Brownell, C. (1996). *Contributions to parenting attitudes and behavior among African American women rearing young infants in poverty.* Unpublished manuscript.

Buccholz, E., Ester, S., & Gol, B. (1986). More than playing house: A developmental perspective on the strengths in teenage motherhood. *American Journal of Orthopsychiatry, 56,* 347–359.

Bumpass, L. L. (1984). Children and marital disruption: A replication and update. *Demography, 1,* 71–81.

Burgess, N. (1994). Gender roles revisited: The development of the woman's place among African American women in the United States. *Journal of Black Studies, 24,* 391–401.

Burns, M. (1995, May). A sexual time bomb: The declining fertility rate of the black middle class. *Ebony* (pp. 76–78).

Burton, L. M. (1990). Teenage childbearing as an alternate life course strategy in multigenerational black families. *Human Nature, 1,* 123–143.

Burton, L. M., & Dilworth-Anderson, P. (1991). The intergenerational family roles of aged black Americans. *Marriage and Family Review, 16,* 311–330.

Burton, L. M., Dilworth-Anderson, P., & Merriwether-de Vries (1995). Context and surrogate parenting among contemporary grandparents. *Marriage and Family Review, 20,* 349–366.

Children's Defense Fund (1993). *Progress and peril: Black children in America.* Washington, DC: Author.

Coleman, S., & Brown, E. (1994). Perceptions of age and parenthood in young adults. Unpublished manuscript, University of Alabama at Birmingham, Civitan International Research Center.

Conner-Edwards, A. F., & Edwards, H. E. (1988). The black middle class: Definitions and demographics. In J. Conner-Edwards & J. Spurlock (Eds.), *Black families in crisis: The middle class* (pp. 1–10). New York: Brunner/Mazel.

Cowan, C. P., Cowan, P. A., Hemming, G., & Miller, N. B. (1991). Transitions from couple to family: Adaptation and distress in parents and children. In P.A.C. Hetherington & E.M. Hetherington (Eds.), *Family transitions* (pp. 79–109). Hillsdale, NJ: Lawrence Erlbaum Association.

Darling, N., & Steinberg, L. (1993). Parenting style as context: An integrative model. *Psychological Bulletin, 113,* 487–496.

Dodson, J. (1988). Conceptualizations of black families. In H. McAdoo (Ed.), *Black families* (pp. 77–90). Newbury Park, CA: Sage Publications.

Duncan, G., & Rodgers, W. (1988). Longitudinal aspects of poverty. *Journal of Marriage and the Family, 50,* 1007–1021.

Farley, R., & Allen, W. R. (1987). *The color line and the quality of life in America.* New York: Russell Sage Foundation.

Franklin, A. J., & Boyd-Franklin, N. (1985). A psychoeducational perspective on black parenting. In. H. P. McAdoo & J .L. McAdoo (Eds.), *Black children: Social, educational and parental environments* (pp. 194–210). Newbury Park, CA: Sage Publications.

Frazier, E. F. (1957). *Black bourgeoisie.* New York: Macmillan Publishing Company.

Furstenberg, F. (1976). The social consequences of teenage parenthood. *Family Planning Perspective, 81,* 48–164.

Furstenberg, F., Brooks-Gunn, J., & Morgan, P. S. (1987). *Adolescent mothers in later life.* Cambridge, MA: Harvard University Press.

Garcia-Coll, C. T. (1990). Developmental outcome of minority infants: A process-oriented look at our beginnings. *Child Development, 61,* 270–289.

Garcia-Coll, C. T., Hoffman, J., & Oh, W. (1987). The social ecology and early parenting of Caucasian adolescent mothers. *Child Development, 58,* 955–963.

Geronimus, A. (1992). Clashes of common sense: On the previous child care experience of teenage mothers-to-be. *Human Organizations, 51,* 318–329.

Goddard, L. L., & Cavil, W. E. (1989). Black teenage parenting: Issues and challenges. In R. L. Jones (Ed.), *Black adolescents* (pp. 373–383). Berkeley, CA: Cobb & Henry.

Hagestad, G. O., & Burton, L. M. (1986). Grandparenthood, life context, and family development. *American Behavioral Scientist, 29,* 471–484.

Hale-Benson, J. (1986). *Black children: Their roots, culture and learning styles.* Baltimore, MD: John Hopkins University Press.

Harrison, A., Serafica, F., & McAdoo, H. (1984). Ethnic families of color. In R. D. Parke (Ed.), *The family: Review of child development research* (pp. 329–371). Chicago: University of Chicago Press.

Harrison, A. O., Wilson, M. N., Pine, C. J., Chan, S. Q., & Buriel, R. (1990). Family ecologies of ethnic minority children. *Child Development, 61,* 347–362.

Hill, R. (1971). *Strengths of black families.* New York: Emerson Hall.

Hill, R. B. (1993). *Research on the African American family: A holistic perspective.* West Point, CT: Auburn House.

Hofferth, S. L. (1985). Updating children's life course. *Journal of Marriage and the Family, 45,* 347–357.

Holliday, B. G., & Curbeam, B. (1981). *The parental belief interview.* Unpublished scale, Peabody College of Vanderbilt University.

Hunter, A. G. (1992). *Beyond the female headed household: Variations in urban Afro-American families.* Paper presented at the Centennial Convention of the American Psychological Association, Washington, DC.

Huston, A. C. (Ed.) (1991). *Children in poverty.* Cambridge, MA: Harvard University Press.

Kelley, M. L. (1989). *Conceptions of parenting in low SES, black urban mothers.* Paper presented at the Biennial Meeting of the Society for Research on Child Development, Kansas City, MO.

Kelley, M. L., Power, T. G., & Wimbush, D. D. (1990). Determinants of disciplinary practices in low-income, black mothers. *Child Development, 63,* 573–582.

Ladner, J. A. (1971). Growing up black. In Ladner, J.A. (Eds.), *Tomorrow's tomorrow: The black woman* (pp. 212–224). Garden City, NJ: Doubleday.

Landy, S., Clark, C., Schubert, J., & Jillings, C. (1983). Mother-infant interactions of teenage mothers as measured at six months in a natural setting. *Journal of Psychology, 115,* 245–258.

Laosa, L. (1977). Socialization, education, and continuity: The importance of the sociocultural context. *Young Children, 32,* 21–27.

Laosa, L. (1981). Maternal behavior: Sociocultural diversity in modes of family interaction. In R. W. Henderson (Ed.), *Parent-child interaction* (pp. 125–167). New York: Academic Press.

Longfellow, C., Zelkowitz, P., & Saunders, E.(1982). The quality of mother-child relationships. In D. Belle (Ed.), *Lives in stress: Women and depression* (pp. 163–176). Beverly Hills, CA: Sage Publications.

Maccoby, E. E., & Martin, J. A. (1983). Children's prosocial dispositions and behaviors. In E. M. Hetherington (Ed.), *Handbook of child psychology: Vol. 4. Socialization, personality and social development* (4th ed., pp. 1–101). New York: J. Wiley & Sons.

MacDonald, K. B., & Parke, R. D. (1984). Bridging the gap: Parent–child play and peer interactive competence. *Child Development, 55,* 1265–1277.

McAdoo, H. P. (1992). Upward mobility and parenting in middle-income black families. In A.K.H. Burlew, W. C. Banks, H. P. McAdoo, & D. A. Ya Azibo (Eds.), *African American psychology: Theory, research and practice* (pp. 63–86). Newbury Park, CA: Sage Publications.

McAdoo, H. P., & McAdoo, J. L. (Eds.). (1985). *Black children: Social, educational, and parental environments.* Beverly Hills, CA: Sage Publications.

McAdoo, H.P. (Ed.). (1988). *Black families.* Beverly Hills: Sage Publications.

McLoyd, V. C. (1990). The impact of economic hardship on black families and children: Psychological distress, parenting and socioemotional development. *Child Development, 61,* 311–346.

McLoyd, V. C., & Randolph, S. M. (1986). Secular trends in the study of Afro-American children: A review of child development. *Monographs of the Society for Research in Child Development, 1936–1980,* 79–92.

McLoyd, V. C., & Wilson, L. (1991). The strain of living poor: Parenting, social support, and child mental health. In A. Huston (Ed.), *Children in poverty* (pp. 105–135). Cambridge, MA: Harvard University Press.

National Center for Health Statistics. (1991). Advance report of the final natality statistics. *1989 Monthly Vital Statistic Report, 38* (3 Suppl.). Hyattsville, MD: Public Health Service.

Nobles, W. W. (1974). Africanicity: Its role in black families. *The Black Scholar, 5*, 10–17.

Nobles, W. W., & Goddard, L. L. (1984). *Understanding the black family: A guide for scholarship and research.* Oakland, CA: Black Family Institute Publications.

Ogbu, J. (1981). Origins of human competence: A cultural ecological perspective. *Child Development, 52*, 413–429.

Ogbu, J. (1985). A cultural ecology of competence among inner-city blacks. In M. B. Spencer, G. W. Brookins, & W. R. Allen (Eds.), *Beginnings: The social and affective development of black children* (pp. 45–66). Hillsdale: Lawrence Erlbaum Associates.

Osofsky, H. J., & Osofsky, J. D. (1971). Adolescents as mothers: Results of a program for low-income pregnant teenagers with some emphasis upon infants' development. *American Journal of Orthopsychiatry, 40*, 825–834.

Osofsky, J. D., Peebles, C. D., & Hann, D. M. (1993). Adolescent parenthood: Risks and opportunities for mothers and infants. In C. Zeanah (Ed.), *Handbook of infant mental health.* New York: Guilford Press.

Patterson, C. J., Kupersmidt, J. B., & Vaden, N. A. (1990). Income level, gender, ethnicity and household composition as predictors of children's school-based competence. *Child Development, 1*, 485–494.

Peters, M. F. (1988). Parenting in black families with young children. In H. McAdoo (Ed.), *Black families* (pp. 228–241). Newbury Park, CA: Sage Publications.

Petit, G. S., & Bates, J. E. (1989). Family interaction patterns and children's behavior problems from infancy to 4 years. *Developmental Psychology, 25*, 413–420.

Phipps-Yonas, S. (1980). Teenage pregnancy and motherhood: A review of the literature. *American Journal of Orthopsychiatry, 50*, 403–431.

Phoenix, A., & Woollett, A. (1991). Introduction. In A. Phoenix, A. Woolett, & E. Lloyd (Eds.), *Motherhood: Meanings, practices and ideologies* (pp. 1–12). Newbury Park, CA: Sage Publications.

Powell, G. (1983). *The psychosocial development of minority group children.* New York: Brunner Mazel.

Radke-Yarrow, M., Zahn-Waxler, C., & Chapman, M. (1983). Children's prosocial dispositions and behaviors. In E. M. Hetherington (Ed.), *Handbook of child psychology: Vol. 4. Socialization, personality, and social development* (4th ed., pp. 469–546). New York: John Wiley & Sons.

Rosenheim, M. K., & Testa, M. F. (1992). *Early parenthood and coming of age in the 1990's.* New Brunswick, NJ: Rutgers University Press.

Sadler, L. S. (1987). Adolescent parents. In M. A. Corbett & J. H. Meyer (Eds.), *The adolescent and pregnancy* (pp. 79–90). Boston, MA: Blackwell Scientific Publishing.

Scott-Jones, D., & LeGall-Nelson, S. (1986). Defining black families past and present. In E. Seidman & J. Rappaport (Eds.), *Redefining social problems* (pp. 83–100). New York: Plenum Press.

Scott-Jones, D., Roland, E. J., & White, A. B. (1989). Antecedents and outcomes of pregnancy in black adolescents. In R. L. Jones (Ed.), *Black adolescents* (pp. 341–371). Berkeley, CA: Cobb & Henry.

Silverstein, B., & Krate, R. (1975). *Children of the ghetto: A developmental psychology.* New York: Praeger Publishers.

Stack, C. (1974). *All our kin: Strategies for survival in the African American community.* New York: Harper & Row.

Staples, R. (1986). *The black family: Essays and studies* (3rd ed.). Belmont, CA: Wadsworth Publishing Company.

Stevens, J. (1988). Social support, locus of control and parenting in three low-income groups of mothers: Black teenagers, black adults and white adults. *Child Development, 59,* 635–642.

Sudarkasa, N. (1988). Interpreting the African heritage in Afro-American family organization. In H. P. McAdoo (Ed.), *Black families* (2nd ed., pp. 27–43). Beverly Hills, CA: Sage Publications.

Taylor, J. (in press). The Pittsburgh project, part III: Toward a purposeful systems approach to parenting. In R. L. Jones (Ed.), *Advances in black psychology.* Richmond, California: Cobb & Henry.

Taylor, J., & Macmillan, M. (1988). Taylor's affiliation and control inventories. In R. L. Jones (Ed.), *Tests and measurements for black populations* (pp. 1–21). Richmond, CA: Cobb & Henry.

U. S. Bureau of the Census (1990). *Statistical abstracts for the United States.* Washington, DC: Government Printing Office.

U. S. Bureau of the Census. (1991). *Statistical abstracts for the United States.* Washington, DC: U.S. Government Printing Office.

U. S. Bureau of the Census. (1992). *Statistical abstracts for the United States.* Washington, DC: U.S. Government Printing Office.

Washington, V. (1988). The black mother in the United States. In B. Birns & D. Hay (Eds.), *The different faces of motherhood* (pp. 185–213). New York: Plenum Press.

Wasserman, G. A., Rauh, V. A., Brunelli, S. A., & Garcia-Castro, M. (1990). Psychosocial attributes and life expectancies of disadvantaged minority mothers: Age and ethnic variations. *Child Development, 61,* 566–580.

Weller, R. H., Eberstein, I. W., & Bailey, M. (1987). Pregnancy wantedness and maternal behavior during pregnancy. *Demography, 24,* 407–412.

Willie, C. V. (1991). *A new look at black families* (4th ed.). Dix Hills, NY: General Hall, Inc.

Wise, S., & Grossman, F. K. (1980). Adolescent mothers and their infants: Psychological factors in early attachment and interaction. *American Journal of Orthospsychiatry, 50,* 454–467.

Young, V. H. (1974). A black American socialization pattern. *American Ethnologist, 1,* 405–413.

CHAPTER 6

Caregiving Roles in Older Women

PEGGYE DILWORTH-ANDERSON
AND LYN RHODEN

Motherhood is a profession by itself, just like school teaching and lecturing.

—IDA B. WELLS

Giving and receiving family support through a mutual aid system, helping to sustain an intergenerational kinship system of care, and serving as primary facilitators in the continuity of family ties are major family caregiving roles of African American women. These roles have fostered and maintained family closeness and connectedness in African American families. Although many adult African American women identify with these roles, they are most often played by middle-aged and older women in the community. Emphasis in this chapter will be placed on the caregiving roles of older women.

CENTRALITY OF WOMEN: DURING SLAVERY

The mutual aid system in which women have played important roles is rooted in a larger cultural context that evolved from a "brothers and sisters" concept in the African American community (Franklin, 1948; Frazier, 1932). This concept emerged from the necessity of survival in a hostile and oppressive society, where African Americans viewed themselves as "making it" only through the concerted efforts of collected individuals. This way of thinking provided a belief system and a context for extended kin relations to emerge. The individual was neither socialized nor afforded the opportunity to "make it" on his or her own either in the underground community or the mainstream society. Historically this can be best observed in the shared planning and execution of escapes from slavery within the underground slave community (Berlin, 1998; Gates, 1987). Other communal efforts such as the sharing of resources within and across households (Escot, 1979), rearing of children (Gates, 1987; Stack, 1974), and quilt-making and other folk arts (Vlach, 1980) were observed in the slave community as a representation of extended familism.

These extended families placed a high value on motherhood and on cooperative approaches to caring for children (Collins, 1990). The idea that African American children belong to the community is rooted in African traditions, which fostered a strong bond in the culture between older women and the young, as well as in cooperative child-care traditions among the women in the slave community. Therefore, blood mothers and "othermothers" could simultaneously and/or separately care for the children. *Othermothers* are women who assist blood mothers by sharing mothering responsibilities, or who take the place of a blood mother by assuming total responsibility for a child. This system of cooperative care by blood mothers and othermothers reflects the centrality of women in African cultures.

The alienating conditions of slavery in America threatened to break down the ties of extended kin networks and community that were pivotal to African tribal life (Martin & Martin, 1978). Although many individual families were separated under slavery, the concept of family survived and was very much a part of slave life (Aschenbrenner, 1975; Gutman, 1976). Slaves were responsible for their own lives: for growing their own food, caring for their own children and burying their own dead. A community-based lifestyle developed out of these actions of daily survival, and family ties began to develop (Berlin, 1998; Martin & Martin, 1978).

Maintaining these family ties in spite of the separation and degradation Africans sometimes suffered under slavery was based on the values and memories the Africans brought with them, and provided a foundation for the future of African American community and family structure (Billingsley, 1992). Billingsley (1992) pointed out two determinants of the survival of stable patterns of family life among Africans under slavery: the strong commitment to family, and the social and economic factors that made family life favorable. The existence and survival of family life is most evident in the large numbers of African families who came forward to register their marriages after the Civil War, providing evidence of the existence of and commitment to family life among slaves.

Further, a part of the creation and survival of family life during slavery was due to the female-centeredness of families. This does not imply, however, that power resided with women, since all the power in the

African American family was vested in the hands of the white slave owner. Under slavery, however, the status of African American men and women was equal as it had never been in African culture. Both men and women were subject to the authority of a white master, worked side by side in the fields and were treated according to their capacity for work and their obedience (Escot, 1979). Within the household, however, women continued to play a central role in the sustainment and stability of the family. Mother-child bonds were paramount as evidenced by the recollections of former slaves, who knew and remembered their mothers more than any other relationship (Billingsley, 1992). Through the bearing of children and the creation and sustainment of the mother-child bond, the African American woman provided the path and the means for establishing and maintaining African American families.

These women, even under extremely adverse conditions of slavery, established some form of homeplace, a hut or shack that represented a physical and psychological space where oppression could be resisted by the reaffirmation of one's humanity (hooks, 1990). The yearning for freedom and the yearning for belonging (Billingsley, 1992) were met within the homeplace where women held families together and provided a context for kinship apart from the harsh realities of slavery. Even women who were separated from their children found ways to maintain some semblance of closeness and connection. In the narrative of his life, Fredrick Douglass (1960) described the care provided by his mother, from whom he was separated at a young age. The only times that Douglass saw his mother after their separation were at night when she would walk the 12-mile journey to see him after having worked all day as a field hand. Despite the risk of a beating, Douglass's mother would come to him, lie down with him while he slept, and leave for her return journey long before he awakened. Clearly, the forced separation of Douglass's mother from her child did not lessen her affection for him or her determination and commitment to give care to him in whatever way was possible. By traveling to him in the night and simply holding him as he went to sleep, Douglass's mother found a way to affirm her role as the nurturer and affirm her son's sense of value as her child. This affirmation of Fredrick Douglass and other slave children was achieved not only through interacting with their mothers, but also through cooperative care provided by othermothers and other fictive kin. Older women were central to this system of extended kin giving care to children. This caring provided a kin place for everyone, and it also allowed children to know that they belonged to someone. Thus, the most common occupation for older female slaves was caring for the children whose mothers were either working in the fields, had been sold to another owner under slavery or had died.

Another way in which women cared for slave children involved protecting them from harm at the hands of their white masters. This protection included suppressing the children, which meant teaching them to control their expressive and inquisitive day-to-day behavior. From this context grew authoritarian child-rearing styles designed to prepare children to survive "the realities of American racism and discrimination" (Scott, 1991, p. 33). Many African American mothers today continue to use an authoritarian parenting style with the objective of "turning out" children who have self-control yet are assertive and strong enough to value themselves in a culture that devalues them.

CENTRALITY OF WOMEN: POSTSLAVERY

During and after the transition from slavery to a postemancipation rural agricultural economy in the South, the status of women as central to family and community continued to be linked to their role as caregivers. The period of tenant farming and sharecropping in the South, which was a part of the transition from slavery, served as a context for women to continue establishing and maintaining the family (Martin & Martin, 1978). Although men were expected and willing to help maintain the family by providing shelter, food and a sense of protection, their roles depended on circumstances that were sometimes beyond their control, such as the availability of work. This resulted in the woman's role within the household becoming even more central to the family as she attempted to insure its continued existence. This was evidenced by the support given to biological mothers by othermothers and female relatives who were able and willing to participate in feeding, nurturing and supervising their children (Collins, 1990; Jones, 1985). The centrality of African American women during this period also included their aid in providing an economic base for the family. Just as in the time of slavery, they worked alongside men in the fields as sharecroppers to maintain their families (Cell, 1982; Lerner, 1972).

The centrality of the African American woman in the family and community remained during the period when African Americans moved from a southern agricultural setting and economy to northern urban industrial areas (Lemann, 1991; Martin & Martin, 1978). As African American families tried to assimilate into this new and unfamiliar way of life, they were in no less need of the support of the extended family and community than they had been under slavery. During this period many white women were dealing with the choice of continuing their wartime work role outside the home, or responding to postwar propaganda emphasizing the need for their return to the traditional homemaker role. This was not a choice that many African American women had to face, however. They continued to work outside the home due to economic necessity and to work within the home as caregivers to husbands and children (Scott, 1991). The children of African American working mothers were usually cared for by trusted neighbors or relatives. The caregiving tradition thus continued, both within the family and the African American community in general. Families continued to survive through the strength and support of mothers, extended family relationships, and women-centered cooperative child-care arrangements.

CENTRALITY OF WOMEN: CONTEMPORARY TIMES

Issues facing contemporary African American women that affect their caregiving roles to children and other family members continue to be reminiscent of those in the past, but there are additional concerns. Unlike many white middle-class women who choose to work outside the home as a liberating alternative to the traditional sex-based caregiver and homemaker role, for most African American women, like other oppressed and poor ethnic groups of women, work outside the home has been and continues to be an economic necessity for their families (hooks, 1990; Scott, 1991). Moreover, for many African American women the necessity to work outside their homes has meant providing daily service to others in the form of domestic labor for white employers. A part of being caregiver and nurturer both to their own families and to those of their employers has meant struggling to maintain balance in their caregiving duties and responsibilities (hooks, 1990).

Although work outside the home is usually an economic necessity outside the realm of their choice, and this work imposes limitations upon their opportunities for self-actualization in other ways, African American women's work expresses an ethic of care on two levels. Work outside the home obviously contributes to the care of children in an immediate economic sense. As a long-term issue, work outside the home represents an ethic of personal accountability, self-reliance and the value of striving for more than one's proscribed place as an African American person in society. Work, then, is not in opposition to motherhood, but an important part of the conceptualization of African American motherhood (Collins, 1990).

This conceptualization of African American motherhood among working women is supported by cultural norms wherein a mother who raises her children is not likely to be the only woman to "mother" these children. Children's blood mothers, or biological mothers, have traditionally been assisted by othermothers and other female members of the family or community. As noted above, this type of shared supervision and cooperative care for children has long served a supportive function for African American women who are attempting to rear children in difficult circumstances. In the stressful and difficult situations that African American families face today, such as those evidenced in distressed inner-city neighborhoods, othermothers and female relatives try to protect and preserve African American community life (Minkler & Roe, 1993). In situations where sick children are present, women-centered cooperative child care does not hinge upon the presence or absence of a father or father figure, but rather reflects the traditional and highly valued centrality of mothering in African American communities (Dilworth-Anderson, 1995; Slaughter & Dilworth-Anderson, 1988).

When providing care in stressful and difficult situations, African American women use few, if any, formal services. Nevertheless, they continue to absorb needy and dependent members.

For example, an increasing number of different generations of low-income single mothers with young children and their grandparents share homes. This sharing of residences was commonplace in the African American community after slavery (Frazier, 1932) and during the migration north in the early 1930s. Sharing of residences is also very prominent in African American communities today (U.S. Bureau of the Census, 1991). As in the past, and as is evident today, economic hardships and other oppressive conditions help shape the need for women to provide care to several generations at the same time. As a result, women in extended African American families provide care and support to children and other needy adult members. Aged African Americans and their adult children, usually daughters, share goods and services with one another (Martin & Martin, 1978; Mutran, 1985; Taylor & Chatters, 1991).

Mutran (1985) reported that aged African Americans give support to, as well as receive it from, their extended families. They give advice and economic support to their adult children more often than do whites, and assist their children by providing services to their grandchildren. In fact, current research shows that African American grandparents—mostly grandmothers—are playing significant roles in the parenting of their grandchildren by serving as surrogate or coparents in their socialization and rearing (Burton, 1992; Minkler, Roe, & Price, 1992). Many of them share homes with their grandchildren and frequently support them financially (Foster, 1983; Hogan, Hao, & Parish, 1990; Wilson, Tolson, Hinton, & Kierman, 1990).

Apfel and Seitz (1991) identified four parenting adaptational models among early childbearing families (parental replacement, supplement, primary parent, and apprentice) that African American grandmothers have used to support their grandchildren. Each model indicates a level of grandparent involvement ranging from the replacement model of taking full responsibility for their grandchildren to the apprentice model, which includes providing only limited care and support. Pearson, Hunter, Ensminger and Kellam (1990) found that grandmothers were important parenting agents for grandchildren regardless of the family structure in which they lived. Grandmothers did, however, vary in the type of involvement they had with their grandchildren according to family structure. For example, the presence or absence of a child's mother or father influenced the type of involvement their grandparents had with them.

REFLECTIONS ON THE MEANING OF CAREGIVING BY AFRICAN AMERICAN WOMEN

The delegation of the caregiver role to women in American society is a reflection of patriarchal, sexist and oppressive sex role norms that structure work and family roles. African American women, however, have long operated outside of these traditional sex-role norms, but have instead negotiated a kind of "tightrope suspended between different but overlapping worlds . . . of being black and being woman" (Scott, 1991, p. 5). From an Afrocentric feminist perspective (Collins, 1990), African American women have taken a conventional role of caregiving and reframed it. Thus, the role assigned to them by patriarchal attitudes regarding women's work has been enhanced to mean self-affirmation, recovery of the wholeness of spirit and a counteraction to the harshness and hardships of racism experienced in the public world.

This reframing of caregiving also reflects the choice to change and expand a traditional role to include a personal commitment to home and community, and a philosophical belief in racial uplift (hooks, 1990).

Within this context of caregiving, African American women provide children with protection, both physically and psychologically (Collins, 1990). During early childhood, protection may mean providing buffers between the child and painful experiences of discrimination in the form of religion, family and community for as long as possible. However, providing protection for a child also includes instruction in independence and self-reliance as means of self-protection (Harrison, Wilson, Pine, Chan, & Buriel, 1990). When an African American woman imposes strong discipline, it is not only to protect her child from immediate danger or to insist upon immediate compliance, but also to teach respect for order in a world where life is threatened on a regular basis. Indeed, respect for self and others must be taught in an environment where these very values are subverted. Mothers, then, may try to keep their children close to home for as long as possible to help build an enmeshed relationship with them (Watson & Protinsky, 1988), in order for children to develop skills necessary for their survival (Aschenbrenner, 1975).

Caregiving provided by African American women to each other, children and their community may be perceived as a "habit of survival" (Scott, 1991) that "give[s] a sense of self-control and offer[s] hope" (p. 7) in a way that alleviates the pain of poverty and racism. From a bicultural perspective, then, caregiving for African American women not only means helping children learn to protect themselves, but also involves teaching them habits of survival. The subtleties which are imparted to African American children by their teachers and caregivers include how to compromise without capitulation and how to cooperate without submission to control or intimidation (Aschenbrenner, 1975). This type of teaching as a means of providing care may be viewed as a form of radicalism that is necessary if one is committed to teaching survival skills that liberate, expand consciousness and challenge domination (hooks, 1990; Scott, 1991).

Teaching habits of survival often creates a paradoxical dilemma for both women and their children (Collins, 1990). This paradox is reflected in the instruction of children in ways to accommodate or find their place in the oppressive system in which they grow up. They must learn to find and keep work, to struggle for an education, to learn the means by which to be economically self-sustaining and to take on responsibilities within family and community. On the other hand, if children are taught only to "fit in" they unwittingly become participants in their own oppression. As teachers and caregivers, then, African American women are faced with the complex challenge of instructing children in the means of survival within the oppressive structure of our society as they also teach ways of "rejecting and transcending those same structures" (Collins, 1990, p. 124).

WHAT'S IN IT FOR A WOMAN?

The positive impact of the African American woman's role of caregiver can be conceptualized as playing itself out on three interlocking levels: the individual, the family and the African American community as a whole. These three levels contribute to the creation of a rich and resilient tapestry representing the complexity of the African American woman's role as caregiver. This tapestry, however, has implications for both the woman and for those to whom she gives care.

On the level of the individual, the African American woman's caregiving represents humanization and the affirmation of the value of the lives and spirits of those she nurtures. Further, through caregiving to each other, to children and to African American men, an emotional framework is created whereby African American women's personal values can be reaffirmed. Within the framework of giving care to others, they may find a context for discovering the "power of self-definition, the importance of valuing and respecting ourselves, the necessity of self-reliance and independence, and a belief in black women's empowerment" (Collins, 1990, p. 119). They can also feel pride in their power as the stabilizing center of the family network, making that network more resilient and so more able to contend with and struggle against the outside pressures of discrimination.

The ethic of care inherent in the role of nurturer also fosters a sense of family. When family members are cared for and encouraged to care for each other, a sense of connectedness is engendered that can yield a feeling of identity, of belonging, of "roots" for the African American woman and others in her family (Martin & Martin, 1978). The security represented by family cohesion holds the assurance of comfort and support in times of need for African American women as well as other for family members.

The African American woman's creation of this context of affirmation of the individual and the family also has political importance for the African American community. The insistence upon care and nurturance in the midst of conditions of racism and often poverty establishes the home and community as sites of "resistance and liberation struggle" (hooks, 1990, p. 43). Within the private space of the home, African American women become agents of social change (Scott, 1991) by enacting the roles of political resistance to oppression and struggle for liberation. Within the community, care extended to children by othermothers represents an ethic of care for children beyond one's own immediate family, and as such serves as a basis for African American women's political activism (Collins, 1990). This activism held by women offers a foundation for the development of strength and solidarity within the community.

Caregiving also has some negative or problematic consequences for African American women. Even when caregiving is a role assumed by choice, there are costs to African American women for whom this role is central to their own lives (Bengston, Rosenthal, & Burton, 1995). As long as the oppressive images of mammy, matriarch and welfare mother are being replaced by equally controlling images of African American women as "mothers of black culture, responsible for the world" (Scott, 1991, p. 8) or as the superstrong African American mother, the costs of the central caregiving role to African American women can still be obscured (Collins, 1990; Dill, 1989). The image of the "invincible strength and genius of the black mother," Patricia Weems warns us, "can be as bogus as the one of the happy slave" (1984, p. 27). Their ability to support others in contending with the oppression of sexism, racism and often poverty does not mean that African American women themselves are invulnerable to these oppressive forces.

African American women may experience contradictory and ambivalent emotional responses to motherhood. Unwanted pregnancies can constitute an oppressive element in a woman's life in and of themselves, especially if she is ill-equipped financially or otherwise to care for children. The adult status that is conferred upon a young woman who has children, and the high value placed on children within the African American community, are factors that contribute to African American mothers' choice to keep their children, despite the cost to self and to their own aspirations for self-actualization (Burton, 1992; Jendrek, 1993). Additionally, because children represent humanity and the future generation, they help reduce the ambivalence women face when they have unplanned children by giving respect and authority to the mother's role as caregiver.

THE FUTURE OF THE CAREGIVING ROLE FOR AFRICAN AMERICAN WOMEN

It may be assumed that the cultural expectation in most African American communities is that adult females, and grandmothers in particular, will continue to occupy their traditional caregiver roles. The ability to maintain this traditional way of responding, however, will be challenged by the problematic status, situations and conditions of women in African

American families (Barresi & Menon, 1990). These situations and conditions include an increase in unemployment, single-parent households, poverty among women and early childbearing families. Although these increases are also evident in white families, African American families experience them at a higher rate (Jaynes & Williams, 1989; Tucker & Mitchell-Kernan, 1995). For example, African American males as compared to white males are almost three times as likely to be unemployed (11 percent and 4 percent, respectively). Further, 40 percent of African American and 25 percent of white families have no employed person in the household (Horton & Smith, 1990).

Among female-headed households, the problem is even more severe. Almost 60 percent of households headed by African American females, as compared to 48 percent headed by white females, have no person employed in them. With slightly over 50 percent (51.8 percent) of African American families headed by females today, the issue of poverty among families with young children, which is related to employment, is an increasing concern. African American mothers in the workforce, many of whom are single and without adequate child care, make 5 percent less money than their white counterparts. Sixty-eight percent of African American female heads of household with children under the age of 18 are living in poverty, as compared to 48 percent of their white counterparts. These adverse conditions facing poor African American women, many of whom are unskilled with low levels of education and more children to take care of as compared to white females, will serve as obstacles to their ability to continue to fulfill their traditional caregiving roles (U. S. Bureau of the Census, 1991).

Given these conditions facing African American families, one of the most viable options available to assure better African American family survival in the future is the extended kin network. This network, from slavery to the present, has included women at its center. In the future, however, there will be a much greater need for this network to develop cooperative caregiving strategies. These strategies, as evidenced by current research, will include an increase in older women providing care to their adult daughters and their grandchildren (Jendrek, 1993). African American grandparents, especially grandmothers, will become increasingly central caregiving figures in the family (Burton, 1992; Minkler et al, 1992). Like African American grandmothers or older othermothers of the past, they may assume roles to protect, nurture and serve as role models for different generations, especially for young children. In addition, the future caregiving roles of African American women will be diverse, dynamic and challenging (Jaynes & Williams, 1989). Thus, survival and coping strategies in extended African American families will need to include both old and new strategies that will enhance caring for and supporting different generations in the family.

Although only limited information is available that discusses the range of responses African American extended families use to address the needs of their members, inferences can be drawn from what is known. Three major inferences are noted here: (1) cultural ways of believing and behaving will encourage the kin network to absorb its needy members; (2) the kin system will probably become increasingly vulnerable in light of the few resources available to it to meet the multiple demands and needs of different generations; and (3) black families will attempt to reshape and redefine themselves to meet the needs of the kin network.

CONCLUSION

African American women's caregiving roles are rooted in a historical context. Such roles have served the family very well from slavery to the present time. Serving in these caregiving roles, however, has had both costs and benefits to women. Regardless of the costs to African American women, traditional caregiving roles with their spiritual, social, economic and psychological outcomes had positive consequences for dependent family members, and have served as part of the core for survival among African Americans in this society.

The ability of African American women to continue in their supportive caregiving roles will be challenged by present and future social and economic conditions in the African American community. A major concern is whether an emerging African American family structure headed by single females, with many of them living in poverty, will be resilient and resourceful enough to address the needs of dependent family members. For example, the increasing life expectancy of the African American elderly and the number of young children being born to childbearing teenagers are presenting challenging caregiving roles for African American families. Presently, elderly African Americans represent about 8 percent of the aged population in American society. This population is growing at a faster rate than the white elderly, especially for African American females. While the total U.S. population is only expected to grow by 18 percent between the years 1980 and 2000, the increase of older African American females is projected to grow by 68 percent. African American females also represent the poorest among the elderly in this society: the majority are widowed and have severe health problems. Given these changing demographic trends in the older population and status of African American families, it is suggested here that women caregivers in the family will have great difficulty maintaining their traditional caregiving system of aid and support.

Competing demands of different dependent generations in the family will greatly challenge African American women's ability to care for their own children, grandchildren and older parents. Many single mothers will be the expected caregivers of the growing older population in the African American community, who themselves will need as much support as, if not more than, the aged for whom they will be caring. It is feasible to surmise, then, that as the structure and composition of the African American family changes, a higher level of flexibility and resilience of female caregivers in the extended kin network will have to be developed.

African American female caregivers will need to develop more diverse ways of addressing dependent members in the future than they have done in the past, and they will need more help from their extended kin network in doing so. Assistance from the kin network will better assure that costs to women caregivers in the family won't always outweigh the benefits to those they support. The extended kin network can assist in this effort by providing support in the form of multiple and substitute caregivers. Both men and women can assist by serving as substitute and replacement caregivers. These types of kin network efforts will help maintain the resilient African American families of the past, support their present existence, and ensure their future strength by enabling female caregivers to serve in roles that address their survival.

REFERENCES

Apfel, N. H., & Seitz, V. (1991). Four models of adolescent mother-grandmother relationship in black inner city families. *Family Relations, 40,* 421–429.

Aschenbrenner, J. (1975). *Lifelines: Black families in Chicago.* New York: Holt, Rinehart & Winston.

Barresi, C. M., & Menon, G. (1990). Diversity in black family caregiving. In Harel (Ed.), *Black aged.* Newberry Park, CA: Sage Publications.

Bengtson, V., Rosenthal, C., & Burton, L. (1995). Parodoxes in families and aging. In R. Binstock & L. George (Eds.), *Handbook of aging and the social sciences* (4th ed., pp. 254–282). San Diego: Academic Press.

Berlin, I. (1998). *Many thousands gone: The first two centuries of slavery in North America.* Boston: Belknap/Harvard Press.

Billingsley, A. (1992). *Climbing Jacob's ladder: The enduring legacy of African American families.* New York: Simon & Schuster.

Burton, L. M. (1992). Black grandparents rearing children of drug-addicted parents: Stressors, outcomes, and social service needs. *The Gerontologist, 32,* 744–751.

Cell, J. W. (1982). *The highest stage of white supremacy: The origins of segregation in South African and the American south.* Cambridge: Cambridge University Press.

Collins, P. H. (1990). *Black feminist thought: Knowledge, consciousness, and the politics of empowerment.* New York: Routledge.

Dill, B. T. (1989). Our mothers' grief: Racial ethnic women and the maintenance of families. *Journal of Family History, 13,* 415–431.

Dilworth-Anderson, P. (1995). The importance of grandparents in the extended kin caregiving of black children with sickle cell disease. *Journal of Health and Social Policy, 5,* 185–202.

Douglass, Frederick. (1960). *Narrative of the life of Frederick Douglass, an American slave: Written by himself.* Cambridge, MA: Belknap Harvard Press.

Escot, P. D. (1979). *Slavery remembered: A record of twentieth century slave narratives.* Chapel Hill: University of North Carolina Press.

Foster, H. J. (1983). African patterns in the Afro-American family. *Journal of Black Studies, 14,* 201–232.

Franklin, J. H. (1948). *From slavery to freedom: A history of American Negroes.* New York: Alfred A. Knopf.

Frazier, E. F. (1932). *The Negro family.* Chicago: University of Chicago Press.

Gates, H. L. (1987). *The classic slave narratives.* New York: Random House.

Gutman, H. (1976). *The black family in slavery and freedom, 1750–1925.* New York: Pantheon Books.

Harrison, A. O., Wilson, M. N., Pine, C. J., Chan, S. Q, & Buriel, R. (1990). Family ecologies of ethnic minority children. *Child Development, 61,* 347–362.

Hogan, D., Hao, L.-X., & Parish, W. (1990). Race, kin networks, and assistance to mother-headed families. *Social Forces, 68,* 797–812.

hooks, b. (1990). *Yearning: Race, gender, and cultural politics.* Boston, MA: South End Press.

Horton, C. P., & Smith, J. C. (1990). *Statistical record of black America.* Detroit, MI: Gale Press.

Jaynes, D. J., & Williams, R. M. (1989). *A common destiny: Blacks in American society.* Washington, DC: National Academy Press.

Jendrek, M. P. (1993). Grandparents who parent their grandchildren: Effects on lifestyle. *Journal of Marriage and the Family, 55,* 609–621.

Jones, J. (1985). *Labor of love, labor of sorrow.* New York: Vintage Books.

Lemann, N. (1991). *The promised land: The great black migration and how it changed America.* New York: Alfred A. Knopf.

Lerner, G. (1972). *Black women in white America.* New York: Vintage Books.

Martin, E. P., & Martin, J. M. (1978). *The black extended family.* Chicago: University of Chicago Press.

Minkler, M., & Roe, K. M. (1993). *Grandmothers as caregivers: Raising children of the crack cocaine epidemic.* Newbury Park, CA: Sage Publications.

Minkler, M., Roe, K. M., & Price, M. (1992). The physical and emotional health of grandmothers raising grandchildren in the crack cocaine epidemic. *The Gerontologist, 32,* 752–761.

Mutran, E. (1985). Intergenerational family support among blacks and whites: Response to culture or to socio-economic differences. *Journal of Gerontology, 40,* 382–389.

Pearson, J. L., Hunter, A. G., Ensminger, M. E., & Kellam, S. G. (1990). Black grandmothers in multigenerational households: Diversity in family structure and parenting involvement in the Woodlawn community. *Child Development, 61,* 431–442.

Scott, K. Y. (1991). *The habit of surviving: Black women's strategies for life.* New Brunswick, NJ: Rutgers University Press.

Slaughter, D. T., & Dilworth-Anderson, P. (1988). Care of black children with sickle cell disease: Fathers, maternal support, and esteem. *Family Relations, 37,* 281–287.

Stack, C. B. (1974). *All our kin: Strategies for survival in a black community.* New York: Harper & Row.

Taylor, R., & Chatters, L. (1991). Extended family networks of older black adults. *Journal of Gerontology, 46,* 210–217.

Tucker, B., & Mitchell-Kernan, C. (1995). *The decline in marriage among African Americans.* New York: The Russell Sage Foundation.

U. S. Bureau of the Census. (1991). *Current population reports,* Series P20, P60.

Vlach, J. M. (1980). Arrival and survival: The maintenance of an Afro-American tradition in folk art and craft. In I. Quimby & S. Swank (Eds.), *Perspectives on American folk art* (pp. 177–217). New York: W. W. Norton.

Watson, M. F., & Protinsky, H. O. (1988). Black adolescent identity development: Effects of perceived family structure. *Family Relations, 37,* 288–292.

Weems, P. (1984). Hush. Mama's gotta go bye bye: A personal narrative. *Sage: A Scholarly Journal on Black Women, 1,* 25–28.

Wilson, M. N., Tolson, T., Hinton, I., & Kiernan, M. (1990). Flexibility and sharing of childcare duties in black families. *Sex Roles, 22,* 409–425.

CHAPTER 7

Social Networks: Community-Based Institutional Supports

CLEOPATRA HOWARD CALDWELL

No matter what accomplishment you make, somebody helps you.

—ALTHEA GIBSON

African American women are exposed to an enormous amount of psychosocial adversity due, in part, to their precarious position within this society. For example, Hatch (1991) found that African American women were more likely than white women to be single, to have more children, to be head of a household and to be part of an extended family network. Despite the high levels of stress African American women face, many have exhibited successful coping and adaptation skills; however, very little is known about the various coping strategies these women employ to maintain their psychological well-being.

One area that has received considerable attention in the scientific literature in the past two decades is the stress-buffering role of social support in coping with a variety of problems (Cobb, 1976; Cohen & Wills, 1985; Kessler, Price, & Wortman, 1985). Much of this work has focused on the structure and function of individuals who form a network of significant interactions (Barrera, 1981; Chatters, Taylor, & Jackson, 1985). Much less work has focused on institutional supports that are available in communities in which African American women live and work. However, several studies have highlighted the importance of community-based institutional supports for the African American elderly (Caldwell, Chatters, Billingsley, & Taylor, 1995; Clemente, Rexroad, & Hirsch, 1975; Taylor & Chatters, 1986; Walls & Zarit, 1991), children (George, Richardson, Lakes-Matyas, & Blake, 1989) and families and communities (Billingsley & Caldwell, 1991; Caldwell, Greene & Billingsley, 1992; Eng, Hatch, & Callan, 1985).

Although it is known that African American women participate in a variety of religious, civic and social organizations (Barnes, 1986; Rodgers-Rose, 1980), there is a paucity of empirical studies on the nature of community-based institutional supports for African American women. Most available works examine the contributions of African American women to the development of voluntary associations from a historical perspective. Thus, this chapter begins with a brief overview of the history of community-based voluntary associations developed by African American women for themselves as background information. Three types of institutional supports (churches, fraternal organizations, and professional mentorships) that are potentially available to assist African American women are then explored. Suggestions for future research and implications for linking formal and informal institutional support networks for African American women are included.

HISTORICAL BACKGROUND: VOLUNTARY ASSOCIATIONS

In a historical analysis of African American women and voluntary associations, Anne Firor Scott (1990) traces the contributions of African American women to the development of welfare organizations, schools, health centers, orphanages and other community-based institutions as far back as the late eighteenth century. She found that the Female Benevolent Society of St. Thomas, founded in Philadelphia in 1793, was one of the oldest groups established by African American women. Through her research she identified other associations resulting in an impressive array of organizational types and functions from 1793 through the early twentieth century. In Philadelphia alone, she found 27 African American female mutual aid societies that were in existence by 1830, which means that even during slavery these organizations were flourishing. The National Association of Colored Women's Clubs (NACW) was founded in 1896 to coordinate many of these groups. By 1914 it had 50,000 members in over 1,000 clubs (Lerner, 1972; Scott, 1990). Resulting from its national organizational approach, the NACW had 850,000 members by 1968 (Lerner, 1972).

These clubs had a wide range of purposes, including social outlets, providing for the poor, encouraging educational pursuits and building community institutions. According to Josephine St. Pierre Ruffin, the convener of the first National Conference of Colored Women in 1895, the need for a national club movement among African American women was as follows (Lerner, 1972, p. 441):

> . . . [W]e need to feel the cheer and inspiration of meeting each other, we need to gain the courage and fresh life that comes from the min-

> gling of congenial souls, of those working for the same ends. Next, we need to talk over not only those things which are of vital importance to us as women, but also the things that are of especial interest to us as colored women. . . .

As expressly black organizations, these groups had the added challenge of meeting community needs that the federal government of the time had ignored and to combat the effects of poverty and prejudice. In some cases, social class dictated the type of community organization to which African American women belonged. Founders of these groups included both working-class women helping each other survive and more elite groups meeting for literary and intellectual endeavors (Scott, 1990). The organizers and leaders of the NACW club movement were usually middle-class women, although their memberships included working-class women (Lerner, 1972).

In an analysis of the involvement of African American women in the community, Barnes (1986) found that middle-class women were typically social activists and members of voluntary associations, while the church provided avenues for such activities for women of lower socioeconomic status. This relationship between social class and volunteerism among African American women was demonstrated on a small scale in a study by Gilkes (1982) in which she defined working-class African American women who were involved in the community as "mobile mothers." The mobile mothers became involved in community service after a personal crisis spurred them to action. She further labeled female community activists who were in positions of privilege within the black community through both educational attainment and professional prestige as "rebellious professionals." These women were middle-class professionals who were protesting unfair expectations in the workplace. This dichotomy defines at least two pathways through which contemporary African American women involve themselves in community-based voluntary associations.

In contrast to the Civil Rights movement, when volunteer activities in the black community encompassed all class levels in a collective effort to achieve social justice, social class is once again an influential factor in the membership of voluntary associations for contemporary African American women. However, the black church continues to be the primary institution in which social class is not the predominant criteria for determining volunteer association membership.

Many voluntary associations have been established within larger institutions such as churches. For example, some groups have an affiliation with black churches because they were first established within a church or because they used church buildings as their base of operation. Additionally, black college campuses have been the site of the establishment of a number of voluntary associations, including fraternal organizations and other women's clubs such as chapters of the YWCA (Giddings, 1988; Scott, 1990). Further, mentoring relationships have also been established to meet the needs of African American career women who continue to battle the effects of racism and prejudice in the workplace. These groups represent places where African American women can experience a sense of shared fate and a mutuality of concern that would not be available in other environments.

This chapter discusses three types of institutionally based voluntary membership organizations that remain prominent sources of support for African American women in contemporary society. These institutions are the black church, university-based black Greek-letter sororities and professional mentorship relationships. In the discussions that follow, we hope to show that an institutional analysis, rather than an interpersonal analysis of the supports available to African American women, could provide additional information for extending conceptual frameworks that attempt to explain the nature of social networks and social support among African American women.

BLACK CHURCHES: INFRASTRUCTURE FOR INSTITUTIONAL SUPPORTS

Religion has historically played a central role in the lives of many African American people (DuBois, 1898; Frazier, 1974; Lincoln & Mamiya, 1990; Mays & Nicholson, 1933). Since their inception in the late eighteenth century, organized black churches have assumed responsibility for the spiritual as well as the instrumental and emotional well-being of African American people (Caldwell, Greene, &, Billingsley, 1992). For African American women of all ages, the black church represents a strong community-based institution that has the potential of providing tremendous support for a variety of problems.

Most of the work on the church as a part of the informal social network of African Americans has examined the importance of social support received from church members by the elderly (Taylor, 1986; Taylor & Chatters, 1986; Walls & Zarit, 1991) or adult populations (Chatters et al., 1985; Taylor & Chatters, 1988). Many of these studies have relied on data from the National Survey of Black Americans (Jackson, 1991), while others have been more regional in focus (Walls & Zarit, 1991).

An overwhelming portion of these samples were female. However, Taylor and Chatters (1988) found consistent gender differences in religious participation. Specifically, African American women were much more likely to be a member of a church and to attend religious services than were African American men. In a surprising result, Taylor and Chatters (1988) found that African American men were more likely than women to receive support from church members. It could be argued that within the context of church members as sources of social support, women are more likely to give than to receive support.

Because the primary focus of social support research has been on interpersonal relationships among church members and women, in general, are more involved in church activities than men, it is unclear why men would be more likely to receive support from church members than women. Nevertheless, black churches can effectively serve as an institutional support for a variety of African American women and their families—not just for church members. An important proposition of this chapter is that black churches as a group can form an infrastructure for providing organized support and social services to the African American community at large.

In an effort to test the plausibility of the contemporary black church functioning as a social service institution, Dr. Andrew Billingsley and his colleagues recently mounted a national study of the family-oriented community-outreach programs sponsored by black churches to assist nonchurch members, called the Black Church Family Project. This study is the first attempt to obtain a national probability sample of black churches in the continental United States. It uses the same sampling frame as the National Survey of Black Americans (Jackson, 1991), and makes the assumption that black churches are distributed in a similar manner as black households.

Since this is an ongoing study, data were only available for the 635 black churches in the northern portion of the country. In an analysis of these data, Caldwell, Green, and Billingsley (1992) found that the contemporary black church continues to provide both instrumental and emotional support to its members as well as to the community at large. Although the black church does not hold the role of primary community center that it once held in black communities, due to better access to some resources of the larger society since the Civil Rights movement (Lincoln & Mamiya, 1990), it can still provide an institutional base for the provision of support, especially for African American women.

Fully 67 percent of the 635 churches in the Black Church Family Project sponsored at least one outreach program for the community. Out of a total of approximately 1,800 church-based support programs offered by 426 black churches, the overwhelming majority (90 percent) were designed to assist community families in need, while 10 percent were designed to meet community development needs. In a reanalysis of these data to explore the nature of church programs that specifically target African American women, we found that women's programs accounted for only 1.5 percent of the 1,685 family programs offered by black churches. These programs were typically general women's support groups, widow support groups, women's resource centers and domestic violence relief efforts. The number of programs for the elderly are not included in this figure since gender-distinct programs for the elderly were not described in the study. However, since we know that the majority of the elderly population of African Americans are females (Manuel, 1988), we feel confident in counting church-based elderly support programs as mostly female programs. In so doing, unique women's programs sponsored by churches would increase to almost 10 percent of all programs offered by northern black churches.

Since most church-based program volunteers and participants were females in the Black Church Family Project (Caldwell, Greene, & Billingsley, 1992), one can assume that most of the programs, at some level, provided support for African American women. For example, since women continue to have the primary responsibility for rearing children in this society, child-care programs and children and youth activities at churches provide a relatively safe place where women can leave their children while assuming other family and work-role responsibilities. Further, family support programs, such as counseling services and aid to the incarcerated, were usually designed to help women deal with family problems. Thus, in this study, most family-oriented community support programs offered by black churches can be viewed as beneficial to African American women.

The black church remains the only social institution in the black community that has successfully survived slavery. In this examination of the role that contemporary black churches can play in supporting African American women, it is evident that many black churches are in a position to be an important institutional support system not only for female church members, but also for female members of the community as well. The challenge for the future is how to effectively link community outreach services provided by black churches to the formal system of service delivery so that a more comprehensive support system for African American women can be provided.

BLACK GREEK-LETTER SORORITIES: COMMUNITY-BASED SUPPORT NETWORKS

A number of prominent social and civic organizations established by African American women within black communities are excellent examples of women working together to help women. The National Council of Negro Women, the Coalition of 100 Black Women, and the Jack and Jill Writings about the formulation of African American female groups are apparent in the literature as far back as 1908 (Scott, 1990). Although these organizations are often thought to provide African American women opportunities for developing leadership skills while actively participating in social movements, some earlier writings presented African American female groups from a deficit perspective (Barnes, 1986). For example, Kardiner and Ovesey (1962) suggested that the members of such groups often engaged in within-group rivalries fueled by the "quest for leadership and prestige." To follow this logic, one would have to assume that such memberships among African American women would lead to more stressful encounters than social support.

Rather than focusing on interpersonal relationships within such groups, this section argues that institutional traits within these organizations are more supportive than earlier literature would suggest. In this section, we examine the structure of university-based fraternal organizations as another example of an effective community-based infrastructure for supporting African American women.

The establishment of Greek-letter organizations for African Americans came early in the twentieth century. In order of initiation, there are four Greek-letter sororities for African American women: Alpha Kappa Alpha (1908), Delta Sigma Theta (1913), Zeta Phi Beta (1920) and Sigma Gamma Rho (1922). They began out of necessity for African American women on college campuses throughout the country due to segregation, sexism and a need for bonding among academically talented women. A historically black institution, Howard University in Washington, D.C. was the site of the inception of all of these sororities, with the exception of Sigma Gamma Rho which was established at Butler University in Indianapolis, Indiana. Thus, even within a predominately African American environment, there was a need for women to come together to support themselves.

From the beginning, these organizations represented mechanisms for African American women to develop a sense of belonging and to be nurtured and mentored for leadership. Initially, these organizations concentrated on transforming the individual. It was not until approximately 20 years after the establishment of the first black sorority that the organizational goals for some were expanded to include involvement in social issues (Giddings, 1988). Ultimately these groups began to integrate the professional aspirations of African American women with the social needs of the black community.

While the birth of most of these sororities occurred on historically black campuses, subsequent chapters became increasingly popular on many predominately white college campuses. The growth of African American sororities both nationally and internationally in the first half of the twentieth century demonstrated the importance of social bonding even among privileged African American women. Although viewed by some as being somewhat elite and separatist at times, the need for such groups continues to flourish in today's society.

Members of the sorority are not the only benefactors of sorority activities. These organizations are socially homogeneous groups with inherent characteristics that are important for providing institutional supports to African American women in general. The early literature on the nature of social networks suggests that in cities, as compared to rural areas, social cohesion at the neighborhood level was often not very strong due to the impact of urbanization (Greenbaum & Greenbaum, 1985). However, the structure of the neighborhood has been the focus of numerous network analyses indicating that neighborhood characteristics can either facilitate or hinder social support (Greenbaum & Greenbaum, 1985). We propose that the use of network analysis of neighborhoods is a perfect strategy for examining organizational traits of sororities that provide a basis for social support among urban African American women.

Greenbaum and Greenbaum (1985) have visually described a network analysis of neighborhoods as "block-level networks linked horizontally to other adjoining block-level networks, and vertically through a system of representations to a variety of larger scale agencies and organizations" (p. 49).

Essentially, a basic infrastructure for sororities is already in place to facilitate social support, both for the individual as well as collectively for the group and for the larger community. All sororities are comprised of a national office that governs the activities and rituals of multiple local chapters. At the national level, community projects as well as social issues for local chapter involvement are coordinated. Local chapters within a sorority can be equated with the block-level networks defined above. Local chapters are further connected to larger community agencies and organizations. Thus, the organizational structure of sororities makes them effective agents for identifying and addressing the concerns of a variety of African American women. They also provide a mechanism for urban African American women to be connected to the community as both providers and recipients of social support.

Several significant features of black sororities make them especially suited for supporting African American women. These include the following: (1) They have an organizational structure that encourages naturally forming social networks for their members; (2) they are a social system that has grown more visible and active over time; (3) group members share a common bond and commitment that make them interdependent on each other and the community in which they exist; and (4) the groups have the potential for expanding and changing to meet the more tangible needs of African American women in general.

In an extensive examination of the history of Delta Sigma Sorority and the black sorority movement, Paula Giddings (1988, pp. 304–305) concluded that:

> . . . [T]he organization's struggle for sisterhood, for identity, for the realization of their obligations as educated black women, has been extraordinary. Delta has made a difference in people's lives . . . Nevertheless, the organization is never satisfied with itself and has never been afraid to engage in the continual "appraisal and reappraisal of its purpose."

The shared experiences of these and other sorority women both individually and collectively, and the commitment to community service, make these groups important institutional resources for African American women.

PROFESSIONAL MENTORSHIP RELATIONSHIPS: ORGANIZATIONAL SUPPORT

African American women have been a part of the workforce in this country since the seventeenth century. The labor force participation of African American women in this society can easily be traced back to slavery. Social support in the workplace is particularly relevant for African American women since research suggests that women often experience social isolation, lack of mentors, tokenism and sex role stereotypes at the office (Bhatnagar, 1988). The African American female professional is caught in a possible conflict by being both black and female in a white male-dominated workforce (Bell, 1990; Denton, 1990; Gilkes, 1982). There is a need for constant adjustments, readjustments and balances between family concerns, community expectations and work responsibilities (Bell, 1990).

Supportive working relationships can reduce the level of job stress experienced by professionals in general. Relationships to enhance career advancement (Thomas, 1990) as well as informal social support from coworkers (Chatters, Taylor, & Jackson, 1985) have been empirically examined. Most research efforts on social support for professional women have focused on mentoring relationships in the work setting. The importance of mentoring relationships for career success as well as psychological well-being have been well documented. For example, Burke and McKeen (1990, p. 318) suggest that:

> Mentoring relationships have the potential to alleviate stress by increasing the protege's self-confidence, forewarning her of career stress, and suggesting ways to deal with it. In addition, it is suggested that female mentors provide unique role models for female proteges because they can relate to the causes of stress unique to female executives.

Race and gender as factors in the formation and effectiveness of the mentor-protege relationship are also important in understanding institutional supports for African American women. In a study of the influence of race and gender on mentoring relationships among corporate managers, Thomas (1990) found that 26 percent of African American women who were proteges had African American women as mentors. Based on sheer numbers, positions and power, most African American female managers had white males as mentors (38 percent). However, they were least likely of any race-gender subgroup to be mentored by white males. African American women were less likely to have white females (19 percent) or African American males (16 percent) as mentors. Based on a review of literature of the mentoring experience and organizational mobility, Scott (1989) concluded that the white female professional is least likely to mentor another female; however, minority female professionals feel obliged to mentor other women, especially other minority women. Thus, the likelihood of professional African American women receiving career support relies heavily on the availability of other African American women in higher-status career positions.

Although white males will continue to play important mentorship roles in the careers of African American professional women, the Thomas (1990) study also found that psychosocial support from mentors of the same race was more beneficial than were cross-race relationships. In general, supportive friendship from other African American women is necessary to help clarify sources of discrimination and help in the selection of appropriate coping behaviors (Denton, 1990; Scott, 1989). Within the work environment, more access to African American women as mentors would serve to improve the work climate for professional African American women. The special bond that can exist between professional African American women across status within the work setting is typically achieved on an informal rather than a formal basis. This means that institutional support for career advancement for professional African American women is not a part of the organizational culture. Barriers to institutional support for African American women continue to exist, based on the disproportionately low numbers of African American women who hold powerful positions within most organizational settings, as well as gender and racial discrimination that may limit opportunities for moving up the organizational hierarchy (Bell, 1990). Until these issues are addressed in a more systematic and sincere way, access to the top of the career ladder will continue to be limited for African American women even with the informal support of mentors.

CONCLUSIONS AND IMPLICATIONS

The resourcefulness of African American women can be documented throughout history (Allen & Britt, 1983). Characteristic of this group is the ability to affiliate with others as an adaptive strategy for survival. A tremendous body of literature supports the idea that African American women are typically embedded within supportive interpersonal social networks. However, far fewer studies have focused on the nature of institutional and community-based supports that African American women have created for themselves and their communities. The all-female African American organization has been in existence at least since the eighteenth century, responding to the social, educational and community-building needs of African American women and their families. Even within prominent volunteer groups that include both men and women, African American women are relied upon to be the providers of instrumental and emotional support. In addition, they are the recipients of vast amounts of support through their participation in various organizations.

Mechanisms through which African American women give and receive support should be explored further to determine both the costs and benefits of community-based affiliative relationships for African American women.

Black churches provide the most extensive network of support for African American women from an array of backgrounds. Churches are the only community-based organizations that can provide support from birth to death. The results of the Black Church Family Project (Caldwell, Greene, & Billingsley, 1992) suggest that the contemporary black church is there to provide not only spiritual and religious guidance but also much-needed social services for African American women. Church membership is not a requirement to receive spiritual or social service, and African American females are the driving force behind volunteer efforts to assist families and the community at large. Thus, black churches remain important institutional support systems for African American women and their families facing a number of challenging issues as we move into the twenty-first century. They also provide the basis for building an infrastructure that can link a multitude of community organizations and voluntary associations to form a web of support that would have far-reaching implications for improving the quality of life for many African American women and their families. Future research in this area should explore which types of churches and essential resource requirements would be necessary to sustain such an infrastructure.

Black Greek-letter sororities have provided social support at the postsecondary educational level for African American women on predominately black and white college campuses since the beginning of the twentieth century. These organizations afford opportunities for African American women to develop a sense of belonging and to be nurtured and mentored for leadership, as well as to provide community service. Although accessible to far fewer women for membership than the black church, the benevolent activities of these groups are aimed at addressing community needs. African American women from any walk of life can benefit from some of these activities. However, community support activities among these groups can be fragmented sometimes. With numerous local chapters throughout the country and national headquarters to provide uniform leadership, these sororities can also form important institutional supports for African American women. Coordinated efforts on the part of several Greek-letter groups could result in a more comprehensive network of support, especially if combined resources were aimed at addressing a prevalent social problem such as substance abuse, AIDS or early childbearing.

Professional African American women are far less likely to receive sufficient social support within a work setting that has few African American women in positions of leadership and power. The old philosophy of the National Association of Colored Women's Clubs holds true even today: that is, that African American women helping other African American women is necessary for survival. Research has shown that, traditionally, African American female mentors were most beneficial to other African American females on the job. However, these arrangements were typically informal in nature. With the tremendous stress experienced by African American women due to the racism and sexism of professional work settings, formal organizational mentoring supports need to be established to address the special concerns of this group.

The purpose of this chapter was to identify the nature of community-based institutional supports available to African American women in a variety of settings. To this end, black churches, Greek-letter sororities and professional mentorship arrangements were highlighted as potential sources of assistance. Black churches and sororities have historically provided assistance, when necessary, to African American women who are aware of these resources through affiliation. Evidence suggests that these organizations are also prepared to provide support to women who are not members. Thus, from a policy perspective, these community-based institutional supports for African American women can be viewed as viable options for a variety of intervention efforts. Through collaborative relations with health, mental health, and social service agencies, the support base for these organizations could be enhanced. For example, the National Cancer Institute's concern about recruiting and maintaining more African American women in clinical trials to improve the breast cancer survival rate of African American women could benefit from involving black churches and sororities. Because of the voluntary nature of these organizations, however, launching large-scaled collaborative initiatives would require mechanisms for obtaining adequate funding to hire necessary staff to coordinate such activities. A major obstacle in this regard is the cumbersome grant-application process that nonprofit agencies must negotiate to acquire funding. Special mechanisms should be developed to provide funding to organizations selected for collaborative work with agencies through formal cooperative arrangements.

The importance of professional mentorship arrangements to the occupational success of African American women is perhaps the easiest institutional support network to understand. Yet it does not exist for most African American women. The mentoring relationships identified in this chapter were informal in nature, with African American women helping each other. The most obvious policy implication is to build on this informal support model and develop organizationally based mentorship initiatives. Emerging literature in this area is beginning to examine the effectiveness of various mentor-mentee combinations on the career advancement of African American women (Blake, 1995). This type of research is essential to provide a conceptual basis for establishing promising mentorship programs for African American women. Recognizing the importance of the mentorship strategy for African American women is the first step toward effective organizational support.

In summary, there are a number of institutional and community-based supports available to African American women. However, access to some of these supports may not be easy. This is particularly true for the less structured career-advancement supports accessible through mentoring relationships within organizations. Yet programmatic activities of community-based institutions such as black churches and Greek-letter organizations are positioned to be of assistance to African American women in a variety of ways. Individuals may benefit from contact with these groups. Moreover, health, mental health and social service agencies working to improve the quality of life for African American women and their families could also benefit from exploring possible advantages of involving one or more of these community-based institutional supports in their service and intervention efforts. Collaborative arrangements between formal and informal institutional systems of support for African American women could form an even stronger web of protection than interpersonal supportive relationships alone. The challenge for the future is to determine how these arrangements could be effectively nurtured and sustained in an effort to improve the psychological well-being of African American women.

REFERENCES

Allen, L., & Britt, D.W. (1983). Black women in American society: A resource development perspective. *Issues in Mental Health Nursing, 5,* 61–79.

Barnes, A. S. (1986). *Black women: Interpersonal relationships in profile.* Bristol, IN: Wyndham Hall Press.

Barrera, M., Jr. (1981). Social support in the adjustment of pregnant adolescents: Assessment issues. In B. H. Gottlieb (Ed.), *Networks and social support* (pp. 69–96). Beverly Hills, CA: Sage Publications.

Bell, E. (1990). The bicultural life experience of career-oriented black women. *Journal of Organizational Behavior, 11,* 459–477.

Bhatnagar, D. (1988). Professional women in organizations: New paradigms for research and action. *Sex Roles, 18,* 343–355.

Billingsley, A., & Caldwell, C. H. (1991). The church, the family, and the school in the African American community. *Journal of Negro Education, 60,* 427–440.

Blake, S. D. (1995, August). *At the crossroads of race and gender: Lessons from the mentoring experiences of professional black women.* Paper presented at the Annual Academy of Management Meeting, Vancouver, British Columbia.

Burke, R. J., & McKeen, C. A. (1990). Mentoring in organizations: Implications for women. *Journal of Business Ethics, 9,* 317–332.

Caldwell, C. H., Greene, A. G., & Billingsley, A. (1992). The black church as a family support system: Instrumental and expressive functions. *National Journal of Sociology, 6,* 21–40.

Caldwell, C. H., Chatters, L. M., Billingsley, A., & Taylor, R. J. (1995). Church-based support programs for elderly black adults: Congregational and clergy characteristics. In M. A. Kimble, S. H. McFadden, J. W. Ellor, & J. J. Seeber (Eds.), *Aging, spirituality, and religion: A handbook* (pp. 306–324). Minneapolis, MN: Augsburg Fortress Publishers.

Chatters, L., Taylor, R. J., & Jackson, J. S. (1985). Size and composition of the informal helpers networks of elderly blacks. *Journal of Gerontology, 40,* 605–614.

Clemente, F., Rexroad, P. A., & Hirsch, C. (1975). The participation of the black aged in voluntary associations. *Journal of Gerontology, 30,* 469–472.

Cobb, S. (1976). Social support as a moderator of life stress. *Psychosomatic Medicine, 38,* 300–314.

Cohen, S., & Wills, T. A. (1985). Stress, social support and the buffering hypothesis. *Psychological Bulletin, 98,* 310–357.

Denton, T. C. (1990). Bonding and supportive relationships among black professional women: Rituals of restoration. *Journal of Organizational Behavior, 11,* 447–457.

DuBois, W.E.B. (1898). The study of the Negro problem. *Annals, 1,* 1–23.

Eng, E., Hatch, J., & Callan, A. (1985). Institutionalizing social support through the church and into the community. *Health Education Quarterly, 12,* 81–92.

Frazier, E. F. (1974). *The negro church in America.* New York: Schocken Books.

George, Y. S., Richardson, V., Lakes-Matyas, M., & Blake, F. (1989). *Saving minds: Black churches and education.* Washington, DC: American Association for the Advancement of Science.

Giddings, P. (1988). *In search of sisterhood: Delta Sigma Theta and the challenge of the black sorority movement.* New York: William Morrow.

Gilkes, C. T. (1982). Successful rebellious professionals: The black women's professional identity and community commitment. *Psychology of Women Quarterly, 6,* 289–311.

Greenbaum, S. D., & Greenbaum, P. E. (1985). The ecology of social networks in four urban neighborhoods. *Social Networks, 7,* 47–76.

Hatch, L. R. (1991). Informal support patterns of older African American and white women: Examining effect of family, paid work, and religious participation. *Research on Aging, 3,* 144–170.

Jackson, J. S. (Ed.). (1991). *Life in black America.* Newbury Park, CA: Sage Publications.

Kardiner, A., & Ovesey, L. (1962). *The mark of oppression.* New York: World Publishing Company, Meridian Books.

Kessler, R. C., Price, R. H., & Wortman, C. B. (1985). Social factors in psychopathology: Stress, social support and coping processes. *Annual Review of Psychology, 36,* 531–572.

Lerner, G. (1972). *Black women in white America: A documentary history.* New York: Pantheon Books.

Lincoln, C. E., & Mamiya, L. H. (1990). *The black church in the African American experience.* Durham: Duke University Press.

Manuel, R. C. (1988). The demography of older blacks in the United States. In J. S. Jackson, (Ed.), *The black American elderly: Research on physical and psychosocial health.* New York: Springer Publishing Company.

Mays, B. E., & Nicholson, J. W. (1933). *The Negro's church.* New York: Russell & Russell.

Rodgers-Rose, L. (1980). *The black woman.* New York: Emerson Hall Publishers.

Scott, A. F. (1990). Most invisible of all: Black women's voluntary associations. *The Journal of Southern History, 56,* 3–22.

Scott, N. E. (1989). Differences in mentor relationships of non-white and white female professionals and organizational mobility: A review of the literature. *Journal of Human Behavior, 26,* 23–26.

Taylor, R. J. (1986). Receipt of support from family among black Americans: Demographic and familial differences. *Journal of Marriage and the Family, 48,* 67–77.

Taylor, R. J., & Chatters, L. (1986). Church-based informal support among aged blacks. *The Gerontologist, 26,* 637–642.

Taylor, R. J., & Chatters, L. M. (1988). Church members as a source of informal social support. *Review of Religious Research, 30,* 193–203.

Thomas, D. A. (1990). The impact of race on managers' experiences of developmental relationships (mentoring and sponsorship): An intra-organizational study. *Journal of Organizational Behavior, 11,* 479–492.

Walls, C. T., & Zarit, S. H. (1991). Informal support from black churches and the well-being of elderly blacks. *The Gerontologist, 31,* 490–495.

CHAPTER 8

The Role of the Black Church and Religion

SHERRY L. TURNER AND CHERIE A. BAGLEY

> *The church among black people has been a social cosmos: it has provided an emotional outlet, a verifiable safety valve for people caught up in the whirling storms of life. She has been a source of inspiration and entertainment, of movements, and plans which have moved the entire nation.*
>
> —KELLY MILLER

The significance of religion in the lives of African American women has been a neglected topic in contemporary psychology. Although the fields of sociology (e.g., Gilkes, 1986, 1987) and theology (e.g., Grant, 1989; Martin, 1991; Weems, 1988, 1991, 1993) have amassed a growing body of literature, fewer psychologists have acknowledged the relevance of religion and church life for African American women. The impact of religion is an important consideration given the potential for it to serve as a buffer against stress. Furthermore, churches may be sources of support for African American women and their families. This chapter explores the role of religion and of the black church in the lives of African American women. The chapter uses a socioecological perspective that examines the social and historical contexts in which African American women live and the extent to which contextual factors influence their lives.[1]

The relevance of spirituality, religion and church life in the lives of black women can be seen in a recent nationwide study of African Americans. Using data from the National Survey of Black Americans (NSBA), Taylor and Chatters (1991) used measures assessing church attendance and membership, exposure to religious reading materials and programs, and prayer. The researchers found that over 90 percent of the 2,107 African American men and women surveyed had attended worship services since the age of 18. Of those who have attended services, 70 percent reported attending at least a few times per month or more frequently, and over 90 percent reported that they viewed church attendance as being either fairly important or very important. Furthermore, three-fourths or more of the respondents reported reading religious materials (74.3 percent), watching or listening to religious programs (82 percent), or praying (93 percent) at least a few times per month or more. Although Taylor and Chatters do not provide specific data for African American women, the researchers do report that black females attend religious services more frequently, view church attendance as more important and describe themselves as being more religious than black males. The results described by Taylor and Chatters (1991) are consistent with those of a recent Gallup survey which reported much higher levels of religiosity among blacks than among whites, and among females than among males (Gallup, 1985). The likelihood of women to report higher levels of religious commitment and involvement than men provides further support for the key role of religion and for our analysis of the impact of religion in their lives.

The spiritual and religious experiences of African American women have been described in a variety of ways. As have Taylor and Chatters (1991), other researchers have used measures such as frequency of church attendance and frequency of prayer to assess religiosity. Because many of the terms describing the religious experiences of individuals are often used rather loosely and sometimes synonymously, it is necessary to distinguish these concepts at the outset of the chapter. Religious *participation* refers to actual behaviors in which the woman participates. These behaviors are external indicants of religiosity and include such things as frequency of church attendance and participation in church-related activities; religious study; and the amount of money, time and other resources given to a church or religious organization. Religious *internalization* refers to the extent to which an African American woman believes that the teachings or doctrines of a particular group influence her on a day-to-day basis. Religious internalization also refers to the degree to which the principles and tenets of a woman's faith guide her behavior.

The distinction between religious participation and religious internalization is essential because it provides a clearer picture of the association between religiosity and other aspects of the woman's life. Religious participation and religious internalization may operate independently of each other. A woman may be deeply committed to a religious doctrine; however, she may not participate in worship or spiritual services and activities for practical reasons such as poor health or limited resources. Similarly, a woman may be actively engaged in religious activities, but she may not hold the teachings as being valuable. Churches are often centers of social and other activities that may be more attractive to African American women than a particular doctrine or social teaching.

African American women are a diverse group who acknowledge the breadth of their religious and spiritual experience. The results of two national surveys (Blackwell, 1991; Taylor & Chatters, 1991), however, suggest that a majority of African American women identify themselves as Protestant Christians and claim membership in one of the seven historically black Christian denominations. In the National Survey of Black Americans, 80 percent of the respondents identified themselves as Protestant Christians, with over 50 percent indicating that they were Baptist and slightly over 10 percent indicating that they were Methodist. Less than 10 percent were Roman Catholic, and 10 percent indicated no religious preference. Only 1 percent of the women indicated that they were either Islamic, Muslim, Jewish, Buddhist or Bahai.

The findings of the National Survey of Black Americans regarding the distribution of blacks among various religious groups are consistent with those reported by Blackwell (1991). Blackwell records that there are approximately 12 million (1,175 million) African Americans who are associated with historically black Baptist churches and approximately 6 million who are affiliated with the three black Methodist denominations. Although accurate figures are not available for the number of African Americans who practice the Muslim religion, it is estimated that approximately 2 million African Americans in the United States are Muslim. The American Muslim Mission (AMM), founded in 1975 by Imam Warith D. Muhammad, has approximately 100,000 followers; the Nation of Islam, led by Minister Louis Farrakhan, reports a membership of 5,000 to 10,000. Relatively few African Americans attend churches that are not racially or ethnically segregated (Hadaway, Hackett, & Miller, 1984).

One difficulty in examining the diversity of religious and spiritual experiences of African American women arises from the lack of research reflecting their various religious and spiritual perspectives. In our own review of literature, we accumulated a wealth of information on the history and role of African American Christian churches and religion in women's lives. Comparatively little information was available about non-Christian and non-Protestant black women. Women who follow Islam and other faiths are either not represented or are underrepresented both in the literature and in research samples. In examining the significance of churches in the lives of African American women, therefore, we have chosen to focus specifically on the contributions of the seven historically black denominations which we refer to collectively as the "black church."

This chapter is divided into three major sections. Initially, we discuss the role of African American women in providing leadership and support for black churches in America. The second section explores the functions of the black church in meeting the needs of African American women and their families. The extent to which African American women and their families are involved in and take advantage of resources provided by the black church is a key consideration in understanding the effects of potential stressors and resources in shaping their lives. The role of personal religiosity or faith in enabling African American women to cope with the demands of their lives is examined in the third section. In this chapter, we explore the function of religiosity in guiding the lives and in mediating stress among African American women.

THE ROLE OF AFRICAN AMERICAN WOMEN IN THE BLACK CHURCH

African American women are an integral part of their churches as evidenced by their membership patterns, participation rates and leadership roles. Many of today's churches (particularly those in the seven major black Christian denominations) are composed of predominately female congregations (Lincoln & Mamiya, 1990).[2] In some denominations, congregations can be over 90 percent female (Gilkes, 1986). Yet, while the composition of black churches has been characteristically female, leadership patterns have been characteristically male. African American women play a myriad of roles and hold a variety of offices in their churches; however, they have traditionally functioned only in the background as providers of supportive services. In some settings, designated roles for women include only such strongly sex-typed activities as cooking, teaching, singing and providing instrumental music, arranging social gatherings, and providing nursing or medical assistance when illness or injury occurs. Women have commonly functioned in traditionally female positions as secretaries, clerks, ushers and youth leaders.

In other churches the role of women has been broadened somewhat and women may serve in more visible and powerful leadership positions as pastors, preachers, evangelists, missionaries, stewards, deacons, lay readers, writers and counselors. In her study addressing the role of women in the "sanctified" church, Gilkes (1986) reports that black women have been responsible for both establishing and maintaining churches. During periods of conflict or transition, black women have been instrumental in holding churches together (Gilkes, 1986). These women have also initiated and managed many church-sponsored programs designed to help meet community needs. These programs include services such as providing housing for college students, organizing political clubs, establishing homes for youth and single mothers, and campaigning for women's suffrage (Gilkes, 1986).

Historically, the struggle for women to participate in all aspects of church life and leadership has been a long, arduous one and it continues to be in some settings. Even when women were involved initially in leadership roles, their contributions were often undocumented. For example, little is mentioned of the role that Amanda Berry Smith, Sarah Gorham and Fanny Coppin played as African missionaries of the African Methodist Episcopal (AME) church during the period from 1885 to 1904. Smith established a church school for Liberian boys; Gorham established a mission in Sierra Leone; and Coppin organized the Women's Christian Temperance Union and Women's Missionary Society in South Africa (Jacobs, 1990).

Increasingly, black women are holding positions of spiritual leadership in black churches and are serving as pastors, evangelists, revivalists, missionaries and educators (Gilkes, 1986, 1987) within their congregations. Although these women have benefited from the examples of historical black female leaders and preachers such as Jarena Lee, Amanda Smith and Sojourner Truth, the role of women in pastoral and other ministerial positions has been very controversial. It is estimated that less than 5 percent of clergy in historically black denominations are female (Lincoln & Mamiya, 1990).

The degree to which women are accepted as clergy depends on a number of factors. In a nationwide study of black clergy in 2,150 congregations in historically black denominations, Lincoln and Mamiya (1990) examined attitudes toward women preachers and pastors. The views regarding women in ministry varied based on demographic factors such as gender, age and education level of the respondents. Individuals who are female, under 30 years of age, and have graduate school training are more favorable in their attitudes toward women clergy than those individuals who are male, over 65 years of age, and who have completed less than high school training (Lincoln & Mamiya, 1990).

Attitudes regarding women in ministry also vary as a function of denominational affiliation. Generally, clergy from the three historically black Methodist denominations express positive views about women as pastors and preachers. This acceptance is consistent with policies within the Methodist churches regarding women in ministry. In each of the Methodist denominations, women may hold any office at the local, district, conference or national levels (Lincoln & Mamiya, 1990).

While Methodist clergy are generally accepting of women in ministry, the same attitudes are not commonly held by their Baptist and Pentecostal counterparts. In Lincoln and Mamiya's study, both Baptist and Church of God in Christ (COGIC) respondents were much more likely than Methodist respondents either to "disapprove" or "disapprove strongly" of having women in ministry. As with Methodist churches, the views of both Baptist and Pentecostal clergy about women in ministry are consistent with their respective denominational policies. The autonomy of the local congregation in the Baptist denominations, however, does provide opportunities for women to be ordained and to serve as pastors despite denominational policies.

The discrepancy between positive attitudes about women in leadership positions and the equitable treatment of women in these positions should be noted. Although Methodist clergy are less likely than Baptist and COGIC clergy to express disapproval of having women serve as pastors, Methodist women are typically not afforded the same opportunities as men to serve in pastoral or other leadership roles. Lincoln and Mamiya (1990) report that female Methodist pastors are often appointed to congregations that are smaller and less prestigious than those of their male peers with similar credentials. Furthermore, unlike their male colleagues who are subsequently promoted to larger congregations, women are often moved laterally to congregations that are similar in size to their previous congregations. Although women may hold any office, as of this writing none of the black Methodist churches had ever elected a female bishop.

The controversy surrounding women's roles and responsibilities within the black church is complex and is closely bound to notions about appropriate gender roles for women. Traditionally, women are perceived as being home-oriented, nurturing, caring and emotional and as not possessing leadership or professional qualities. Conversely, men are perceived as being independent and aggressive, and as possessing mechanical, business and leadership acumen (Ruble, 1983). Occupational roles considered appropriate for men and women, both inside and outside church settings, are consistent with sex-role expectations (Deaux & Lewis, 1984). The effects of sex-segregated positions and limited opportunities for leadership on females' personal, professional and spiritual development is not yet fully understood. The fact that many individuals cite religious or biblical reasons for excluding women from leadership positions may be a source of stress among black church women, who may desire to achieve and develop to their fullest potential and yet also wish to adhere to traditional interpretations of scripture that sanction women's leadership. Additionally, reliance upon biblical interpretations that limit women's participation in church affairs may also alleviate stress. This is an area deserving greater attention.

The controversy over women in ministry also reflects the struggle for power among African Americans in this society. The black church has often been viewed as one of the few places in which African Americans maintain autonomy and are allowed to exercise power (Blackwell, 1991). Mirroring patterns of male domination in white society, African American men have often excluded African American women from positions of leadership. A challenge for African American women has been managing the tension between being supportive of black men and rejecting oppression and discrimination at the hands of black men. In meeting this challenge, women in black churches have often developed alternative ways of obtaining and gaining authority within the male-oriented black church structure. For example, many churches have a viable women's department that allows women to have their own autonomy (Gilkes, 1986). Furthermore, women often pursue alternative forms of ministry and leadership within black churches. Rather than preaching, women function effectively as teachers and missionaries.

Despite the difficulty women have had in achieving equal status with men in the black church, women remain committed to service within this prominent institution. The black church often provides opportunities for women to develop leadership skills that they may not otherwise have received (Blackwell, 1991). Furthermore, the church provides valuable resources to African American women and their families. These resources are discussed below.

THE BLACK CHURCH AS A RESOURCE FOR AFRICAN AMERICAN WOMEN

The role of the black church in America has been very distinct from that of its white counterpart. From its earliest inception, the black church has offered a response to slavery and to the discrimination that has been prevalent in many white churches (Hopkins, 1993; Hopkins & Cummings, 1991; Paris, 1985). The enslaved Africans who first arrived in this country practiced their own ancestral religions which included a view of a just, compassionate God who was concerned about the poor and oppressed in society (Hopkins, 1993). Although Christianity was initially employed by white slave owners as a means of enforcing slavery, the Christianity adopted by the slaves included traditional African themes of freedom and liberation from bondage (Bagley & Carroll, 1995; Hopkins, 1993).

The earliest organized black church was the African Methodist Episcopal Church, founded in 1787 by Richard Allen in Philadelphia, Pennsylvania (AME Church, 1988; Lincoln & Mamiya, 1990). The AME church was organized after Richard Allen and other African Americans were told that they could not pray with whites at the altar of the white Methodist Society of Philadelphia. At that time, strict social codes prohibited African Americans from praying simultaneously with whites. Richard Allen and his followers departed from this church and organized the AME church which addressed both the spiritual concerns (e.g., brotherhood, charity and social justice) as well as the physical needs (e.g., food, clothing, shelter, and education) of black Americans (Lincoln & Mamiya, 1990).

Like the AME church, other black churches and congregations were formed and have continued to be counteractive forces against racism and discrimination as well as against many other societal ills with which African Americans must contend. These churches have been essential to the economic survival of African Americans and to the survival of black families (Hill, 1972). Blackwell (1991) asserts that, aside from the family, the black church is the most important social institution in the black community. For African American women, their families and their communities, the black church has performed several crucial functions, some of which are outlined below.

The Black Church and Civil Rights

The black church has played an integral role in the struggle for civil rights for African Americans. This influence has been largely due to the fact that the black church has received support from and maintains contact with more African Americans than any other social institution (Paris, 1985). Lincoln and Mamiya (1990) found that a large percentage (44 percent) of black churches have worked cooperatively with civil rights organizations such as the National Association for the Advancement of

Colored People (NAACP) and the Southern Christian Leadership Conference (SCLC) in dealing with community problems. The churches were also involved in local community crisis events such as school desegregation. Based on findings from the NSBA study, Taylor and Chatters (1991) found that many black Americans believe that the church has "actively encouraged social progress for black Americans." The importance of civil rights and the condition of African Americans may also be clearly seen in many of the teachings of the black church.

Though not widely acknowledged, the contributions of African American church women were vital to the success of the civil rights movement. In a study of black female civil rights leaders from rural Mississippi, Payne (1990) found that African American women often reported becoming involved in the movement because of their religious beliefs. A group of black church women organized the Montgomery bus boycott (Burks, 1990). Additionally, women such as Fannie Lou Hamer, Septima Clark and Ella Baker were actively involved in the Student Nonviolent Coordinating Committee (SNCC) and the SCLC (Crawford, 1990; Locke, 1990; McFadden, 1990; Mueller, 1990).[3]

The Black Church and Women's Rights

Although the black church has actively engaged in the struggle for equality for African Americans, it has more slowly embraced the struggle for women's rights. In her review of the work of black Baptist women, however, Brooks (1983) reports that as early as the 1880s black women were actively working both inside and outside the church to promote female equality. These women often united with white women to demonstrate the biblical basis for women's leadership in the home and the church, for social reform, and in the labor force. In their speeches and writings, these black female leaders often rejected the helpless, fragile, and passive images of womanhood that were typically espoused by both black and white men, and they portrayed women as being both powerful and influential.

Contemporary writers such as Katie Cannon (1993), Jacqueline Grant (1989, 1993), Cheryl Townsend Gilkes (1986, 1987, 1993), Clarice Martin (1991, 1993) and Renita Weems (1988, 1991, 1993) highlight both Afrocentrism and black feminism in theological discourse. Such an approach, referred to as *womanist theology*, embodies writings about the culture and history of African American women from their own perspective. Womanist theorists identify with their black male counterparts in their struggle against white racism and with their white female counterparts in their struggle against sexism. At the same time, however, womanists distinguish themselves both from white feminists who fail to acknowledge racism and from black liberation theologians who fail to acknowledge patriarchy (Grant, 1993). As in liberation theology and feminist theology, a central theme in womanist theology is freedom from oppression (Brown-Douglass, 1993). A major goal of womanists has been to promote survival by advocating justice, jobs, education, health care and housing for poor black women, men and children (Williams, 1993).

Womanists also acknowledge the relationship between Christianity and the values and traditions of the dominant Western society. Womanists recognize that Africans, Asians and Latin Americans who convert to Christianity are often expected to abandon their own cultural practices and to adopt Western traditions that may support oppressive social and political structures (Grant, 1993). Although the church is often viewed as being less male-dominated and oppressive of women than other social institutions, some authors (e.g., Sanders, 1992) argue that churches also subjugate females. Womanist theology provides a framework within which the oppression of black women and other individuals can be confronted.

The Black Church as a Cohesive Institutional Structure

Black churches are also beneficial because they foster unity within families and within diverse communities of African Americans. According to Blackwell (1991), the black church promotes social cohesion by stressing family unity, mutual aid and responsibility. Paris (1985) further asserts that the church promotes a common set of fundamental ideals, rituals, symbols and beliefs. The black church often serves as an equalizer among persons from different stations in life: the affluent have an opportunity to share resources with others and to receive spiritual fulfillment; in turn, the poor also have an opportunity to receive needed material and spiritual resources.

The Black Church as a Resource for Families

In addition to their role as promoters of equality for blacks, churches also provide valuable resources for African American women and their families and for African American communities (Bronfenbrenner, Moen, & Garbarino, 1984; Hill, 1972; Taylor & Chatters, 1988; Taylor, Thornton,

& Chatters, 1987). Churches may serve as a buffer against stress because they often provide (1) financial assistance and material goods such as food and clothing; (2) emotional support, companionship and opportunities for social interaction among members; (3) information about needed services; and (4) an advocacy base for better jobs, housing and schooling for the larger African American society (Taylor et al., 1987). In their review of the NSBA data, Taylor and Chatters (1988) reported that the most essential type of assistance received by African Americans from their churches came in the form of social and emotional support. The respondents reported that when they experienced difficulties, church members offered advice and encouragement, companionship and moral support. Instrumental support most often came in the form of money and financial assistance, transportation and other goods and services.

The black church also supports African American women and families by sharing in the training of children (Levin, 1984; Nobles, Goddard, Cavil, & George, 1987). In fact, the role of the church and the role of the family in shaping children's lives are frequently seen as analogous (Levin, 1984; Nobles et al., 1987). African American women frequently receive support from black churches in raising their children. Lincoln and Mamiya (1990) report that many churches place special emphasis on services and support for children and youth.

RELIGIOSITY, FAITH AND COPING AMONG AFRICAN AMERICAN WOMEN

Countless successful African American women acknowledge the influence of religiosity and the church in their lives. Marian Wright Edelman (1992), founder and president of the Children's Defense Fund, has acknowledged the role of her religious upbringing in shaping her social and political convictions. Renowned performing artists such as Leontyne Price, Aretha Franklin and Gladys Knight trace their roots and musical training to their experiences in black churches (Blackwell, 1991). Susan Taylor, editor of *Essence* magazine, has a regular column focusing on spirituality. Similarly, Dr. Vanessa Gamble (1990), a young African American physician, has written about the challenges she faced in medical school, in coping with her mother's illness and about the role of her faith in helping her and her family to cope with difficulties. The influence of religious participation and internalization on the mental health of African American women is an area worthy of greater attention. We turn now to a discussion of the influence of personal religiosity and faith in helping African American women to cope with the demands of their lives.

Religiosity, Faith and Mental Health

Several studies have demonstrated a positive relationship between religiosity and African American women's physical and mental health (Ellison, 1990; Ellison & Gay, 1990; Griffith, English, & Mayfield, 1980). In recent surveys of black Americans, Ellison (1990; Ellison & Gay, 1990) found that frequency of church attendance was a significant predictor of life satisfaction and personal happiness. Similarly, a study of a diverse group of African American women in St. Louis showed an inverse relationship between religiosity and psychological distress (Handal, Black-Lopez, & Moergen, 1989). Using the Langer Symptom Survey and a subscale of the Personal Religiosity Survey, Handal et al. (1989) found that low levels of religiosity were correlated with high levels of psychological distress. Conversely, high levels of religiosity were related to better adjustment and an absence of psychological distress. Although the results of the Handal study are exploratory, the research provides some empirical support for many African American women's subjective reports that their religion "provides direction, emotional sustenance, and motivation" for their lives and for their reports of "feeling better" and "more positive" after attending worship services.

African American women may perceive discipline and spirituality as being related to economic, social and occupational benefits. A disciplined, religious lifestyle may also result in a sense of inner peace and contentment. Prayer, in particular, may be perceived as yielding positive benefits in the lives of African American women. Taylor and Chatters (1991) report that prayer may be seen in two ways. First, it may be viewed as a means of changing one's situation and of obtaining help with a particular problem. A woman suffering from financial burdens may use prayer as a way of acquiring money, employment or a release from financial difficulties. Chatters and Taylor (1989) report that one in six adult African Americans participating in their survey reported using prayer to cope with financial difficulties.

African American women, alternatively, may use prayer to help bring about changes in themselves (Chatters & Taylor, 1989). Rather than praying for material and tangible resources, a woman experiencing financial difficulties may pray to be better equipped to handle her financial burdens, or to change the way in which she views her financial situation and priorities. Additional research is needed which examines more closely the use of prayer and other expressions of religiosity as coping strategies among African American women. The relationship between religiosity and mental health may have significant implications for counseling and other therapeutic interventions with African American women. These implications are discussed below.

Linking Religiosity, Church Life and Mental Health: Implications for Practice

African Americans have generally not used traditional mental health centers when distressed and are less likely than whites to use psychological services for personal difficulties (Cheatham, Shelton, & Ray, 1987; Neighbors, 1985). African American women may not seek out and receive needed mental health care because they do not want to disclose information about their personal lives, they perceive counseling services as being relevant for white women only, they have little time to focus on themselves, or they rely upon their faith to help them handle difficulties (Hicks, 1991). Furthermore, black women may lack familiarity with traditional mental health settings or may view the settings negatively. Because of the familiarity of black women with churches and because of role of the church in their lives, many social scientists and practitioners argue that the church may be better equipped than traditional mental health facilities to provide assistance for African American women (Richardson, 1991; Thomas & Dansby, 1985). Ministers and other members of the woman's informal support network may help moderate physical or mental distress (Neighbors, 1985). Reliance upon trained clergy and collaboration between mental health practitioners and the church may facilitate the counseling process (Richardson, 1991) and, in turn, empower black women.

Recovery and healing are often promoted through religion or spirituality (Hicks, 1991). Richardson (1991) maintains that during counseling sessions, clients often acknowledge the influence of religion in their lives. Knowing about and responding to a client's religious beliefs can inform the counselor's decisions regarding treatment, referral and implementation strategies (Worthington, 1992) and thereby facilitate mental health.

IMPLICATIONS FOR POLICY

There is a pressing need for an increased awareness of the status of black women in the United States. This knowledge should be followed by a commitment to removing barriers which stifle the progress of black women and their families. The United Nations Commission on the Status of Women (United Nations, 1991) has identified several key areas for national action that might be useful in shaping the social agendas of black churches. Of chief concern are "obstacles to the advancement of women in education, employment and health," to equality in political participation and decision-making, and to alleviating economic and social inequality. Special attention should be given to "problems faced by women living in extreme poverty, rural women and women in the informal sector of the economy" (United Nations, 1991, p. 3).

Poor black women and children are often unfairly targeted in efforts to reform health care and welfare. Recently proposed policies have resulted in the curtailment of essential medical and social services that might benefit black women and children ("Empowerment Key to Black Women's and Girls' Health," 1995). Because of the black church's powerful historical role as a catalyst for change, the institution must continue to strive to shape public policy and must begin to advocate forcefully for the rights of black women and children.

Because of the prominence of the black church in the African American community, it is also critical for secular organizations, policymakers and service providers to rely upon the black church for support in their efforts to serve black women and their families. Consultation regarding policies and practices affecting African Americans should occur with black religious leaders. Organizations such as the Black Community Crusade for Children, coordinated by the Children's Defense Fund, have enlisted the help of black churches in advocating support for poor women and children and also in creating programs to intervene when government funding has been cut short. More collaboration between secular and nonsecular institutions is needed.

The resolution of gender inequities within black churches is requisite for addressing black women's needs. Because the involvement of black women in shaping the policies and social agendas of the church is critical, black churches need to recognize and encourage women's leadership.

The emergence of womanist theological perspectives may be instrumental in shaping the social agenda of the black church. The reexamination of biblical texts that have been traditionally interpreted by whites and males may result in less rigid, restrictive sex-role expectations for black women. Furthermore, the emphasis on freedom from oppression may challenge churches to reconsider their policies concerning the status of black women.

SUGGESTIONS FOR FUTURE RESEARCH

We have attempted to provide a review of current research examining the role that religion and church life play in the lives of African American women. We support Wilmore's (1972) assertion that although religion has always been one of the most important aspects of the life of black persons in the United States, it has been woefully neglected as an area of serious study by black and white scholars alike. Although sociologists, theologians and psychologists have devoted some attention to understanding the impact of religion for African Americans, additional research is needed that is multidisciplinary in its approach.

Research is also needed that is multifactorial in focus. Often when religion is used as a variable in social science research, it has been included as a demographic variable and is very simplistic in nature. Many researchers use a single indicator of religiosity, often denominational affiliation or frequency of church attendance. A more careful analysis of complex spiritual and religious processes is necessary. Important, yet not fully understood, is the development of African American women's religious identity. Regardless of a woman's specific religious beliefs, the process by which she internalizes religious principles has not been clearly delineated.

The development of African Americans within the context of limited social and economic opportunities is insufficiently understood. We propose that future researchers should assess more systematically the impact on black women of racism, sexism and classism and the effectiveness of religion and church life in mediating the effects of oppression. There is currently no comprehensive body of knowledge that clearly delineates how oppression within American society influences the development of African Americans and affects relationships among and between African American males and females. American society has often excluded African Americans from leadership positions and social opportunities. During times of crisis, however, churches have often been accessible and have provided the milieu necessary to strengthen individuals and to allow inclusion. The black church in America was initiated to meet the comprehensive needs of black culture and it continues to promote the development of individuals, families and communities.

Although many African American women perceive the church and religion as having positive influences on people's lives, this is not universally true. Taylor and Chatters reported that at least some respondents feel as though the church has had a negative impact on African Americans because of its emphasis on money and because of their perceptions of the origins of Christianity—the religion most frequently practiced by African Americans—in white culture. In examining the role of religion, it is necessary also to acknowledge the deleterious effects that religiosity may have on African American women.

Although many African American women perceive their own spirituality as beneficial to their lives, additional research is needed to understand empirically the effects of religion (Neighbors, 1990). The reports of many women regarding the value of their religious beliefs cannot be ignored, and both authors of this chapter affirm the positive expression of religion in their lives.

NOTES

[1] For a review of research examining religion and mental health, the reader is referred to a special issue of *The Counseling Psychologist, 17*(4), 1992, which focuses on religious faith, and to the journal *Psychology and Christianity*. These works do not focus specifically on African American women.

[2] The seven major historically black denominations include the African Methodist Episcopal (AME) Church; the African Methodist Episcopal Zion (AMEZ) Church; the Christian Methodist Episcopal (CME) Church; the National Baptist Convention, U.S.A., Incorporated (NBC); the National Baptist Convention of America, Unincorporated (NBCA); the Progressive National Baptist Convention (PNBC); and the Church of God in Christ (COGIC).

[3] For an excellent review of the contributions of these women, please refer to Crawford, V. L., Rouse, J. A., & Woods, B. (1990), *Women in the Civil Rights Movement: Trailblazers and Torchbearers 1941–1965,* Bloomington, IN: Indiana University Press.

REFERENCES

African Methodist Episcopal Church (1988). *The book of discipline.* Nashville: AMEC Sunday School Union.

Bagley, C. A., & Carroll, J. (1995). Healing forces in African American families. In H. I. McCubbin, E. A. Thompson, A. I. Thompson, & J. A. Futrell (Eds.), *Resiliency in ethnic minority families: African American families* (Vol. 2, pp. 117–142). Madison: University of Wisconsin, Center for Family Studies.

Blackwell, J. E. (1991). *The black community: Diversity and unity.* New York: HarperCollins.

Bronfenbrenner, U., Moen, P., & Garbarino, J. (1984). Child, family, and community. In R. D. Parke (Ed.), *Review of child development research: Vol. 7. The family* (pp. 283–328). Chicago: University of Chicago Press.

Brooks, E. (1983). The feminist theology of the black Baptist church, 1880–1990. In A. Swerdlow & H. Lessinger (Eds.), *Class, race and sex: The dynamics of control* (pp. 31–59). Boston: G. K. Hall.

Brown-Douglass, K. D. (1993). Womanist theology: What is its relationship to black theology? In J. H. Cone & G. S. Wilmore (Eds.), *Black theology: A documentary history: Volume Two. 1980–1992* (pp. 290–299). Maryknoll, NY: Orbis Books.

Burks, M. F. (1990). Trailblazers: Women in the Montgomery bus boycott. In V. L. Crawford, J. A. Rouse, & B. Woods (Eds.), *Women in the civil rights movement: Trailblazers and torchbearers 1941–1965* (pp. 71–83). Bloomington: Indiana University Press.

Cannon, K. G. (1993). Hitting a straight lick with a crooked stick: The womanist dilemma in the development of a black liberation ethic. In J. H. Cone & G. S. Wilmore (Eds.), *Black theology: A documentary history: Volume Two: 1980–1992* (pp. 300–308). Maryknoll, NY: Orbis Books.

Chatters, L. M., & Taylor, R. J. (1989). Life problems and coping strategies of older black adults. *Social Work, 34,* 313–319.

Cheatham, H. E., Shelton, T. O., & Ray, W. J. (1987). Race, sex, causal attribution and help-seeking behavior. *Journal of College Student Personnel, 28,* 559–568.

Crawford, V. L. (1990). Beyond the human self: Grassroots activists in the Mississippi civil rights movement. In V. L. Crawford, J. A. Rouse, & B. Woods (Eds.), *Women in the civil rights movement: trailblazers and torchbearers 1941–1965* (pp. 13–26). Bloomington: Indiana University Press.

Deaux, K., & Lewis, L. L. (1984). Structure of gender stereotypes: Interrelationships among components and gender label. *Journal of Personality and Social Psychology, 46,* 991–1004.

Edelman, M. W. (1992). *The measure of our success: A letter to my children and yours.* Boston: Beacon Press.

Ellison, C. G. (1990). Family ties, friendships, and subjective well-being among black Americans. *Journal of Marriage and Family, 52,* 298–310.

Ellison, C. G., & Gay, D. A. (1990). Religion, religious commitment, and life satisfaction among black Americans. *The Sociological Quarterly, 31,* 123–147.

"Empowerment key to black women's and girls' health." (1995, Summer). *Necessary, 2,* 12–13.

Gallup. G., Jr. (1985). Religion in America. *Annals AAPSS, 480,* 167–174.

Gamble, V. N. (1990). On becoming a physician: A dream not deferred. In E. C. White (Ed.), *The black women's health book* (pp. 52–64). Seattle: Seal Press.

Gilkes, C. T. (1986). The role of women in the sanctified church. *The Journal of Religious Thought, 43,* 24–41.

Gilkes, C. T. (1987). Some mother's son and some father's daughter: Gender and biblical language in Afro-Christian worship tradition. In C. Atkinson, C. Buchanan, & M. Miles (Eds.) *Shaping new vision: Gender and values in American culture* (pp. 73–99). Ann Arbor: UMI Research Press.

Gilkes, C. T. (1993). Womanist ways of seeing. In J. H. Cone & G. S. Wilmore (Eds.), *Black theology: A documentary history: Volume Two. 1980–1992* (pp. 321–324). Maryknoll, NY: Orbis Books.

Grant, J. (1989). *White women's Christ and black women's Jesus: Feminist Christology and womanist response.* Atlanta: Scholars Press.

Grant, J. (1993). Womanist theology: Black women's experience as a source for doing theology, with special reference to Christology. In J. H. Cone & G. S. Wilmore (Eds.), *Black theology: A documentary history: Volume Two. 1980–1992* (pp. 273–289). Maryknoll, NY: Orbis Books.

Griffith, E., English, T., & Mayfield, V. (1980). Possession, prayer, and testimony: Therapeutic aspects of the Wednesday night meeting in a black church. *Psychiatry, 43,* 120–128.

Hadaway, C. K., Hackett, D. G., & Miller, J. F. (1984). The most segregated institution: Correlates of interracial church participation. *Review of Religious Research, 25,* 204–219.

Handal, P. J., Black-Lopez, W., & Moergen, S. (1989). Preliminary investigation of the relationship between religion and psychological distress in black women. *Psychological Reports, 65,* 971–975.

Hicks, I. D. (1991). *For black women only.* Chicago: African American Images.

Hill, R. B. (1972). *The strengths of black families.* New York: Emerson Hall.

Hopkins, D. N. (1993). *Shoes that fit our feet: Sources for a constructive black theology.* Maryknoll, NY: Orbis Books.

Hopkins, D. N., & Cummings, G. (1991). *Cut loose your stammering tongue: Black theology in the slave narratives.* Maryknoll, NY: Orbis Books.

Jacobs, S. M. (1990). Three Afro-American women missionaries in Africa, 1882–1904. In D. C. Hine (Ed.), *Black women in U.S. history* (Vol. 2, pp. 693–707). Brooklyn: Carlson Publishing.

Levin, J. S. (1984). The role of the black church in community medicine. *Journal of the National Medical Association, 76,* 477–483.

Lincoln, C. E., & Mamiya, L. H. (1990). *The black church in the African American experience.* Durham: Duke University Press.

Locke, M. E. (1990). Is this America? Fannie Lou Hamer and the Mississippi Freedom Democratic Party. In V. L. Crawford, J. A. Rouse, & B. Woods (Eds.), *Women in the civil rights movement: Trailblazers and torchbearers 1941–1965* (pp. 27–37). Bloomington: Indiana University Press.

Martin, C. (1991). The *haustafeln* (Household codes) in African American biblical interpretation: "Free slaves" and "subordinate women." In C. H. Felder (Ed.), *Stony the road we trod: African American Biblical interpretation* (pp. 206–231). Minneapolis: Fortress Press.

Martin, C. (1993). Womanist interpretations of the New Testament: The quest for inclusive translation and interpretation. In J. H. Cone & G. S. Wilmore (Eds.), *Black theology: A documentary history: Volume Two: 1980–1992* (pp. 225–244). Maryknoll, NY: Orbis Books.

McFadden, G. J. (1990). Septima P. Clark and the struggle for human rights. In V. L. Crawford, J. A. Rouse, & B. Woods (Eds.), *Women in the civil rights movement: Trailblazers and torchbearers 1941–1965* (pp. 85–97). Bloomington: Indiana University Press.

Mueller, C. (1990). Ella Baker and the origins of "participatory democracy." In V. L. Crawford, J. A. Rouse, & B. Woods (Eds.), *Women in the civil rights movement: Trailblazers and torchbearers 1941–1965* (pp. 51–70). Bloomington: Indiana University Press.

Neighbors, H. W. (1985). Seeking professional help for personal problems: Black Americans' use of health and mental health services. *Community Mental Health Journal, 21,* 156–166.

Neighbors, H. W. (1990). Clinical care update: Minorities. The prevention of psychopathology in Africans: An epidemiologic perspective. *Community Mental Health Journal, 26,* 167–177.

Nobles, W. W., Goddard, L. L., Cavil, A. E., & George, P. Y. (1987). *African American families.* Oakland, CA: Black Family Institute.

Paris, P. J. (1985). *The social teaching of the black churches.* Philadelphia: Fortress Press.

Payne, C. (1990). Men led, but women organized: Movement participation of women in the Mississippi delta. In V. L. Crawford, J. A. Rouse, & B. Woods (Eds.), *Women in the civil rights movement: Trailblazers and torchbearers 1941–1965.* Bloomington: Indiana University Press.

Richardson, J. (1991). Utilizing the resources of the African American church: Strategies for counseling professionals. In C. C. Lee & B. L. Richardson (Eds.), *Multicultural issues in counseling: New approaches to diversity.* Alexandria, VA: American Association for Counseling and Development.

Ruble, T. L. (1983). Sex stereotypes: Issues of change in the early 1970s. *Sex Roles, 9,* 397–402.

Sanders, C. J. (1992). Afrocentrism and womanism in the seminary. *Christianity and Crisis, 52,* 123–126.

Taylor, R. J., & Chatters, L. M. (1988). Church members as a source of informal social support. *Review of Religious Research, 30,* 193–203.

Taylor, R. J., & Chatters, L. M. (1991). Religious life. In J. Jackson (Ed.), *Life in black America* (pp. 105–123). Newbury Park: Sage Publications.

Taylor, R. J., Thornton, M. C., & Chatters, L. M. (1987). Black Americans' perceptions of the sociohistorical role of the church. *Journal of Black Studies, 18,* 123–138.

Thomas, M. B., & Dansby, P. G. (1985). Black clients: Family structures, therapeutic issues, and strengths. *Psychotherapy, 22,* 398–407.

United Nations (1991). *Women: Challenges to the year 2000.* New York: Author.

Weems, R. J. (1988). *Just a sister away: A womanist vision of women's relationships in the Bible.* San Diego: Luramedia.

Weems, R. J. (1991). Reading her way through the struggle: African American women and the Bible. In C. H. Felder (ed.), *Stony the road we trod: African American biblical interpretation* (pp. 57–77). Minneapolis: Fortress Press.

Weems, R. J. (1993). Womanist reflections on biblical hermeneutics. In J. H. Cone & G. S. Wilmore (Eds.), *Black theology: A documentary history. Volume Two: 1980–1992* (pp. 216–224). Maryknoll, NY: Orbis Books.

Wilmore, G. (1972). *Black religion and black radicalism: An interpretation of the religious history of Afro-American people.* Maryknoll, NY: Orbis Books.

Williams, D. S. (1993). Womanist theology: Black women's voices. In J. H. Cone & G. S. Wilmore (Eds.), *Black theology: A documentary history: Volume Two: 1980–1992* (pp. 265–272). Maryknoll, NY: Orbis Books.

Worthington, E. L., Jr. (1992). Religious faith across the life span: Implications for counseling and research. *Counseling Psychologist, 17,* 555–612.

CHAPTER 9

Stress, Coping and the Mental Health of African American Women

FRANCES M. CHRISTIAN, CHERYL S. AL-MATEEN, CARMEN T. WEBB, AND LUCIA S. DONATELLI

Stress is central in the lives of African American women and they are at risk for experiencing the physiological and psychological by-products of stress. This chapter identifies common stressful external influences on the mental health of African American women. We discuss how societally derived processes such as racism, sexism and classism may combine to impede the positive mental health of African American women, and identify the typical coping resources employed by African American women to help them maintain their families and positive mental health. Finally, this chapter reviews the current state of knowledge about the mental health problems of African American women as well as their experiences in the mental health system, and provides recommendations for conducting gender- and culture-sensitive mental health treatment for them.

CHRONIC STRESSES

Pearlin (1982) acknowledged the importance of the social context in studying sources of stress: "The sources of stress extend from the most immediate contexts of people's lives to the outermost boundaries of societies and cultures" (p. 369). The literature reviewed suggests that race, sex, class and their derivatives (racism, sexism and classism) are crucial variables that shape the social context of African American women. In addition to routine daily encounters and universally stressful life events, African American women confront stresses due to their position and status in American society. Thus, the potential sources of stress in African

American women's lives and their coping responses cannot be fully understood apart from their sociocultural environment.

Financial Stress

While white women, with whom African American women are most often compared, may experience stressors as a result of their gender and class, African American women are disproportionately poor. African American women, as a group, have a more vulnerable economic resource network than white women (Allen & Britt, 1983; McNair & Roberts, 1998; Nichols-Casebolt, 1989; Simms, 1987). Future earnings of African American women will probably constitute an even greater percentage of total family income in comparison to white women, due to the widening earning gap between African American males and white males (Geschwender & Carroll-Seguin, 1990). Thus, increasing numbers of African American women and their families will be at risk for encountering economic or financial stress.

Chronic stressful environmental conditions such as poor housing and discrimination, as well as acute stressors such as crime and violence, often accompany financial stress. A number of studies have shown that chronic financial stress is associated with depression (Makosky, 1982; Dressler, 1985; Dressler, Milburn, Brown, & Gary, 1988; Fellen, 1989) as well as other mental health problems (Belle, 1990; Bennett, 1987). Social support networks of low-income African American women may not buffer them against stress and may contribute to a "contagion of stress" if network members are also experiencing a number of financially related life events and stressful ongoing conditions (Belle, 1982, p. 94). Feelings of helplessness and powerlessness to remove major stressors for low-income African American women have been found to contribute to self-medication with drugs and alcohol, and palliative coping strategies such as overeating, daytime sleeping and suppression of thoughts about problems (Belle, 1982).

Multiple Role Stress

Multiple social roles, associated with competing demands leading to role overload and strain (McBride, 1990), have been identified in the literature as another potential source of stress for African American women of all socioeconomic groups. Although most individuals perform multiple roles, the stress-coping research relevant to women tends to focus on how they balance the roles of worker, wife and mother. A number of researchers have noted that historically, African American women have combined the roles of worker, wife and mother (Beckett, 1976; Burgess & Horton, 1993; Harrison & Minor, 1978; Hoffman & Hale-Benson, 1987; Lewis, 1989; Rodgers-Rose, 1980). A fundamental difference in the lives of African American and white women is the experience of African American women as paid workers. African American women are more likely than white women to work after marriage and childbirth, irrespective of their husbands' education, occupation or income (Allen & Britt, 1983).

Research on sex-role attitudes has shown that African American women expect to combine work and family roles (Grump, 1975; Malson, 1983; Thomas, 1986). Although multiple social roles tend to characterize the lives of many African American women, there is conflicting research with regard to whether they experience role-strain problems. Some researchers have suggested that, as a part of their socialization process, African American women have developed effective coping strategies for managing conflicting role demands (Katz & Protrokowski, 1983). These coping strategies include obtaining social support from family members, extended kin and female friends (Brown & Gary, 1985), as well as positive cognitive appraisals of stressful events (Lindball-Golberg, Dukes, & Lasley, 1988). Also, older children are likely to assist with household chores and rearing of young children (Malson, 1983).

By contrast, other researchers have found that African American women do experience role strain and they tend to choose the least effective coping strategies for managing their multiple roles (McAdoo, 1986). Research has also suggested that African American females, due to their increased likelihood of having both family and work responsibilities, are more dissatisfied with their leisure activities than their white female counterparts (Brown, 1988).

Also, professional African American women have been identified as often having considerable ambivalence about hiring other African Americans for domestic help. On one hand, they may realize they need help, but on the other, they feel as if they are exploiting African American women (Comas-Diaz & Greene, 1994). Professional African American women may have the added role expectation of giving back to their community. Those who have some measure of success may be expected to help others, a stress that may impinge on their financial and emotional resources (Comas-Diaz & Greene, 1994).

Romantic Relationship Stress

Research suggests that the greater resources of middle-class and higher educated African American women (financial, social, educational) may present many disadvantages, resulting in stress (Bell, 1990; Comas-Diaz & Greene, 1994). For example, their higher income, educational achievements and social mobility may not protect them from stress arising from the lack of availability of compatible male partners (Tobin, 1980; Comas-Diaz & Greene, 1994). This research underscores that middle-class and highly educated African American women who desire an intraracial relationship may especially have difficulty finding and maintaining intimate and supportive heterosexual relationships. African American men may not find educated African American women appealing as mates. The greater a woman's educational level and income, the less desirable she is to black males (Comas-Diaz & Greene, 1994).

If a romantic relationship with a professional is important to the African American woman, she soon realizes that further advancement means more limited access to similarly employed African American males. She may be tempted to delay or even curtail professional advancement. If relationships with professionals are not important, she may find herself marrying "down," then volleying with her family's and society's reactions to her nonprofessional/non-middle-class husband (Comas-Diaz & Greene, 1994).

If the African American woman is a lesbian, she is likely to struggle with different kinds of stresses in romantic relationships. In addition to racism and sexism, lesbian African American women have to cope with internalized and externalized homophobia (Miller, 1989). An African American lesbian couple may face dual social censure and alienation from the African American and the gay community (Greene, 1994). An African American woman in a lesbian couple may also be torn between the needs of her partner, the gay community, her family of origin, and the African American community. Because the desire for acceptance and social support from the family of origin may be stronger than such needs from the lesbian community, this may be a source of conflict between couples who have different needs (Falco, 1991).

Work Stress

The middle-class African American woman who defines herself as: (1) successful/middle class apart from her husband, or (2) the primary financial contributor to the middle-class status, may feel guilt for surpassing her husband. This guilt stressor may operate fairly often, since Willie (1986) and McAdoo (1980) show that African American females are often better educated than African American males.

Research has also suggested that middle-class and professional African American women may experience stress as a result of having to confront racism and sexism in the workplace. In an investigation of African American professional women, Leggon (1980) identified the problem of status discrepancy for African American female professionals as a potential source of stress. The women in Leggon's study reported that the discrepancy between their high-achieved status as professionals and their low-ascribed status as women and African Americans in American society was a significant source of stress for them. Thus, there is no "double advantage" to the dual status of being African American and female (Fulbright, 1986). A dual status simply leads to a dual vulnerability to racism and sexism. African American professional women are likely to experience a pressure to compensate for both race and gender in the workplace. Stress may occur when the African American woman must constantly prove her worth to compensate for both race and gender. She may also feel guilt about taking on alien characteristics of the corporate world. She may use coping skills of vigilance and caution, carefully not revealing parts of her true self—with the payoff being even greater stress (Spurlock, 1985).

Although African American women with professional positions have increased in the labor force, African American women as a group are disproportionately positioned in the lower strata of the working class (Rix, 1987; U.S. Department of Health and Human Services, 1992). The majority of African American women are overrepresented in low-status occupations and are concentrated in a few low-paying, traditionally female occupations (Rix, 1987; Zambrana, 1987). In addition to low pay or erratic income, if the African American woman is a single head of household, her struggle for economic survival may result in "intense, continuous and unabating stress" (Bennett, 1987, p. 223). These African American women are particularly vulnerable to the negative health effects or diseases often linked to lower socioeconomic status (SES) (e.g., diabetes, lung disease cerebrovascular disease and cirrhosis of the liver [McNair & Roberts, 1998]).

Upward-Mobility Stress

Research has shown that upward-mobility stresses for middle-class African American women may extend beyond the workplace. For example, the African American woman's presence in the middle class may bring varied responses from members of her family of origin. Some family members may feel envious, and react with anger, calling her "uppity" or accusing her of "forgetting where she came from." In contrast, especially if she is first-generation middle class, they may place her on a pedestal and hold her up as a shining example to others in the African American community. She may feel great pressure to live up to this image. Likewise, one who is second- or third-generation middle class may feel the pressure of living up to familial role models. McAdoo (1982) has shown that those who had been middle class for three generations reported higher stress levels than those who had risen in status over the same time period. Upward-mobility stress for an African American woman may be associated with pressure or "reciprocal obligations" from kin to continue help exchange patterns (McAdoo, 1978). They may depend on her to help the rest of the family out of poverty or through school. Although research shows that some African American women do not consider this an excessive responsibility (McAdoo, 1978), others may prefer to spend their emotional and financial capital in career-advancing or status-building areas. The result is an African American woman who feels guilt about her success and confusion about whether she is betraying her roots (Spurlock, 1985). The immediate or extended family may therefore serve as a significant stressor or a support.

COPING STRATEGIES

The transactional stress-coping theoretical model of Lazarus and Folkman (1984) has been especially influential in recent years. This model proposes that how an individual appraises and copes with stress may be more important than specific life events or demands. Additionally, the model posits that when secondary appraisals (e.g., "I can manage this") are adequate, the experience of stress is not likely to occur, irrespective of the severity or chronicity of the stressor.

However, the transactional model can be seen as reflecting a largely Eurocentric perspective grounded in the experience of the white majority culture. White or Eurocentric culture has been described as oriented toward individualistic goals and individual mastery (Nobles, 1978). In contrast, African American culture has been described as emphasizing harmony, survival of the family or group and having kinships organized around consanguinity (blood ties and affinity) rather than conjugality (marriage) (Sudarkasa, 1981).

The transactional model appears to minimize the influence of such concepts as social structures and culture in the stress-coping process. These concepts are viewed as "distal" variables while individual perception, expectations and beliefs are viewed as more important "proximal" variables (Lazarus & Folkman, 1984, p. 231). Researchers have recently begun to advocate that more culturally relevant concepts such as "mundane extreme environmental stress" (Peters & Massey, 1983), manufactured "incompetence" (Myers, 1982), "contagion of stress" (Belle, 1982) and "acculturative stress" (Anderson, 1991) be incorporated into future expansion of theoretical and empirical research on stress-coping in minority populations. Thus, we will provide an overview of culturally derived coping strategies often used by African American women.

Reliance on Family and Extended Kin

The moderating influence of social support and social networks on the effects of stress has been the focus of considerable research (for reviews, see Cohen & Willis, 1985; Dunston, 1990; Leavy, 1983; Milburn, 1986; Snapp, 1989; Varux, 1985). Reliance on family and extended kin is a primary coping strategy of African American women.

Whether an African American woman experiences poverty or is affluent, social support from family and extended kin has been shown to be a culturally rather than an economically based coping strategy (McAdoo, 1982). Traditionally, African Americans have utilized their families and informal support networks to help them cope with life stressors: "The will to simply 'keep on keeping on' in the midst of difficulty begins with support, protection and encouragement by loved ones" (Baker, 1987, p. 627). In the National Survey of Black Americans (NBSA) study conducted between 1977 through 1980 (Neighbors, Jackson, Bowman, & Gurin, 1983), 2,107 African American adults were surveyed about many issues of concern to African Americans. The findings showed that African American women did use professional help systems, but usually in conjunction with informal help systems. They combined this formal/informal support network more than African American men did (Neighbors, 1988; Neighbors et al., 1983).

Family and extended kin support date back to African traditions (Elam, 1968; Felton, 1980; Greathouse & Miller, 1981) in which care and support centered around kinship bonds. Interdependence with members of the group was emphasized. Children learned their responsibilities to the family at an early age, and an individual could depend on resources from the family, the clan or even the tribe.

In contemporary African American families, adoption/absorption of a child into the extended family may occur if the child is born out of wedlock, if finances are a problem, if abuse or neglect is prevalent, or if it is simply the most stable living arrangement for the child. The extended family, whether or not they are under the same roof, may also offer material resources to meet the child's wants and needs, such as food, shelter or school tuition. Many young professionals have pointed to the hard, self-sacrificing work of their relatives as their motivation to stay in school and keep working. Further, the extended family can provide alternative nurturing figures if one or both parents are unavailable. The elderly may offer the wisdom of oral history, valued greatly in the African community; children may provide companionship to family members living alone. Older children teach and guide younger children, providing both male and female role models. This fact is often neglected in literature that is focused on the absence of the African American male parent.

Thus, extended family care can be helpful by allowing the individual to pursue his or her goals with a base of material, cognitive and emotional resources. The knowledge and assurance of that support may teach one early on that despite the outside forces of society, there is security within the family.

Sisterhood

In addition to family and extended kin, African American women turn to one another for social support. However, this sense of sisterhood or closeness among African American women can be impeded by differences in age, skin color, class, education, career, marital status and lifestyle. Also, competition for, or fear of rejection by, African American men may be a major cause of distance and lack of trust among African American women. Judgements may be made about the "good and righteous" versus the "bad and fallen" and then barriers may be erected between the two groups (Mays, 1985).

Despite the aforementioned impediments to sisterhood, research has suggested that the common experience of oppression is often a cohesive factor that draws African American women together from diverse backgrounds. In informal support groups, African American women tend to form strong supportive bonds despite differences (Mays, 1986). Brown and Gary (1985, 1987) found that along with social support from family members, reliance on female friends is an important coping strategy for African American women, irrespective of their marital status. McAdoo (1980a) obtained similar findings in a survey of African American women. The majority of the women stated that they received equal amounts of help from family and female friends. Single parents as well as married suburban women were likely to rely on female friends for emotional more than financial support. Middle-class African American women are actively participating in self-help groups, commonly known as "sister circles" (Neal-Barnett & Smith, 1997). The central themes of sister circles are affirmation, self-discovery and healing. Spirituality is often an important aspect of these groups and also the focus of the next section.

Religiosity

African culture assumes wholeness and unity of body and spirit, rather than stressing individualism. The role of religion in contemporary African American culture has a long history dating back to its African roots. Although scant attention has been given in the literature to the use of spiritual beliefs and religious practices as a strategy for coping, general surveys suggest this to be an important strategy for coping with major life events as well as the daily management of stressful situations (George & McNamara, 1984; Gurin, Veroff, & Feld, 1960; Neighbors et al., 1983).

One might well view the African American church as a type of extended family (Felton, 1980). The pastor, as a surrogate father, may be called to intervene, not just on a spiritual level, but in societal problems as well. For example, he may intervene as an advocate at the workplace, or be called upon to mediate disputes between nuclear family members. The church membership, the "brothers and sisters," may also act as sources of support and encouragement. The sense of being among one's church family may provide one with a feeling of security within which to exercise one's talents: "For many blacks, there is no place to use their very best and to be approved and applauded for it, save the church" (Felton, 1980, p. 25). For example, as a member becomes involved in church activities, she may begin to recognize leadership and public speaking abilities by teaching a Bible study class or reading announcements. A head of a committee may develop skills in budget-planning, fund-raising tactics, organization of activities and delegation of tasks. This member is now equipped with the experience of using her skills and talents when she pursues positions in other areas of society. An African American woman may not find such patience and support of her professional development elsewhere in American society.

Most African Americans turn to religion as a solution to their problems before they think of psychotherapy (McGoldrick, 1982). Similarly,

Smith (1981) noted that "belonging to and participating in church and religious activities may prove to be more supportive of their mental health than psychotherapy" (p. 266). Religion is a "retained cultural trait" that enables African Americans to cope realistically with change and day-to-day stressors. These notions have received support in the research. African American women, more than African American men, view prayer as helpful in coping with stressful problems (Neighbors et al., 1983); African American females have higher religious involvement than African American males (Brown, Ndubuisi, & Gary, 1990); and there is an inverse relationship between religiosity and depression for both African American males and females (Brown et al., 1990). Also, research shows that the church service itself may provide an emotional outlet. Affirmation of faith during the sermon is used to overcome despair and anxiety. Through music, one can express emotion that cannot be expressed elsewhere. The congregation that participates with clapping, waving, standing and shouts of "amen" benefit from the catharsis. Those who have written extensively on the therapeutic elements of the worship service of the African American church note its group cohesiveness, universality, altruism and social learning, which have been recognized as curative elements in group process (Griffith, English, & Mayfield, 1980; Griffith, Young, & Smith, 1984).

Adaptive External Locus of Control

Rotter (1966) viewed locus of control as an element of personality and theorized that people are predisposed to view their own behavior as either internally or externally controlled. A person with internal locus of control would believe that the course of human behavior is governed by the individual, whereas a person with external locus of control would believe that the environment (fate, chance, powerful others or luck) exercises the major influence in her behavior (Rotter, 1966). The locus-of- control theory predicts that individuals who perceive themselves as having control over stressors in their lives will cope more effectively than individuals who place luck or fate in charge.

Locus of control is closely related to Seligman's (1975) description of "learned helplessness," which leads an individual to believe that he or she has no means of escape from adverse situations. The reformulated learned-helplessness model (Abramson, Seligman, & Teasdale, 1978) expands the theory to incorporate "explanatory styles" or habitual ways in which individuals explain the occurrence of events. Individuals who attribute events in their lives to stable, global and internal causes are at greater risk for heightened stress or depression.

Historically, internal locus of control has been viewed as a more positive psychological coping strategy than external locus of control. However, researchers have recently criticized the notion that only internal locus-of-control beliefs mediate adaptive coping behaviors (see Folkman, 1984, and Rothbaum, Weisz, & Snyder, 1982, for reviews). Individuals who realistically appraise a stressful situation or event as personally uncontrollable may adopt what Rothbaum et al. (1982) refer to as "secondary control"—the use of adaptive emotion-focused coping mechanisms (e.g., avoidance, withdrawal, denial, distraction) to respond to the stressful situation or event. Therefore, people who appear to be giving up due to external locus-of-control beliefs may actually be controlling disappointment (Folkman, 1984). A coping response seemingly motivated by generalized external locus-of-control beliefs may in fact be a reaction to a realistically appraised uncontrollable stressful encounter and indicate adaptive emotion-focused coping.

Recently, researchers have begun to examine external locus of control as a positive psychological coping strategy, particularly for African Americans and other oppressed groups. Studies have shown that locus of control may operate differently for African Americans than for whites. Although African Americans tend to feel personally responsible for what happens to them individually, they also see the "system's" restrictive opportunity structure as a major determinant of what happens to African American people (Barbarin, Maish, & Gooden-Shorter, 1981). Thus, external locus of control may, in some situations, be an adaptive attributional strategy for African Americans. Barbarin et al. (1981) concluded that although internal locus of control alone may be related to positive mental health among whites, both internal and external locus-of-control attributes seem to be involved in the effective functioning of African Americans.

Similarly, Lefcourt (1986) hypothesized that groups whose social position is one of minimal power either by class or race tend to have a higher external locus of control. Thus, the ability of African American women to attribute individual failure to social-system barriers when dealing with racism and chronic stressors may constitute a coping resource (Neff, 1985). Similarly, Veroff, Douvan, and Kulka (1981) concluded from the Inner American survey that "blacks manage to assign problems accurately to the reality in which they live or at least to limit their disruptive effects . . . without allowing them to pervade the sense of self and identity" (p. 437).

The possible adaptive functions of external locus of control as a coping strategy for African American women is still unclear since there is limited research available with them as subjects. In an extensive review of cross-cultural research with the locus-of-control construct, Dyal (1984) noted that the most consistent finding is that African Americans tend to be more external than American whites, "which can be interpreted as reflecting the ecological validity . . . of different opportunity structures available to the two groups" (p. 282). Obviously, external locus of control may, in some cases, be beneficial to African American women for coping with chronic stressors and institutional practices such as racism, sexism and discriminatory stressful events.

AFRICAN AMERICAN WOMEN'S MENTAL HEALTH: DIAGNOSTIC AND TREATMENT ISSUES

Despite the use of a variety of coping strategies and cultural resources to manage stress and maintain their positive mental health, African American women do develop psychological problems. The literature summarized in this section represents a review of the mental health literature over the past two decades related to research, treatment and intervention strategies for African American women. Characterized as scarce at best, the psychological consequences of being African American and female is one of the most neglected topics in mental health theory, research and clinical practice, as well as the emerging field of psychology on women. Although African American women may encounter a number of mental healt–related problems as a result of their race, gender and structural position in American society, their psychological and behavioral problems have rarely been studied.

Little is known about the incidence and prevalence of mental illness among African American women, as epidemiological data is rarely analyzed for the interaction effects of race and gender (Olmedo & Parron, 1981; Powell, 1982). The epidemiological research does show that socioeconomic status is a more powerful predictor of the incidence and prevalence of mental illness than race (Belle, 1990; Neighbors, 1984, 1990; Williams, 1986). The highest rate of mental disorder has been found among persons falling within this group; African American women "still comprise the most destitute group—educationally, economically, and politically" (Rodgers-Rose, 1980, p. 40). Research also shows that gender is a more powerful predictor of professional help-seeking behavior than is race. African American women are more likely than African American men to utilize professional mental health providers (Neighbors & Howard, 1987). However, the traditional health care sector (doctors, hospitals) and ministers are more often used than mental health services or professionals (Broman, 1987; Neighbors, 1985; Neighbors & Jackson, 1984). Research shows that by the time African American women seek professional mental health services, their problems have escalated to a critical stage (Mays, 1996). They generally do not seek professional help for their psychological problems except when problems become severe (Mays, 1996). The pathway to professional mental health services for these women almost always includes input from their social network (Caldwell, 1996).

African American women tend to avoid the mental health agencies and professionals, and perhaps for good reasons. Research shows they are likely to be given a misdiagnosis of schizophrenia, particularly paranoid schizophrenia, rather than affective disorders (Adebimpe, 1981; Jones & Gary, 1986; Mukherjle, Shukla, Woodle, Rosen, & Olarte, 1983; Olmedo & Perron, 1981; Simon, Joseph, Barry, Stiller, & Sharpe, 1973; Wilkinson, 1980). Also, African American women are more likely to be institutionalized for mental illness (Smith, 1981) and receive different and less preferred forms of treatment than whites (Atkinson, 1985; Gross, Herbert, Knatterud, & Donner, 1969; Krebs, 1971).

In addition to the possibility of receiving an inaccurate diagnosis and having unequal quality of care, agency policies and practices may present barriers to African American women seeking mental health services. According to Copeland (1982), these policies and practices include long waiting lists, rigid scheduling and intake procedures, inflexible hours, discrimination in hiring practices, inconvenient geographic location, and the use of irrelevant or inappropriate modes of treatment. Belle (1984) found that difficulties with transportation to and from services and difficulties arranging child care often prevented low-income African American women from keeping their mental health appointments. Recently, managed care restrictions and the increased cost of private mental health treatment place middle-class African American women in jeopardy for access to mental health services. As more restrictions are placed on public mental health treatment, both middle- and lower-class African American women are likely to be barred from access to a variety of mental health treatment options (Dunston, 1990).

Most of the clinical practice literature that does exist on African American women consists of single case reports and descriptions. Since minimal systematic attention has been devoted to the psychological problems or well-being of African American women, no literature is available on them for many of the discrete psychological disorders in the *Diagnostic and Statistical Manual IV.* Research and clinical practice literature is virtually nonexistent on African American women who have major psychological disorders, such as personality, affective, or anxiety disorders or schizophrenia. Other disorders such as anorexia (Pumariega, Edwards, & Mitchell, 1984; Robinson & Anderson, 1985; Root, 1990), bulimia (Gray, Ford, & Kelly, 1987) and transsexualism (Lothstein & Roback, 1984) have been mentioned in the literature, but the prevalence of these disorders is reported as infrequent in African American women. Nevertheless, little attention has been given to uncovering the sociocultural factors that may inhibit the occurrence of certain psychological disorders in African American women. Also, little attention has been given to research and clinical practice issues that address facilitating African American women's ability to cope with their realities (e.g., racism, sexism and classism) and improving the quality of their lives. Relatively little is known about the similarities or differences that may exist in the psychological problems experienced by various subgroups (e.g., middle class versus low income, married versus single) of African American women.

Although there is a limited amount of literature for many of the major psychological disorders, the literature that does exist notes that in therapy, African American women often present painful psychological experiences that are derived from their status in American society, based on devaluation of both their race and gender. These experiences include concerns about discriminatory experiences resulting from racism and sexism (Collins & McNair, 1986; Copeland, 1982; Evans & Kerr, 1991; Gray & Jones, 1987; Greene, 1986; Smith & Steward, 1983; Trotman, 1984), self-concept and self-esteem (Brown-Collins & Sussewell, 1986; Copeland, 1977; Ford, 1978; McCombs, 1986; Myers, 1975), and physical/facial features and hair texture (Boyd-Franklin, 1987; Hughes & Hertel, 1990; Neal & Wilson, 1989; Trotman, 1984).

IMPLICATIONS FOR MENTAL HEALTH PRACTICE

Despite the incipient status of mental health literature on African American women, and the need for more stress-coping research, some consistent themes relevant to their psychological treatment have appeared in the available literature.

The clinical practice literature frequently advises therapists to become aware of their own biases and stereotypes and become familiar with the psycho-historical background of African American women (Helms, 1979; Olmedo & Parron, 1981). There is consensus in the clinical practice literature that issues related to trust and willingness to self-disclose are potential barriers when African American women are treated by white therapists (Franklin, 1985; Nickerson, Helms, & Terrell, 1994; Ridley, 1984). It is frequently mentioned that clinical assessments should incorporate an understanding of the social, environmental, economic and vocational conditions that influence the psychological functioning of African American women (Copeland, 1982; Holahan, Betax, Spearly, & Chance, 1983; Jenkins, 1985). Also, the clinical practice literature cautions therapists from viewing all the problems that African American women may bring to the therapy situation as stemming from their oppression based on race or sex (Ford, 1978; Helms, 1979). The task of the therapist is to disentangle the effects of racism and sexism from unique individual maladaptations or pathology (Thompson, 1987). Therapists should avoid overemphasizing or underemphasizing the importance of race and/or gender as the primary determinant of psychological problems of African American women.

However, therapists have been encouraged to adopt an empowerment perspective to help African American women make individual and community change (Gutierrez, 1990). Although there is an emerging literature on the appropriateness of cognitive-based interventions (Lewis, 1994; Randall, 1994; Satterfield, 1998), there is no consensus in the clinical practice literature that any one intervention strategy is more effective with African American women. Group therapy, particularly with other African American women, is most frequently written about as an appropriate and effective intervention strategy (Boyd-Franklin, 1987, 1991; Mays, 1985, 1986; Moore, 1982; Nayman, 1983). Even if there is great diversity among African American women based on differences in education, occupation, and socioeconomic and marital status, the presence of other African Americans in a group setting appears to facilitate the development of trust, self-disclosure and feelings of sisterhood.

CONCLUSIONS

Stress is inherent in living and recognized as an important factor in determining one's physical and mental well-being. African American women are likely to encounter stressful events and situations due to their race, sex and social class. Societal and cultural factors influence the types of stressful events and situations that African American women encounter as well as their choice of coping strategies. Racism and sexism have been identified as sources of stress for African American women of all socioeconomic classes. Poverty is an important source of stress for those in lower socioeconomic groups, whereas status discrepancy in the workplace and upward mobility may be unique stressors for those in higher socioeconomic groups. Multiple role strain and lack of availability of romantic partners may be sources of stress for all classes of African American women.

African American women have developed creative coping strategies and resources for dealing with their stressful experiences. These strategies and resources especially include extended family and social network supports, a sense of sisterhood or closeness and reliance on female friends, a strong sense of religiosity, and adaptive use of external locus-of-control beliefs to help them identify forces outside of their personal control.

Despite the use of a variety of coping strategies and resources to manage stress and maintain their positive mental health, African American women do develop psychological disorders. Future research should address the many still-unanswered questions with regard to the incidence and prevalence of discrete psychological disorders among African American women. Future research could also give attention to uncovering the sociocultural factors that may inhibit the occurrence of certain psychological disorders in African American women. Comparative studies offer fertile ground for new insights among African American women since relatively little is known about the similarities or differences that may exist in the psychological problems experienced by various subgroups (e.g., middle class versus low income, married versus single). However, it is clear that an African American woman's psychological symptoms cannot be fully understood as merely an individual dysfunction or maladaptation. Practitioners need to include consideration of an African American woman's social ecology in order to provide culturally sensitive mental health services.

REFERENCES

Abramson, L. Y., Seligman, M. E., & Teasdale, J. D. (1978). Learned helplessness in people: Critique and reformulation. *Journal of Abnormal Psychology, 87,* 49–74.

Adebimpe, V. R. (1981). Overview: White norms and psychiatric diagnosis of black patients. *The American Journal of Psychiatry, 138,* 279–285.

Allen, L., & Britt, D. W. (1983). Black women in American society: A resource development perspective. *Issues in Mental Health Nursing, 5,* 61–79.

Anderson, L. P. (1991). Acculturative stress: A theory of relevance to black Americans. *Clinical Psychology Review, 2,* 685–702.

Atkinson, D. R. (1985). A meta-review of research on cross-cultural counseling and psychotherapy. *Journal of Multicultural Counseling and Development, 1,* 139–153.

Baker, F. M. (1987). The Afro-American life cycle: Success, failure, and mental health. *Journal of the National Medical Association, 79,* 625–633.

Barbarin, O. A., Maish, K. A., & Gooden-Shorter, K. (1981). Mental health among blacks: The relevance of self-esteem, commitment to social change, and paradoxical attribution. In A. Barbarin, P. R. Good, M. Pharr, & J. A. Siskind (Eds.), *Institutional racism and community competence* (DHHS Publication No. 81–907, pp. 114–124). Rockville, MD: National Institute of Mental Health.

Beckett, J. O. (1976). Working wives: A racial comparison. *Social Work, 21,* 463–476.

Bell, E. L. (1990). The bicultural life experience of career-oriented black women. *Journal of Organizational Behavior, 2,* 459–477.

Belle, D. (1982). The impact of poverty on social networks and social support. *Marriage and Family Review, 5,* 89–103.

Belle, D. (1984). Inequality and mental health: Low income women. In L. E. Walker (Ed.), *Women and mental health policy* (pp. 135–150). Beverly Hills, CA: Sage Publications.

Belle, D. (1990). Poverty and women's mental health. *American Psychologist, 45,* 385–389.

Bennett, M.B.H. (1987). Afro-American women, poverty and mental health: A social essay. *Women and Health, 12,* 213–228.

Boyd-Franklin, N. (1987). Group therapy for black women: A therapeutic support model. *American Journal of Orthopsychiatry, 57,* 394–401.

Boyd-Franklin, N. (1991). Recurrent themes in the treatment of African American women in group psychotherapy. *Women & Therapy, 11,* 25–40.

Broman, C. L. (1987). Race differences in professional help seeking. *American Journal of Community Psychology, 15,* 473–489.

Brown, D. R. (1988). Socio-demographic vs. domain predictors of perceived stress: Racial differences among American women. *Social Indicators Research, 20,* 517–532.

Brown, D. R., & Gary, L. E. (1985). Social support network differentials among married and nonmarried black females. *Psychology of Women Quarterly, 9,* 229–241.

Brown, D. R., & Gary, L. E. (1987). Stressful life events, social support networks, and the physical and mental health of urban black adults. *Journal of Human Stress, 13,* 165–174.

Brown, D. R, Ndubuisi, S. C., & Gary, L. E. (1990). Religiosity and psychological distress among blacks. *Journal of Religion and Health, 29,* 55–68.

Brown-Collins, A. R, & Sussewell, D. R. (1986). The Afro-American's emerging selves. *Journal of Black Psychology, 3,* 1–11.

Burgess, N. L., & Horton, H. (1993). African-American women and work: A sociohistorical perspective. *Journal of Family History, 18,* 53–63.

Caldwell, C. H. (1996). Predisposing, enabling and need factors related to patterns of help seeking among African-American women. In H. W. Neighbors & J. S. Jackson (Eds.), *Mental health in black America* (pp. 146–160). Thousand Oaks, CA: Sage Publications.

Cohen, S., & Willis, T. A. (1985). Stress, social support and the buffering hypothesis. *Psychological Bulletin, 98,* 310–357.

Collins, R. L., & McNair, L. D. (1986). Black women and behavior therapy: Exploring the biases. *The Behavior Therapist, 1,* 7–10.

Comas-Diaz, L., & Greene, B. (1994). Women of color with professional status. In L. Comas-Diaz & B. Greene (Eds.), *Women of color: Integrating ethnic and gender identities in psychotherapy* (pp. 347–388). New York: Guilford Press.

Copeland, E. J. (1977). Counseling black women with negative self-concepts. *Personal and Guidance Journal, 55,* 397–400.

Copeland, E. J. (1982). Oppressed conditions and the mental health needs of low-income black women: Barriers to services, strategies for change. *Women & Therapy, 1,* 13–26.

Dressler, V. G., Milburn, N. G., Brown, D.R., & Gary, L. E. (1988). Social support and depressive symptoms among blacks. *The Journal of Black Psychology, 144,* 35–45.

Dressler, W. W. (1985). Extended family relationships, social support, and mental health in a Southern black community. *Journal of Health and Social Behavior, 26,* 39–48.

Dunston, P. J. (1990). Stress, coping, and social support: Their effects on black women. In D. S. Ruiz (Ed.), *Handbook of mental health and mental disorder among black Americans* (pp. 133–147). Westport, CT: Greenwood Press.

Dyal, J. A. (1984). Cross-cultural research with the locus of control concept. In H. M. Lescourt (Ed.), *Research with the locus of control construct: Vol. 3. Extensions and limitations* (pp. 206–306). New York: Academic Press.

Elam, H. (1968). Psycho-social development of the African child. *Journal of the National Medical Association, 60,* 104–109.

Evans, K., & Kerr, E. (1991). The influence of racism and sexism in the career development of African American women. *Journal of Multicultural Counseling and Development, 19,* 130–135.

Falco, K. L. (1991). *Psychotherapy with lesbian clients: Theory into practice.* New York: Brunner/Mazel.

Fellen, P. (1989). Perspectives on depression among black Americans. *Health and Social Work, 14,* 245–252.

Felton, C. (1980). *Care of souls in the black church: A liberation perspective.* New York: Martin Luther King Press.

Folkman, S. (1984). Personal control and coping processes: A theoretical analysis. *Journal of Personality and Social Psychology, 46,* 339–352.

Ford, D. J. (1978). Counseling for the strengths of the black woman. In L. Harmon, J. Birk, L. Fitzgerald, & M. Tanney (Eds.), *Counseling women* (pp. 186–192). Montery, CA: Brooks/Cole.

Franklin, D. L. (1985). Differential clinical assessments: The influence of class and race. *Social Services Review, 59,* 41–61.

Fulbright, K. (1986). The myth of the double-advantage: Black female managers. In M. C. Simms & J. M. Malveaux (Eds.), *Slipping through the cracks: The status of black women* (pp. 33–45). New Brunswick, NJ: Transaction Books.

George, A. S., & McNamara, P. H. (1984). Religion, race and psychological well-being. *Journal for the Scientific Study of Religion, 23,* 351–363.

Geschwender, J. A., & Carroll-Seguin, R. (1990). Exploring the myth of African American progress. *Signs, 15,* 115–129.

Gray, B. A., Jones, B. E. (1987). Psychotherapy and black women: A survey. *Journal of the National Medical Association, 79,* 177–181.

Gray, J. J., Ford, K., & Kelly, L. M. (1987). The prevalence of bulimia in a black college population. *International Journal of Eating Disorders, 6,* 733–740.

Greathouse, B., & Miller, V. G. (1981). The black American. In A. Clark (Ed.), *Culture and childrearing* (pp. 69–93). Philadelphia, PA: F. A. Davis Company.

Greene, B. A. (1986). When the therapist is white and the patient is black: Considerations for psychotherapy in the feminist heterosexual and lesbian communities. *Women & Therapy, 5,* 41–65.

Greene, B. A. (1994). Lesbian women of color: Triple jeopardy. In L. Comas-Diaz & B. Greene (Eds.), *Women of color: Integrating ethnic and gender identities in psychotherapy* (pp. 389–427). New York: Guilford Press.

Griffith, E. E., English, T., & Mayfield, V. (1980). Possession, prayer, and testimony: Therapeutic aspects of the Wednesday night meeting in a black church. *Psychiatry, 43,* 120–128.

Griffith, E. E., Young, J., & Smith, D. (1984). The black church service as a mental health resource. *Hospital and Community Psychiatry, 35,* 464–469.

Gross, H. S., Herbert, M. R., Knatterud, G. K., & Donner, L. (1969). The effect of race and sex on variation of diagnosis and disposition in a psychiatric emergency room. *Journal of Nervous and Mental Disease, 3,* 638–642.

Grump, J. P. (1975). Comparative analysis of black women's and white women's sex role ideology. *Journal of Consulting and Clinical Psychology, 43,* 858–863.

Gurin, G., Veroff, J., & Feld, S. (1960). *Americans view their mental health: A nationwide survey.* New York: Basic Books.

Gutierrez, L. M. (1990, March). Working with women of color: An empowerment perspective. *Social Work* (pp. 149–153).

Harrison, A. O., & Minor, J. H. (1978). Interrole conflict, coping strategies, and satisfaction among black working wives. *Journal of Marriage and the Family, 40,* 799–805.

Helms, J. E. (1979). Black women. *The Counseling Psychologist, 8,* 40–41.

Hoffman, P. H., & Hale-Benson, J. (1987). Self-esteem of black middle-class women who choose to work inside or outside the home. *Journal of Multicultural Counseling and Development, 15,* 71–81.

Holahan, C. J., Betax, J. F., Spearly, J. L., & Chance, B. J. (1983). Social integration and mental health in a biracial community. *American Journal of Community Psychology, 11,* 301–311.

Hughes, M., & Hertel, B. R. (1990). The significance of color remains: A study of life chances, mate selection, and ethnic consciousness among black Americans. *Social Forces*, 69, 1105–1119.

Jenkins, Y. M. (1985). The integration of psychotherapy and vocational intervention: Relevance for black women. *Psychotherapy, 22,* 394–397.

Jones, B. E., & Gary, B. A. (1986). Problems in diagnosing schizophrenia and affective disorders among blacks. *Hospital and Community Psychiatry, 37,* 61–65.

Katz, M. H., & Protrokowski, C. S. (1983). Correlates of family role strain among employed black women. *Family Relations, 32,* 331–339.

Krebs, R. L. (1971). Some effects of a white institution on black psychiatric outpatients. *American Journal of Orthopsychiatry, 41,* 589–596.

Lazarus, R. S., & Folkman, S. (1984). *Stress, appraisal, and coping.* New York: Springer Publishing.

Leavy, R. L. (1983). Social support and psychological disorders: A review. *Journal of Community Psychology, 10,* 409–426.

Lefcourt, H. M. (1986). Internal-external control of reinforcement: A review. *Psychological Bulletin, 65,* 206–220.

Leggon, C. (1980). Black female professional dilemmas and contradictions in status. In L. Rodgers-Rose (Ed.), *The black woman* (pp. 189–202). Beverly Hills, CA: Sage Publications.

Lewis, E. A. (1989). Role strain in African American women: The efficacy of support networks. *Journal of Black Studies, 20,* 155–169.

Lewis, S. (1994). Cognitive behavioral approaches. In L. Comas-Diaz & B. Greene (Eds.), *Women of color: Integrating ethnic and gender identities in psychotherapy* (pp. 223–238). New York: Guilford Press.

Lindball-Goldberg, M., Dukes, J. L., & Lasley, J. H. (1988). Stress in black low-income, single parent families. *American Journal of Orthopsychiatry, 58,* 104–120.

Lothstein, L. M., & Roback, H. (1984). Black female transsexuals and schizophrenia: A serendipitous finding. *Archives of Sexual Behavior, 13,* 371–386.

Makosky, V. P. (1982). Sources of stress: Events or conditions. In D. Belle (Ed.), *Lives in stress* (pp. 35–53). Beverly Hills, CA: Sage Publications.

Malson, M. R. (1983). Black women's sex roles: The social context for a new ideology. *Journal of Social Issues, 39,* 101–113.

Mays, V. M. (1985). Black women working together: Diversity in same sex relationships. *Women's Studies International Forum, 8,* 67–71.

Mays, V. M. (1986). Black women and stress: Utilization of self-help groups for stress reduction. *Women & Therapy, 4,* 67–79.

Mays, V. M. (1996). Mental health symptoms and service utilization patterns of help seeking among African-American women. In H. W. Neighbors & J. S. Jackson (Eds.), *Mental health in black America* (pp. 161–176). Thousand Oaks, CA: Sage Publications.

McAdoo, H. P. (1978). Factors related to stability in upwardly mobile black families. *Journal of Marriage and the Family, 40,* 761–776.

McAdoo, H. P. (1980a). Black mothers and the extended family support network. In L. Rodgers-Rose (Ed.), *The black woman* (pp. 125–145). Beverly Hills: Sage Publications.

McAdoo, H. P. (1980b). Patterns of upward mobility in black families. In L. Rodgers-Rose (Ed.), *The black woman* (pp. 155–172). Beverly Hills: Sage Publications.

McAdoo, H. P. (1982). Stress absorbing systems in black families. *Family Relations, 31,* 479–488.

McAdoo, H. P. (1986). Strategies used by black single mothers against stress. In M. C. Simms & J. M. Malveaux (Eds.), *Slipping through the cracks: The status of black women* (pp. 153–166). New Brunswick, NJ: Transaction Books.

McBride, A. B. (1990). Mental health effects of women's multiple roles. *American Psychologist, 45,* 381–384.

McCombs, H. G. (1986). The application of an individual/collective model to the psychology of black women. *Women and Therapy, 5,* 67–80.

McGoldrick, M. (1982). Normal families: An ethnic perspective. In F. Walsh (Ed.), *Normal family processes* (pp. 395–424). New York, New York: Guilford Press.

McNair, L. D., & Roberts, G. W. (1998). African-American women's mental health. In E. A. Blechman & K. D. Brownell (Eds.), *Behavioral medicine and women: A comprehensive handbook* (pp. 821–825). New York: Guilford Publications.

Milburn, N. G. (1986). Social support: A critical review of the literature as it applies to black Americans (Occasional Paper No. 26). Washington, DC: Howard University, Institute of Urban Affairs and Research.

Miller, N. (1989). *In search of gay America: Women and men in a time of change.* New York: Atlantic Monthly Press.

Moore, H. B. (1982). Black sisterhood: A second look. *Women & Therapy, 1,* 39–50.

Mukherjle, S., Shukla, S., Woodle, J., Rosen, A. M., & Olarte, S. (1983). Misdiagnosis of schizophrenia in bipolar patients: A multiethnic comparison. *The American Journal of Psychiatry, 140,* 1571–1574.

Myers, H. F. (1982). Stress, ethnicity, and social class: A model for research with black populations. In E. E. Jones & S. J. Korchin (Eds.), *Minority mental health* (pp. 118–148). New York: Praeger.

Myers, L. W. (1975). Black women: Selectivity among roles and reference groups in the maintenance of self-esteem. *Journal of Social and Behavioral Sciences, 2,* 39–46.

Nayman, R. L. (1983). Group work with black women: Some issues and guidelines. *Journal for Specialists in Group Work, 8,* 31–38.

Neal, A. M., & Wilson, M. L. (1989). The role of skin color and features in the black community: Implications for black women and therapy. *Clinical Psychology Review, 9,* 323–333.

Neal-Barnett, A. M., & Smith, J. S. (1997). African-Americans. In S. Friedman (Ed.), *Cultural issues in the treatment of anxiety* (pp. 154–174). New York: Guilford Press.

Neff, J. A. (1985). Race and vulnerability to stress: An examination of differential vulnerability. *Journal of Personality and Social Psychology, 49,* 481–491.

Neighbors, H. W. (1984). The distribution of psychiatric morbidity in black Americans: A review and suggestions for research. *Community Mental Health Journal, 20,* 169–181.

Neighbors, H. W. (1985). Seeking professional help for personal problems: Black Americans' use of health and mental health services. *Community Mental Health Journal, 21,* 156–166.

Neighbors, H. W. (1988). The help-seeking behavior of black Americans: A summary of findings from the national survey of black Americans. *Journal of the National Medical Association, 80,* 1009–1012.

Neighbors, H. W. (1990). Clinical care update: The prevention of psychopathology in African Americans. *Community and Mental Health Journal, 26,* 167–179.

Neighbors, H. W., & Howard, C. S. (1987). Sex differences in professional help seeking among adult black Americans. *American Journal of Community Psychology, 15,* 403–415.

Neighbors, H. W., & Jackson, J. S. (1984). The use of informal and formal help: Four patterns of illness behavior in the black community. *American Journal of Community Psychology, 12,* 629–644.

Neighbors, H. W., Jackson, J. S., Bowman, P. J., & Gurin, G. (1983). Stress, coping, and black mental health: Preliminary findings from a national study. *Prevention in Human Services, 2,* 5–29.

Nichols-Casebolt, A. M. (1989). Black families headed by single mothers: Growing numbers and increasing poverty. *Social Work, 33,* 306–313.

Nickerson, K. J., Helms, J. E., & Terrell, F. (1994). Cultural mistrust, opinions about mental illness and black students' attitudes toward seeking professional help from white counselors. *Journal of Counseling Psychology, 41,* 378–385.

Nobles, W. W. (1978). Toward an empirical and theoretical framework for defining black families. *Journal of Marriage and the Family, 40,* 679–688.

Olmedo, E. L., & Parron, D. L. (1981). Mental health of minority women: Some special issues. *Professional Psychology, 12,* 103–111.

Pearlin, L. I. (1982). The social contexts of stress. In L. Goldberger & S. Brezvitz (Eds.), *Handbook of stress: Theoretical and clinical aspects* (pp. 357–379). New York: Free Press.

Peters, M. F., & Massey, G. (1983). Mundane extreme environmental stress in family stress theories: The case of black families in white America. *Marriage and Family Review, 6,* 193–218.

Powell, G. J. (1982). Overview of the epidemiology of mental illness among Afro-Americans. In B. A. Bass, G. E. Wyatt, & G. J. Powell (Eds.), *The Afro-American family: Assessment, treatment, and research issues* (pp. 155–163). New York: Grune & Stratton.

Pumariega, A. J., Edwards, P., & Mitchell, C. B. (1984). Anorexia nervosa in black adolescents. *Journal of the American Academy of Child Psychiatry, 23,* 111–114.

Randall, J. (1994). Cultural relativism in cognitive therapy with disadvantaged African-American women. *Journal of Cognitive Psychotherapy,* Vol. 8 (3), 195–207.

Ridley, C. R. (1984). Clinical treatment of the non-disclosing black client: A therapeutic paradox. *American Psychologist, 39,* 1234–1244.

Rix, S. (1987). *The American women, 1987–1988.* New York: W. W. Norton & Company.

Robinson, P., & Anderson, A. (1985). Anorexia nervosa in American blacks. *Journal of Psychiatric Research, 19,* 193–198.

Rodgers-Rose, L. F. (1980). Some demographic characteristics of the black woman: 1940–1975. In L. F. Rodgers-Rose (Ed.), *The black woman* (pp. 29–41). Beverly Hills, CA: Sage Publications.

Root, M.P.P. (1990). Disordered eating in women of color. *Sex Roles, 22,* 525–536.

Rothbaum, F., Weisz, J. R, & Snyder, S. S. (1982). Changing the world and changing the self: A two-process model of perceived control. *Journal of Personality and Social Psychology, 42,* 5–37.

Rotter, J. B. (1966). Generalized expectations for internal versus external control for reinforcement. *Psychological Monographs, 80,* 1–28.

Satterfield, J. M. (1998). Cognitive behavioral group therapy for depressed low-income minority clients: Retention and treatment enhancement. *Cognitive and Behavioral Practice, 5,* 65–80.

Seligman, M. E. (1975). *Helplessness: On depression, development and death.* San Francisco, CA: Freeman.

Simms, M. C. (1987). Black women who head families: An economic struggle. In M. C. Simms & J. Malveaux (Eds.), *Slipping through the cracks: The status of black women* (pp. 141–151). New Brunswick, NJ: Transaction.

Simon, R. J., Joseph, L. F., Barry, J. G., Stiller, P. R, & Sharpe, L. (1973). Depression and schizophrenia in hospitalized black and white mental patients. *Archives of General Psychiatry, 2,* 509–512.

Smith, A. S. (1981). Religion and mental health among blacks. *Journal of Religion and Health, 20,* 264–287.

Smith, A. S., & Steward, A. (1983). Racism and sexism in black women's lives. *Journal of Social Issues, 39,* 11–15.

Snapp, M. B. (1989). *Toward race, class, and gender inclusive research on stress, social support, and psychological distress: A critical review of the literature* (Research Paper 10.) Memphis, TN: Memphis State University, Center for Research on Women.

Spurlock, J. (1985). Survival guilt and the Afro-American of achievement. *Journal of the National Medical Association, 77,* 29–32.

Sudarkasa, N. (1981). Interpreting the African heritage in Afro-American family organization. In H. P. McAdoo (Ed.), *Black families* (pp. 37–53). Beverly Hills, CA: Sage Publications.

Thomas, V. G. (1986). *Sex roles: A synthesis and critique of selective measurement and research.* Washington, DC: Howard University, Mental Health Research and Development Center, Institute for Urban Affairs and Research.

Thompson, C. (1987). Racism or neuroticism: An entangled dilemma for the black middle class patient. *Journal of the American Academy of Psychoanalysts, 15,* 395–405.

Tobin, M. (1980). *The black female Ph.D.* Washington, DC: University Press of America.

Trotman, F. K. (1984). Psychotherapy of black women and the dual effects of racism and sexism. In C. M. Brody (Ed.), *Women therapists working with women: New theory and process of feminist therapy* (pp. 96–107). New York: Springer.

U.S. Department of Health and Human Services. (1992). *Statistical Abstracts of the United States.* Washington, DC: U. S. Government Printing Office.

Varux, A. (1985). Variations in social support associated with gender, ethnicity, and age. *Journal of Social Issues, 41,* 889–1100.

Veroff, J., Douvan, E., & Kulka, R. A. (1981). *The inner American: A self-portrait from 1957–1976.* New York: Basic Books.

Wilkinson, D. Y. (1980). Minority women: Socio-cultural issues. In A. M. Brodsky and Hare-Mustin (Eds.), *Women and psychotherapy* (pp. 285–304). New York: Guilford Publications.

Williams, D. H. (1986). The epidemiology of mental illness in Afro-Americans. *Hospital and Community Psychiatry, 37,* 42–49.

Willie, C. (1986). The black family and social class. In R. Staples (Ed.), *The black family: Essays and studies* (pp. 224–294). Belmont, CA: Wadsworth Publishing Co.

Zambrana, R. (1987). A research agenda and issues affecting poor minority women: A model for understanding their health needs. *Women and Health, 12,* 137–160.

CHAPTER 10

Health Care Delivery for African American Women

LORNA H. HARRIS AND AUDREYE E. JOHNSON

Health is a human right, not a privilege to be purchased.

—SHIRLEY CHISHOLM

African customs and traditions have survived in America over the centuries and remain visible in health and other behaviors (Dennis, 1985; Watson, 1984; Williams, 1975). Africans adapted their pharmacopoeia to a foreign environment. They adapted plants that were similar to those used in their homeland for medication and treatment of illness and disease. Whether healers practiced openly or clandestinely was dependent upon the brutality and repression of the slaveholders in the New World.

African American women have faced double jeopardy in the pursuit of a healthy existence and in receiving health care services. Before the Mayflower (1620), blacks came to this country as Europeans did, with the explorers and as indentured servants. Women did not have rights in colonial America and did not receive the vote in the United States until 1920. Chattel slavery was legalized by Massachusetts in 1641, and in the next 25 years was adopted with racial and religious caveats by the other 12 colonies. The enslaved were expected to be cared for by their owners, and racism interfered with consistent health care even for free African Americans who were able to pay. The health of the enslaved, either in transport to the Americas or afterwards, was of scant concern. Into this breach came the healers (medicine men, conjure women, hoodoo doctors, doctoresses, midwives, "pharmacists") who used their African medicinal heritage to provide health care to enslaved and free African Americans alike (Watson, 1984). Many of these roles can still be identified in communities today, and for some African Americans these healers still serve as the first point of contact with the health care system in time of illness (Gary, 1981, 1983; Tomes & Shaw-Nickerson, 1987).

The growth of the plantation system produced healers who treated both races. The healers used various concoctions of roots and herbs, called on the spirits, and practiced laying on of hands as part of the ritualism of health care delivery. Some became well known for their cures or their specialties. These healers prevented the further decimation of free and slave African Americans.

Caucasian physicians who treated the plantation enslaved developed racist theories of difference and inferiority (this carried over from their thinking about and treatment of free African Americans) and promoted the idea that only Southern doctors could treat African Americans (Morais, 1976). The quality of life of the enslaved was not considered by these plantation physicians as affecting their health. The enslaved were thought of as non-Christian, good only for labor, and not on the same human level as Caucasians. Living in overcrowded, substandard houses, the enslaved worked under poor conditions starting at an early age (8 years), from sunup to sundown, and had inadequate diets and clothing that led to illness and high mortality rate. The "peculiar institution" produced a significant health gap between African Americans and Caucasians, and created a negative health status for African Americans, the legacy of which remains until today (Johnson, 1988; Morais, 1976).

African American women were affected by societal restrictions against women as well as by their race. These demeaning tactics did not prevent them from fulfilling the needs of their communities and families as caregivers and healers. They worked along with the men in meeting health care needs, and they nurtured the family. They were willing to challenge racist and sexist barriers to seek professional education despite the risks and rejections they faced.

JEOPARDIES OF HEALTH CARE

The legal end of slavery after the Civil War did not bring racial equality to the lives of African Americans. Laws passed during Reconstruction to enhance the health and welfare of African Americans were quickly placed in limbo or outlawed by the passage of Black Codes, which regulated African American conduct to such an extent that it amounted almost to reenslavement. Further erosion of civil rights for African Americans was sealed in the compromise election of Rutherford B. Hayes as president of the United States in 1877 (Bennett, 1988; Franklin & Moss, 1988). The decline continued, and the era ended with the Supreme Court decision of *Plessy* v. *Ferguson* in 1896. This decision encompassed states' rights, the doctrine of "separate but equal," and Jim Crow as the law of the land, and dictated race relations into the middle of the 20th century. Disease was allowed to take its toll among African Americans, who were excluded by law from the health care facilities controlled by Caucasians (Rabinowitz, 1974).[1]

Hospitals were needed for African American patients and health care providers alike. Caucasian hospitals either denied admission outright or placed African Americans in segregated, often inferior wards. African American doctors were denied hospital privileges to attend their patient if that patient was admitted. With the exception of the federally supported Freedmen's Hospital (physical medicine) in Washington, D.C., separate hospitals for African Americans were opened in most of the Southern states, and a few west of the Mississippi River. These hospitals were financed by African American health personnel, churches, and communities. St. Elizabeth's, a federally funded psychiatric hospital in Washington, D.C., admitted African Americans to segregated wards. The need for health facilities to serve African Americans with dignity was great because the poverty-level incomes of most African Americans did not adequately finance needed facilities, personnel, or services, nor did they allow for equal access to facilities.

Surgical experimentation without anesthesia on African American women was cruel and inhuman (*Sage*, 1985). Various types of gynecological invasive surgeries, such as episiotomy and uterine repair, could be considered forms of genital mutilation deserving of a Nuremburg Tribunal as was held following World War II in response to Nazi atrocities. Like Jews in the Nazi period, enslaved African Americans were used as test subjects without their consent and without consideration of their value or their feelings as human beings.

African American women usually put the health of others before their own, suffering in silence or hoping that their illness would go away with self-medication. Recognition that African American women face unique health care issues impacted by racism and sexism brought into existence the National Black Women's Health Project and resulted in a conference on this subject in 1983 that has continued on a yearly basis (Avery, 1990; Johnson, 1988).

Some of the different health issues of African American women in society have been discussed at length in White (1990). A conspiracy of silence about these issues has been used as a protective mechanism against the outer world as well as with family members. Keeping one's business to oneself has characterized African Americans' behavior. Because they have been and remain vulnerable, silence is an automatic response to protect self and family. These conditions become barriers to health care, for ". . . health is influenced by individual, family, and societal conditions, or stated another way by socio-economic status and position" (Johnson, 1988, p. 38; Watkins & Johnson, 1985). The intersection of health (physical and mental), status (citizenship rights), and class (socioeconomic position) was recognized as converging to influence the life chances of African Americans. This multifaceted interface was seen by African Americans in how they developed mutual aid and self-help systems to obtain civil, social, and human rights. African American women were involved in social welfare and social work development to serve the bio-psycho-social needs of African Americans. In the 19th and 20th centuries, African American women, via club groups, began to address many health-related problems in African American communities of the North and South with their energy, money, and time.

SOME HEALTH ISSUES

Research on the health of women in America has been scant. In fact, most studies conducted on disease and illness have been done on Caucasian men. The health issues of African American women have been virtually ignored. The Society for the Advancement of Women's Health Research was established in 1990 to improve research on women's health.

The milestone study of African American health resulted in the *Report of the Secretary's Task Force on Black and Minority Health* (U.S. Department of Health and Human Services [HHS], 1985). An important finding was excess deaths among African Americans—death rates that were different from the death rates of the Caucasian population for the same age and sex groupings. The *Report* concluded that several steps could be taken to control the health disparity, among them better health care accessibility, information, and education, as well as development of sensitivity and understanding among health care providers. Other areas of concern related to policymaking, program implementation, data development, private and federal partnership, and a research agenda focused on African Americans (HHS, 1985).

The overall excess mortality for African Americans was 80 percent from: (1) heart disease and stroke, (2) homicide and accidents, (3) cancer, (4) infant mortality, (5) cirrhosis, and (6) diabetes (Table 10.1). The excess death rate for African American females was significantly higher than for Caucasian females, 631.1 per 100,000 for blacks versus 411.1

Table 10.1. Ten Leading Causes of Death for Black Females, 1996

Disease	Deaths
Heart disease	40,306
Cancer	27,293
Stroke	10,509
Diabetes	6,668
Injuries	4,013
Pneumonia/influenza	3,793
HIV	3,668
Lung disease	2,996
Nephritis, nephrotic syndrome, and nephrosis	2,271
Septicemia	2,152
All causes	132,617

Source: U.S. Department of Health and Human Services, 1998.

for whites (HHS, 1985, p. 67). Other diseases often found among African Americans under age 45 were TB and anemia. These diseases were associated with socioeconomic conditions (HHS, 1985), and recently TB has been on the rise because of the increase of acquired immune deficiency syndrome (AIDS) among African Americans. African American females were twice as likely to have hypertension, diabetes, and anemia as white women. These diseases begin to surface early in life, ". . . and several health conditions responsible for the disparities are known risk factors for cardiovascular disease" (HHS, 1985, p. 75).

Thirty percent of those with AIDS are African American, who make up only 12 to 13 percent of the U.S. population. African American women account for over 50 percent of females diagnosed with AIDS.

> African American women are contracting AIDS from their sexual partners and from the use of contaminated or shared needles in IV drug use. These women are having babies who are already infected with the disease, which will in turn further affect the infant mortality rate in the

> African American community. . . . the disease has no boundaries related to race, sex, socio-economic status, or age. . . . diseases affect not only bodily function but the psychological and social aspects of life. (Johnson, 1988, p. 43)

AIDS as a health issue in the African American community or among other people of color was not recognized by the Centers for Disease Control and Prevention (CDC&P) until 1987. African Americans provided health education and dissemination of information to their communities via their organizations and media (Johnson, 1988). Since 1988 CDC&P has funded a National Alumni AIDS Prevention Project housed at Jackson State University in Jackson, Mississippi, a historically black university. The Project provides technical services and information to individuals, organizations, and groups.

SOCIAL INDICATORS OF HEALTH

Of the factors that influence health care access, income and purchasing power lead the list. Money determines such health-related issues as housing, clothing, and food. The rise in African American female household heads has caused a lower standard of living. Women remain the lowest paid group and, with their lower incomes, they have primary responsibility for care of their children and of older adults.

Poverty has been a meaningful factor in health service availability and care for African American women. The impact of poverty on their ability to access and receive adequate health care has been explored in areas such as prenatal services (Curry, 1990; Libbus & Stable, 1991; May, McLaughlin, & Penner, 1991; Polednak, 1991); cancer screenings (Calle, Flanders, Thun, & Martin, 1993; Roetzheim et al., 1992); coronary heart disease (Wiist & Flack, 1990; Goldberg, Hartz, Jacobson, Krakauer, & Rimm, 1992); and diagnosis and treatment of HIV infection (Shayne & Kaplan, 1991).

Healthy People 2000 (HHS, 1990) found African American women to have higher rates of coronary disease and diabetes. Their risk as homicide victims was four times that of Caucasian women. Obesity was a problem for 44 percent of those 20 years and older. While their birth rate has slowed, and the Caucasian birth rate has increased, African American women between the ages of 15 and 17 and those younger than 15 years were three and five times, respectively, more likely to give birth. These dismal data do not bring to life the bio-psycho-social existence of African American women. The pattern of health care for the enslaved and the exclusion of free African Americans from health services have been replicated in part by the system of care available to African American women today. Poor nutrition, inadequate and substandard housing, inadequate income, limited child care resources, high levels of stress, lack of education, limited access to health information, fear and mistrust of the health care system, limited social outlets, and poor working conditions when employed have all had an impact on healthy life outcomes for African American women.

HEALTH PROVIDERS

Scant attention has been given to the education of health care providers in awareness of the cultural proclivities of different patient groups, and, especially in sensitivity to African American women. Thus, barriers abound between the patient and the provider, which must be overcome (Watkins & Johnson, 1985). Acceptance of the patient as an equal able to engage in problem solving about health issues is often absent in the treatment relationship. This disrespect leads to miscommunication between provider and patient, and influences the patient–provider relationship for effective health care. The different perspectives of patient and provider dictate their approaches to the patient's illness. Patient and provider are from different worlds, and most often the two separate realities will not meet; there may be a fundamental disagreement about the nature of illness. These differences become pronounced when paired with the provider's lack of racial/ethnic and/or gender respect, understanding, and appreciation.

Even African American women who regularly utilize the health care system may not be given the information needed to make sound decisions about the services they need or should demand, nor can they be assured of receiving quality health care that will result in improved health outcomes (Goldberg et al., 1992). The end result is that African American women often receive care that is racially and sexually biased.

CONCLUSION

The jeopardies of race, gender, health, age, family status, and income combine to affect the bio-psycho-social aspects of African American women's lives. These areas have their roots in the past social and civil status (whether free or slave) of African Americans in this country. Conditions of their lifestyles continue to be fed by societal benign neglect, racism, sexism, ignorance, low wages, and unintended self-abuse influenced by ignorance, fear, and mistrust, based on real perceptions of maltreatment, lack of education, and poverty that influence self-esteem and self-determination. African American women as a group are affected by these issues, and few are able to escape the damaging effects of the brutality of racism and sexism on their lives.

The delivery of health care to African American women should be influenced by respect, understanding, and appreciation of their many-faceted roles as women who have always shared in and contributed to the cohesiveness of family and community life. They are capable of becoming involved in their own health care. The active participation of women in the patient–provider interaction should be sought and secured via the linking of modern and folk medicine remedies, based on knowledge of the individual patient. It is important to begin at a level where the patient can feel comfortable. The patient's health belief system, medication rituals, and trust level are all important avenues to explore and to use in the treatment of all African American women. This diagnostic assessment tool should be applicable to all women regardless of race, ethnicity, or socioeconomic class.

African American women will need to make a commitment to learn more about the health issues that are apt to impact their existence. They will need to become knowledgeable about their health, and take responsibility for the influences of their lifestyles and those of their communities. The conspiracy of silence will need to be overcome in favor of open discussion, learning, and treatment of health problems. The caregiving role will have to be placed into proper perspective; taking care of others without taking care of oneself does not serve the best interests of either the caregiver or the recipient of care.

More research about women is needed. There is a special need for research to be directed to the health issues that are already known to face African American women. The risk factors that have been identified as affecting the African American community should be explored in the context of race, sex, and age. The common denominator of health problems that confront women must not overshadow their heterogeneity or obscure those factors that make all groups of women distinctly different even as they maintain their common thread of femininity.

NOTES

[1] To provide health care and health providers for African Americans, it was necessary to develop training and service facilities for these purposes. Howard University Medical College began in 1869, and Meharry Medical College was founded in 1876 at Central Tennessee College to educate black physicians. Six other medical schools developed: Leonard Medical School of Shaw University,

Raleigh, NC, 1882; Louisville National Medical College, Louisville, KY, 1888; Flint Medical College of New Orleans University, New Orleans, LA, 1889; Knoxville Medical College, Knoxville, TN, 1900; University of West Tennessee, Medical Department, Memphis, TN, 1900; Chattanooga National Medical College, Chattanooga, TN, existed 1903–1904. These six schools were recommended to be closed by the *Flexner Report* of 1910. Only Howard and Meharry were considered worth retaining. By 1923 all of the other medical schools had closed. Howard and Meharry Medical Schools educated between 1910 and 1947 ". . . 3,439 students, 101 of whom were women" (Morais, 1976, pp. 93–94). These physicians made major contributions to medical science which helped all people.

REFERENCES

Avery, B. Y. (1990). Breathing life into ourselves: The evolution of the National Black Women's Health Project. In E. C. White (Ed.), *The black women's health book: Speaking for ourselves.* Seattle, WA: Seal Press.

Bennett, L., Jr. (1988). *Before the Mayflower: A history of black America* (6th ed.). Chicago: Johnson.

Calle, E. E., Flanders, W. D., Thun, M. J., & Martin, L. M. (1993, January). Demographic predictors of mammography and pap smear screening in US women. *American Journal of Public Health.* 83(1): 53–60.

Curry, M. A. (1990). Factors associated with inadequate prenatal care. *Journal of Community Health Nursing,* 7(4): 245–252.

Dennis, R. E. (1985). Health beliefs and practices of ethnic and religious groups. In E. L. Watkins & A. E. Johnson (Eds.), *Removing cultural and ethnic barriers to health care* (pp. 12–28). Chapel Hill: University of North Carolina, Schools of Public Health and Social Work.

Franklin, J. H., & Moss, A. A., Jr. (1988). *From slavery to freedom: A history of Negro Americans* (6th ed.). New York: McGraw-Hill.

Gary, L. E. (1981). The health status of black Americans. In A. E. Johnson (Ed.), *The black experience: Social, cultural, and economic considerations.* Chapel Hill: University of North Carolina at Chapel Hill, School of Social Work.

Gary, L. E. (1983). Utilization of network systems in the black community. In A. E. Johnson (Ed.), *The black experience: Considerations for health and human services.* Davis, CA: International Dialogue Press.

Goldberg, K. C., Hartz, A. J., Jacobson, S. J., Krakauer, H., & Rimm, A. A. (1992, March 18). Racial and community factors influencing coronary artery bypass graft surgery rates for all 1986 medicare patients. *Journal of the American Medical Association, 267*(11): 1473–1477.

Johnson, A. E. (1988). Health issues and African American women: Surviving but endangered. In John S. McNeil & S. E. Weimstein (Eds.), *Innovations in health care practice.* Silver Spring, MD: National Association of Social Workers.

Libbus, M. K., & Stable, M. R. (1991). Prenatal education in a high risk population: The effect on birth outcomes. *Birth, 18*(2): 78–82.

May, K. M., McLaughlin, F., & Penner, M. (1991). Preventing low birth weight: Marketing and volunteer outreach. *Public Health Nursing, 8*(2): 97–102.

Morais, H. M. (1976). *The history of the Afro-American in medicine.* The Association for the Study of Afro-American Life and History. Cornwells Heights, PA: Publishers Agency.

Polednak, A. (1991, November). Black–white differences in infant mortality in 38 standard metropolitan statistical areas. *American Journal of Public Health, 81*(11): 1480–1482.

Rabinowitz, H. N. (1974, September). From exclusion to segregation: Health and welfare services for southern blacks, 1865–1890. *Social Service Review.*

Roetzheim, R. G., Vandurme, D. J., Brownlee, H. J., Herold, A. H., Pamies, R. J., Woodard, L., & Blair, C. (1992, September 1). Reverse targeting in a media-promoted breast cancer screening project. *Cancer, 70*(5): 1152– 1158.

Sage. (Fall 1985). II, Special Issue on Health.

Shayne, V. T., & Kaplan, B. J. (1991). Double victims: Poor women and AIDS. *Women and Health, 17*(1): 21–35.

Tomes. E. K., & Shaw-Nickerson, E. (1987). Predecessor of modern black nurses: An honored role. *Journal of National Black Nurses Association,* Winter, Vol. 1, No. 2, pp. 72–78.

U.S. Department of Health and Human Services. (1985). *Report of the Secretary's Task Force on Black and Minority Health* (Vol. 1). Washington, DC: U.S. Government Printing Office.

U.S. Department of Health and Human Services. (1990). *Healthy people 2000: National health promotion and disease prevention objectives.* DHHS Publication No. (PHS) 91–50213. Washington, DC: U.S. Government Printing Office.

Watkins, E. L., & Johnson, A. E. (Eds.). (1985). *Removing cultural and ethnic barriers to health care.* Chapel Hill: University of North Carolina, Schools of Public Health and Social Work.

Watson, W. H. (Ed.). (1984). *Black folk medicine: The therapeutic significance of faith and trust.* New Brunswick, NJ: Transaction Books.

White, E. C. (Ed.). (1990). *The black women's health book: Speaking for ourselves.* Seattle, WA: Seal Press.

Wiist, W. H., & Flack, J. M. (1990, July–August). A church-based cholesterol education program. *Public Health Report, 105*(4): 381–388.

Williams, R. A. (1975). *Textbook of black related diseases.* New York: McGraw-Hill.

CHAPTER 11

Career and Family

AUDREY J. MURRELL

One of the sad commentaries on the way women are viewed in our society is that we have to fit one category. I have never felt that I had to be in one category.

FAYE WATTLETON

It has been well documented that both sex and race have an influence on the performance and the outcomes of work. Sex discrimination has been well documented to exist in the workplace (Larwood & Gutek, 1987; Larwood & Wood, 1995; Nieva & Gutek, 1981) and concepts such as comparable worth (Feldberg, 1984; Madden, 1985; Powell, 1988) and the "glass ceiling" (Collins, 1989; Irons & Moore, 1985; Morrison & Von Glinow, 1990) have brought the discussion of sex discrimination into the forefront of research. Literature on both the historical and contemporary effects of racial inequity in the workplace has also been substantial (Bowman, 1988; Davis & Watson, 1982; Dickens & Dickens, 1982; Ferman, Kornbluh, & Miller, 1968; Fernandez, 1975; Vatter & Palm, 1972).

As Nkomo and Cox (1989) noted, investigations into the dual effect of racism and sexism on the economic lives of African American women have fallen into an empirical and theoretical void, caught between the issues of race and gender. Most theorists simply select either race or sex and speculate as to which is most valid in explaining results for African American women. This perspective ignores the unique contribution that both factors in combination make in explaining economic outcomes for African American women.

Recent revelations in future demographic trend projections suggest the folly in this type of omission. As indicated by the report issued by the Hudson Foundation (Johnston & Pacher, 1988), the future workforce will see the greatest growth of women and people of color by the year 2000. The number of African American women in the workforce will increase by 2.1 million, representing 16 percent of the 47 percent of women in the workforce (U.S. Bureau of the Census, 1991). To the extent that understanding the unique effect of racism and the separate effect of sexism provides an incomplete picture of the lives of African American women, we are lacking an important understanding of a rapidly growing segment of the U.S. workforce.

This chapter focuses on the dual effect of racism and sexism on the economic lives of African American women, with a special emphasis on African American women in management. General management fields represent the sixth largest growing area projected into the year 2005 and the second fastest growing professional field (U.S. Bureau of the Census, 1991). While a great deal has been written on the effects of race (e.g., Bowman, 1988) and gender (e.g., Feldberg, 1984) on employment, and within management (e.g., Morrison & Von Glinow, 1990), very little has been written on the dual effects of these two factors for African American women. Some have argued that simply adding together the existing knowledge about race and gender is an insufficient approach for understanding the combined effect of race and gender. This type of additive approach ignores the interactive effect of race and gender as a unique source of influence on the economic lives of African American women (Essed, 1992).

The theoretical perspective encompassing the combined effect of race and gender produces a unique phenomenon that can be labeled an *ethgender* effect (Ramsford & Miller, 1983). Ethgender effects should be examined in conjunction with the unique effects of race and gender much like the process of examining both interactive as well as main effects in factorial analysis of variance models (Bock, 1975). Thus, it is insufficient simply to examine whether race or gender in isolation has the greater influence for African American women. This type of main-effects-only model suggests that in some way, African American women can prioritize. This is much like assuming that only interactive effects exert influence over economic outcomes for African American women. The limitation of examining race by sex exclusively is that it leads to the expectation that the combination of race and gender will produce an effect, regardless of the criterion. Often when race by sex effects are insignificant, they are generalized to be of no importance in other aspects of work outcomes. As a result, very little is discovered which provides a holistic picture for African American women as to those areas in which race, sex and race by sex affect their economic and social well-being. While the degree of overlap between sex and race may vary, its presence in any model to explain outcomes for African American women is necessary, but not sufficient.

Examining race, sex and ethgender effects also directs our attention away from previous comparative models that are both limited and divisive. These comparative models usually attempt to determine whether race or gender is most important or whether African American women have it better or worse because of their dual status. Much of the previous work that addresses African American women in management focuses on either providing support for whether race or gender is a stronger factor (e.g., Almquist, 1975; Nkomo & Cox, 1989) or supporting the idea that the effect of race by gender produces either a double advantage (Epstein, 1973) or a double negative (Beale, 1970; Ladner, 1971). This type of comparative perspective invariably leads to conclusions concerning supremacy such as that offered by Bock (1969). He concluded that African American women have an unnatural superiority over African American men in professional employment. The implications of the conclusions derived from comparative analyses are that the answer for African American women will always be subordinated either to the issue of sex or the issue of race. This subordination retards understanding the implications of maintaining what King (cited in Collins, 1989) has labeled a "both/or orientation," or the consequences of simultaneously being part of a racial and gender group, yet also being different from it.

Conversely, examining ethgender effects necessitates taking into account both the unique effect of race and of sex as well as the combined effect of race by sex in accounting for the economic outcomes of African American women. Thus, understanding the total effect of these factors becomes more important than partitioning out which individual factors exert the greatest influence or simply looking at the interactive effects in isolation. This approach should lead to the development of a holistic picture of the race and sex and ethgender effects across a variety of the outcomes and rewards of work.

While a discussion of factors that affect the economic lives of African American women may include a variety of variables (see Cox & Nkomo, 1991; McGuire & Reskin, 1992; Reid, 1988; and Simms & Malveaux, 1986, for some of these variables), this chapter will focus on three specific areas related to work: earnings, occupational segregation and family composition. These factors were selected because they comprise a representation of the individual, structural and social factors that have been noted to influence economic attainment and career mobility. This chapter uses a combination of previous work and national census data to accomplish this goal. In order to provide a holistic view of the implication of these factors for the economic outcomes of African American women in the workforce, we must examine the unique effect of sex, the unique effect of race, and then the combined effects of sex by race as they affect the work lives of African American women.

PARTICIPATION AND EARNINGS

The participation of women in the workforce has grown over the last several decades. In 1970, women comprised 38 percent of the labor force; by 1991, women made up about 46 percent of the workforce, representing a growth of some 35 million women over this 10-year period. However, despite this dramatic increase in labor force participation, sex differences in the rewards of work, such as pay, mobility and sex segregation, remain alarmingly disparate.

There are several indicators that the gender gap in outcome factors of work remains, and consequently has an important effect on African American women. While differences in earnings between men and women have decreased considerably between 1979 and 1990, current figures indicate that, regardless of race, women employed full-time year round earn 72 percent of a man's salary, a difference of nearly $8,000 annually (U.S. Bureau of the Census, 1991).

This difference cannot be attributed to individual merit-based factors such as education or work experience. College-educated women who are employed full time earn slightly more on average than men with a high school diploma. Within management fields, Olson and Frieze (1987) found that, regardless of work experience, women's current salaries were about $2,900 lower than men's salaries. In fact, a Stanford University study of 172 people who had sex-change operations found that every person who had undergone a sex-change operation from male to female experienced a drop in earnings (cited by Reskin, 1992). Thus, the effect of gender on overall earnings for African American women, although having decreased somewhat since the 1970s, remains considerable.

Since the civil rights movement of the mid-1960s, a small percentage of upward mobility has occurred for African American workers into jobs previously not held by African Americans, such as management, engineering, law and in computer technology and other technical fields (Bowman, 1988). Current figures, however, indicate that African Americans remain underpaid and overrepresented in unskilled occupations despite comparable education attainment and workforce experience. In 1991, over 13 million African Americans were employed in the labor force. Of these numbers, African Americans comprised 10.8 percent of the total labor force and 12 percent were unemployed, making the unemployment rate for African Americans twice that for whites. Unemployment rates are especially disparate between African Americans and whites between 25 and 34 years old (5.9 percent for African Americans and 12.6 percent for whites), which has implications for future earnings by limiting important factors such as work experience and exposure to training. Thus, race has a dramatic effect by lowering the participation rates of African American women through overrepresentation among the nation's unemployed.

Research has demonstrated that across a variety of occupations, ethnic minority members suffer in terms of salary and career attainment as a result of their minority status (Ehrenberg & Smith, 1982; Gwartney & Long, 1978). African Americans earned 58 percent of whites' income in 1991, while more African Americans than whites lived below the poverty line (34.2 percent for African Americans versus 11.1 percent for whites). Greenhaus, Paramuraman, and Wormley (1988) found that not only did African American workers have lower salaries and fewer promotions than their white counterparts, but dramatic race differences also exist with regard to access to training and development activities, performance evaluations, integration into the organization and job discretion.

While the number of years of education is positively associated with earning power, 71 percent of African Americans with 4 years of high school earned under $20,000 per year. The median income for African Americans with 4 or more years of college was $30,766. White median income earned for 5 years of high school was $15,570, with 10 percent fewer people under the $20,000 income mark compared to African Americans. Thus, education has a greater effect on earnings for the average income of whites. This suggests that for African American women, additional education does not have the same return in terms of salary when compared to their white female counterparts (U.S. Bureau of the Census, 1991).

Race appears to play a unique role in restricting entrance into the workforce for African American women. Unemployment rates for African American women are almost as high as those for African American men (12.9 percent for men and 11.9 percent for women) and are significantly higher than for white women (5.5 percent) and white men (6.4 percent). The disparity in unemployment may be exacerbated by current downsizing trends within organizations. For example, the stalling of upward mobility of African American managers has been attributed to the effects of corporate restructuring and the easing of government pressures on companies to maintain a critical mass of minorities (Johnson, 1987). The effects of organizational transformation and workforce changes create dual barriers to the entry of African American women into the work force.

While the disparity in earnings based on either race or sex alone is substantial, the combined effects of race by sex place African American women in a unique position. Both white females and African American males must work about 8 months to earn a salary equal to what white males earn in 6 months (see Table 11.1). However, African American

Table 11.1. 1991 Participation Rates and Median Income Levels by Race and Sex[a]

	FEMALES		MALES	
	African American	**White**	**African American**	**White**
Labor force	5,983	45,482	5,880	55,557
Percentage	88.1	94.5	87.1	93.6
% Race[b]	50.4	45.0	49.6	55.0
% Sex[c]	11.6	88.4	9.6	90.4
Unemployed	805	2,672	874	3,775
Percentage	11.9	5.5	12.9	6.4
% Race	47.9	41.4	52.1	58.6
% Sex	23.2	76.8	18.8	81.2
Earnings total	18,838	20,759	22,176	30,598
1–3 years high school	12,783	13,298	16,832	19,560
4 years high school	16,521	17,552	20,271	26,526
4 years college	28,094	29,109	32,145	41,661

[a]Based on data from U. S. Bureau of the Census, 1991. All participation figures shown in 1,000s. Income figures reflect median income of full-time, year-round workers 25 years old and over.

[b]Reflects percentage within racial group (holding sex constant).

[c]Reflects percentage within gender group (holding race constant).

women must work about 10 months to make a comparable salary. Thus, in comparison to African American males and white females, African American women must earn an extra month's wages to have comparable earnings. Although women earn 74 percent of a man's salary, African American women earn significantly less than their African American male or white female counterparts (about 86 percent for each). The combined effect of race and sex produce unique disparities on earnings for African American women. Thus, not only are African American women overrepresented among the nation's unemployed, but once employed, they earn lower wages because of this dual status.

OCCUPATIONAL SEGREGATION

The extent of differences in earnings between men and women are somewhat masked by the profound effect that occupational sex segregation has on earnings and occupational status (Feldberg, 1984; Reskin & Hartmann, 1986; Rytina & Bianchi, 1984). The degree of occupational sex segregation declined somewhat during the 1970s. However, further decline has remained stagnant well into the 1990s. As King (1992) observed, 55 out of every 100 women would have to change from a female-dominated to a male-dominated occupation for all occupations to be sex-integrated.

Women tend to be employed in clerical and service jobs, while men are more likely to be employed as managers, craft workers, laborers and farmers (Blau & Ferber, 1985). These service and clerical jobs are low-paying, low-status jobs that often provide little room for mobility and advancement. Women comprise 60 percent of those in service jobs and 80 percent of those in administrative support positions (e.g., clerical, secretarial, record processing). Forty percent of women in managerial positions are employed in fields such as personnel, public administration and health-related fields. Work by Olson, Frieze, and Good (1987) showed some differences in management areas (such as line and staff positions) and industry type (with women overrepresented in staff positions and underrepresented in technical areas such as manufacturing).

The implications of this profound sex segregation can be seen both in differences in overall earnings of those employed in male- versus female-dominated jobs and in differences in earnings of women in traditionally male-dominated professions. In 1991, women in managerial positions earned almost $15,000 less than men in those same positions (see Table 11.2). Earnings for women in both professional specialty

Table 11.2. 1991 Participation Rates and Median Income Levels by Sex, Race, and Industry[a]

	FEMALES		MALES		PERCENT[b]	
	African American	White	African American	White	African American	White
Managerial	346	4,095	312	7,058	40.6	5.7
Income	26,566	26,257	32,553	41,706	—	—
Professional	459	4,132	293	5,477	51.6	6.7
Income	27,249	29,831	36,587	41,466	—	—
Technical	146	972	103	1,288	49.4	8.9
Income	22,299	24,419	25,792	31,750	—	—
Sales	185	2,420	199	4,860	48.8	6.6
Income	13,486	18,898	25,066	31,168	—	—
Administrative	1,075	7,272	357	2,031	80.0	11.4
Income	20,115	19,010	25,229	28,994	—	—
Service[c]	692	2,147	421	1,610	59.8	17.2
Income	12,554	12,187	14,537	17,020	—	—
Pv. household	23	121	1	6	96.0	21.0
Income	11,643	7,339	—	13,422	—	—
Protective sv.	48	131	187	1,112	15.2	16.8
Income	24,475	22,709	21,404	31,367	—	—
Mac. operators	349	1,475	401	2,761	40.1	14.8
Income	13,738	15,308	17,330	25,103	—	—
Transportation	28	130	455	2,530	9.0	15.6
Income	23,546	16,088	21,555	25,905	—	—
Equi. handlers	95	256	316	1,313	17.5	6.4
Income	13,704	14,818	15,587	20,756	—	—
Farming/fishing	3	207	77	1,441	16.1	6.4
Income	—	9,673	10,725	15,608	—	—
Craft/repair	91	603	706	7,602	8.6	7.8
Income	19,575	19,067	24,619	28,291	—	—

[a]Based on data from the U.S. Bureau of the Census, 1991. All participation figures shown in 1,000s. Income figures reflect a median income of full-time, year-round worker, 25 years old and over.

[b]Percentages reflect within-category percentages (e.g., percent of African Americans in job industry).

[c]Excluding household service jobs.

Abbreviations: pv = private, sv = service, mac = machine; equi = equipment.

occupations and skilled craft occupations were 71 percent of men's earnings. Interestingly, in administrative support occupations where women outnumber men by more than three to one, women earn 71 percent of the salary awarded to men and represent only 58 percent of supervisors in these areas. Olson et al. (1987) found that having a staff position significantly lowered salary, while positions in heavy manufacturing (e.g., primary and fabricated metals) raised starting salaries. Overall, occupational sex segregation has been shown to account for about 40 percent of the wage gap between men and women employed full time (England & Farkas, 1986; Treiman & Hartmann, 1981).

Interestingly, the discussion of occupational segregation has been somewhat limited to the issue of sex segregation. One earlier study demonstrated that race segregation in occupations substantially reduced African Americans' earnings relative to those of whites (Lyson, 1985). Similar to the situation for women, African Americans are likely to be relegated to occupations that have low-paying, low-status jobs primarily in service areas (Bowman, 1988). However, the lower employment rates of African Americans compared to whites somewhat masks the effect of race segregation in employment. African Americans are overrepresented in lower-stratum jobs, primarily governmental and public administration occupations, a phenomenon some have suggested is because of the protection afforded to them by stronger governmental regulations (e.g., Bowman, 1988).

Fernandez (1975) conducted a study of 115 African American managers at predominately white corporations. These managers were found to be in mostly lower management positions, relegated to duties targeted toward African Americans such as marketing for African American customers or human resource management specialists dealing with diversity and affirmative action issues. Similarly, Bowman (1988) found that equal proportions of African American women and African American men were located in secondary sector jobs such as service, operatives, and unskilled workers. Thus, for African American women, the effect of race on occupational segregation operates in much the same manner as occupational sex segregation does for white women. African American women are overrepresented in secondary sector jobs that offer little opportunity for advancement, and which provide low salaries, low status and little authority or power within organizations.

The amount of African American female managers grew only 1 percent between 1974 and 1984. Some have argued that the earnings of African American men in management positions come closer to the earnings of white males than do the earnings of African American females (Plowski & Williams, 1983). As Bowman (1988) found, despite the position of African Americans in low-paying secondary sector jobs, African American women within the National Sample of Black Americans (NSBA) were twice as likely to be service workers; African American men were more likely to be employed as operators, craftsmen and other unskilled workers (e.g., handlers, laborers and material-moving workers).

Although service occupations are among the fastest-growing occupations projected for the future workforce, the overrepresentation of African American women within these jobs is alarming. Lower-stratum occupations such as service jobs are among the lowest-paying, lowest-status occupations and are likely to involve part-time rather than full-time work. In addition, they provide few benefits, with only 30 percent of those employed in service jobs in 1991 provided with health care benefits compared to 58 percent for craftsman and those in other skilled positions (U.S. Bureau of the Census, 1991). African American women are also more likely than white women to work in service positions, especially in private household work. These positions are projected to continue to decline by the year 2005, are the lowest paying of the major job categories, and offer the fewest benefits (only 4 percent with health care coverage [see Table 11.2]).

FAMILY SIZE AND COMPOSITION

Family size and composition play an important role in overall economic status and mobility. For example, the unemployment rate for women maintaining a family in 1991 was 7.2 percent, above the average for women overall (6.3 percent). Labor force participation rates for married women are lower than their single counterparts (66.5 percent for single women and 58.5 percent for married women). This rate increases sharply for married women with children between the ages of 6 and 17 (64.8 percent for single and 73.6 percent for married women).

Women who head families earn about $4,500 a year less than men who head households. Adding multiple earners to female-headed families has a dramatic effect on income of these female-headed families, up 50 percent for women and 45 percent for men (see Table 11.3). In fact, a wife and one other family member earn slightly more than a husband alone ($30,628 for wife and one other family member, and $27,664 for husband alone). In addition to the effect of additional earners within the family, the presence of a spouse or children within the home has a greater

Table 11.3. 1991 Participation Rates and Median Income by Sex, Race, and Family Type[a]

	African American	White	Ratio
MARRIED COUPLES			
Percentage	47.8	82.8	—
Income	33,784	47,014	.84
Wife working	2,349	27,008	—
Income	40,038	47,247	.85
Wife not working	1,220	20,006	—
Income	20,333	30,781	.66
SPOUSE NOT PRESENT			
Male head	472	2,276	—
Income	21,848	30,570	.71
Female head	3,430	7,512	—
Income	12,125	19,528	.62
AVERAGE HOUSEHOLD SIZE	2.9	2.6	—
NUMBER OF EARNERS			
None (%)	18.8	13.9	—
Income	6,309	17,369	.36
One (%)	34.7	26.7	—
Income	16,308	27,670	.59
Two (%)	35.6	45.8	—
Income	34,050	43,036	.79
Three (%)	8.0	10.2	—
Income	43,813	54,632	.80
Four + (%)	2.9	3.7	—
Income	59,983	67,753	.89

[a]Based on data from the U.S. Bureau of the Census, 1991. All participation figures are shown in 1,000s. Income figures reflect median income of full-time, year-round workers, age 25 years old and over.

direct effect on the income of males as compared to females. Olson and Frieze (1987) have found that for starting MBAs, the presence of a spouse adds about $3,000 for men's salaries and a child adds about $1,600, but has no appreciable effect for women's salaries.

While the number of African American families has increased over the past several decades, the income disparities between African American and white families continue to grow. Median income for white families was $15,000 more than for African American families in 1991 ($36,920 for white families and $21,420 for African American families). Some of this difference is attributable to the greater contribution that a working wife makes to overall family income among whites compared to African American families. For African American families, a working wife contributes an additional 51 percent to the total family income, compared to 65 percent for white families (U.S. Bureau of the Census, 1991).

The median income of African American couples in which both spouses work is twice that for African American families in which only the husband works. White families with the wife in the paid workforce gain more than one and a half times what the husband earns alone. However, income differences between African Americans and whites are significantly less between married couples in which the wife works, or between families with three or more earners (see Table 11.3). Conversely, income disparities are greatest for families with no earners or for those families with a female head of the household and no spouse present. Thus for African American women, multiple earner families help to abate the negative effect of racial disparities on total family income.

Evidence of the combined effect of race and sex can be seen in the income differentials of female compared to male heads of households for white compared to African American families (see Table 11.3). Female-headed African American families earn about $7,400 less than their white female and African American male counterparts. African American families headed by men have incomes that are circa $9,700 more than those headed by African American women. In addition, of those maintaining households, African American women earn only 40 percent of the salary of white males.

One factor underlying the disparity is that the median income for African American families maintained by a woman has remained virtually unchanged since 1967 ($11,800 in 1967 and $12,130 in 1990), while the median income for African American men with no wife present has risen by about 23 percent ($17,710 in 1967 and $21,850 in 1990). However, a wife in the paid labor force brings total family income of African Americans significantly closer to that of white families (up to 85 percent). This confirms earlier research that for African American families, income derived from a wife in the paid workforce is an integral part of total family income and well-being.

CONCLUSIONS AND FUTURE DIRECTIONS

The effects of race and sex have traditionally been examined separately. Many have recently argued that for African American women, the economic effects of racism cannot be discussed separately from the gender-specific effects of sexism. Many African American feminists agree that race, gender and also class are inextricably tied to each other, providing an interlocking systemic effect on the economic experiences of African American women (Collins, 1989; hooks, 1989). Instead of debating the positive versus negative influence of the dual status effect of racism and sexism on the economic lives of African American women, this chapter has sought to define a holistic approach to the study of the effect of race, sex and ethgender effects on participation, earnings, segregation and family income for African American women.

The majority of investigations on the gender gap in earning and occupational status ignore the effect of race differences. Many of these studies relegate the discussion of race effects to a sideline within their discussion of sex differences. The general conclusion offered from this research is that the effect of factors such as occupational sex segregation and the glass ceiling have a negative effect for both African American and white women. The unique nature of this effect for African American women is left for future research to explore. As McGuire and Reskin (1992) have noted, African American women are dramatically affected by the greater disadvantaged status that women face regardless of their color as well as by sharing the disadvantaged status that African American men encounter because of their race.

In terms of labor force participation and earnings, it appears that the race differentials in unemployment provide a strong barrier for African American women. Racial disparities in unemployment rates significantly lower the presence of African American women in the labor force. Regardless of gender, African Americans are twice as likely to be unemployed as whites, a trend that has increased substantially over the past decade. Thus, in terms of participation in the labor force for African Americans, there appears to be a "glass door" that denies access to employment opportunities for African American women. Obviously, this "glass door" serves to prohibit African American women from gaining the necessary work experience and training for future advancement and earnings.

One area of future research concerns the implications of both short-term and long-term unemployment for African American women. While much has been written concerning the economic and psychological effects of work stoppage for whites (see Leana & Feldman, 1992) and sex differences in reactions to unemployment for whites (see Leana & Feldman, 1991), very little has been written concerning the effects of work stoppage for African American women or sex differences among African Americans in reactions to job loss. A few exceptions have been the interest in labor force dropout rates of African American men and the effect of these dropout rates on African American family income (e.g., Bowman, 1988; Farley & Allen, 1987). Given the increasing number of African American women in the paid labor force as well as their representation as heads of households, a more systematic exploration of the effect of unemployment for these women would be a fruitful area for future research.

Although race differentials appear to overshadow sex or ethgender effects in overall labor force participation rates, the effect of occupational sex segregation places African American women in a unique position comparable to that of white women. African Americans are overrepresented in lower-stratum, secondary jobs, and the effect of sex segregation relegates African American women to sex-typed jobs within those secondary-stratum occupations. These female-dominated occupations are low-status, low-paying jobs with little opportunity for advancement (Treiman & Hartmann, 1981).

African American and white women share the effects of occupational sex segregation, but the combined ethgender effect along with the primary race effect place African American women in a unique position. While African American women are more likely than African American men to hold managerial titles, they are often employed in low-level, female-dominated positions with low status and little authority (Almquist & Wehrle-Einhorn, 1987; Fulbright, 1985; Irons & Moore, 1985). Hartmann (1987) and others (Mueller, Parcel, & Tanaka, 1989) assert that African American women are more likely to be given supervisory roles over other minorities or advocacy roles such as affirmative action officer or diversity specialist.

One implication of ethgender occupational segregation concerns the area of negotiation and conflict resolution within organizations. As Kolb (1992) has written, the overrepresentation of women in support roles within organizations suggests that many women are likely to be important behind-the-scenes peacemakers or arbitration specialists. African American women's overrepresentation in supervisory positions such as administrative support, human resources and customer service suggests that

African American women may be hidden peacemakers within important organizational conflicts such as professional-staff, labor-management, or customer-employee. African American women may also serve as behind-the-scenes peacemakers of racial conflicts over given their supervisory roles of other ethnic minorities within organizations.

These speculations suggest that African American women have an important yet hidden role to play within organizations. Individual specialists who intervene in organizational conflicts are often outsiders and less likely to be trusted or familiar with the organization. Nonetheless, these specialists are considered professional well-paid experts in conflict resolution. By exploring the role that African American women play in resolving conflict within these sex- and race-typed positions, organizations should discover an untapped resource for dealing with some of these critical sources of conflict. In addition, this type of examination may add an important and innovative understanding to the psychology of conflict resolution.

While race and sex make differential contributions to earnings and occupational segregation, the ethgender effect appears most prominently when one examines the effect that family composition has on overall family income. Much has been written concerning the overrepresentation of female-headed households within African American families (Bianchi & Farley, 1983; Spain, Bianchi, & Bartos, 1988). Much of this previous discussion centers around the disadvantaged state that children of these households face (Moynihan, 1986), while more recent debate has focused on systemic factors such as the feminization of poverty (McAdoo, 1988). These approaches face the following limitations: they either ignore the effect that systemic factors have on economic outcome for female-headed African American families or overemphasize the role that either race or sex plays in affecting these outcomes. Ethgender effects substantially decrease the income potential afforded to an African American female head of household to a greater degree than predicted by either sex or race alone.

Contemporary thought concerning resolutions of the unique problems faced by African American females who maintain households has focused on the positive effect that multiple earners, social support and extended family networks have for these families (Taylor, 1986; Taylor, Jackson, & Quick, 1982; Taylor, Chatters, Tucker, & Lewis; 1990). Indeed, the gap between African American–headed and white female–headed families decreases with multiple earners within the family. While multiple earners within the family may not totally eliminate the difference in family income between African American female-headed families and other family types, they do substantially raise the economic status of these families above poverty. However, the success of multiple-earner households is contingent upon the coordination of a variety of additional factors such as child care, household chores, parental authority and spousal relationships (McAdoo, 1988). The discussion of the work-family interface has increased with the dramatic changes in gender composition in the workforce (see Lobel, 1991). Models of work and family investment have neglected the unique concerns that the women in African American female-headed households face in the work environment. Research in the field of management has been particularly limited in its understanding of the issues that these families, and African American women in particular, face (see Bell, 1990).

Discussions of work-family conflict and balance abound; very little research uses adult African American female-headed households as a model for working women dealing with dual-investment conflict. However, African American women, because of their long history of labor force participation and dual career and family roles, would provide an interesting group for study on the issue of work-family interface. These women have traditionally seen little conflict with combining the roles of work and family (Davis, 1981; Dill, 1979; Ladner, 1971). A valuable area of future research would be the variety of ways African American women cope with potential conflict between multiple identities and achieve a balance between work and family roles.

One idea suggested by Lobel (1991) and derived from social identity theory (Tajfel & Turner, 1985) is that the importance of a given identity is determined by the salience or accessibility of that identity in a given situation coupled with the relevance of that identity to the individual. Further study into the social identity of African American women who maintain families both with and without additional earners should reveal a variety of techniques for dealing with potential identity conflicts. In addition, this type of focus may lead to an emphasis on the positive aspects of this dual status rather than a continued preoccupation with its negative aspects.

For example, while evidence concerning the double negative effect for African American women abounds, African American women maintain higher career aspirations than their white female and African American male counterparts (Murrell, Frieze, & Frost, 1991). Both adolescents and young college students desire careers in traditionally male-dominated fields and plan more for more education than is generally required for these careers. This type of career realism (Pelham & Fretz, 1982; Rotberg, Brown, & Ware, 1987) and preparation for the negative effects of race and gender should provide valuable insight into effective coping strategies for these women once they are in the workforce. A worthwhile area for future research would be longitudinal studies addressing these issues.

One additional implication of this self-imposed realistic preview is the increase in African American women seeking alternatives to traditional labor force participation. Recent figures show that African American women own about one-third of all African American–owned businesses, a total of about 100,000 companies (U.S. Bureau of the Census, 1991). This number reflects a 40 percent increase since 1977, and the Small Business Association reports that this percentage continues to increase. Thus, many African American women are seeking opportunities outside traditional labor force roles and have established themselves as successful entrepreneurs. These efforts have also expanded African American women beyond the boundaries of traditional female-dominated fields into areas such as high technology and manufacturing.

In addressing the total contribution of race, sex and ethgender effects, many African American women have left traditionally male-dominated organizations to structure their own work environment. These entrepreneurs have also established networks to assist others in future endeavors. However, very little has been written about this group of African American female business owners. Given their history of dealing with the unique and combined effects of race and sex, future research examining these entrepreneurs may reveal some innovative techniques for how organizations may achieve balance between racial and gender groups in both the opportunities and the outcomes of work.

REFERENCES

Almquist, E. (1975). Untangling the effects of race and sex: The disadvantaged status of black women. *Social Science Ouarterly, Vol 56,* 129–142.

Almquist, E., & Wehrle-Einhorn, J. L. (1987). Doubly disadvantaged: Minority women in the labor force. In A. Stromberg & S. Harkess (Eds.), *Women working.* Palo Alto, CA: Mayfield.

Beale, F. (1970). Double jeopardy: To be black and female. In T. Cade, (Ed.), *The black woman.* New York: Signet.

Bell, E. L. (1990). The bicultural life experience of career-orientated black women. *Journal of Organizational Behavior, 11(b),* 459–477.

Bianchi, S. M., & Farley, R. (1983). The growing gap between blacks. *American Demographics, 5*(7), 14–20.

Blau, F. D., & Ferber, M. A. (1985). Women in the labor market: The last twenty years. In L. Larwood, A. H. Stromberg, & B. A. Gutek (Eds.), *Women and work: An annual review* (Vol. 1, pp. 19–49). Beverly Hills, CA: Sage Publications.

Bock, E. W. (1969). Farmer's daughter effect: The case of the Negro female professional. *Phylon, 30,* 17–26.

Bock, R. D. (1975). *Multivariate statistical methods in behavioral research.* New York: McGraw-Hill.

Bowman, P. J. (1988). Work life. In J. S. Jackson (Ed.), *Life in Black America* (pp. 124–155). Newbury Park, CA: Sage Publications.

Collins, P. H. (1989). The social construction of black feminist thought. *Signs: Journal of Women in Culture and Society, 14*(4), 1–29.

Cox, T. H., & Nkomo, S. M. (1991). A race and gender-group analysis of early career experience of MBAs. *Work and Occupations, 18*(4), 431–447.

Davis, A. (1981). *Women, race, and class.* New York: Random House.

Davis, G., & Watson, C. (1982). *Black life in corporate America.* Garden City, NY: Doubleday.

Dickens, F., & Dickens, J. (1982). *The black manager: Making it in the corporate world.* New York: Amacom.

Dill, B. T. (1979). The dialectic of black womanhood. *Signs: Journal of Women in Culture and Society, 4,* 535–555.

Ehrenberg, R. G., & Smith, R. S. (1982). *Modern labor economics.* Glenview, IL: Scott, Foresman & Company.

England, P., & Farkas, G. (1986). *Households, employment and gender.* New York: Aldine.

Epstein, C. (1973). Positive effect of the multiple negative: Explaining the success of black professional women. *American Journal of Sociology, 78,* 913–935.

Essed, P. (1992). Alternative knowledge sources in explanations of racist events. In M. L. McLaughlin, M. L. Cody, & S. J. Read (Eds.), *Explaining one's self to others: Reason-giving in a social context.* Hillsdale, NJ: Lawrence Erlbaum Associates.

Farley, R., & Allen, W. R. (1987). *The color line and the quality of American life.* New York: Russell Sage.

Feldberg, R. L. (1984). Comparable worth: Toward theory and practice in the United States. *Signs, 10,* 311–328.

Ferman, L. A., Kornbluh, J. L., & Miller, J. A. (1968). *Negroes and jobs.* Ann Arbor: University of Michigan.

Fernandez, J. P. (1975). *Black managers in white corporations.* New York: John Wiley & Sons.

Fulbright, K. (1985). The myth of the double-advantage: Black female managers. *Review of Black Political Economy, 14,* 33–45.

Greenhaus, J. H., Paramuraman, S., & Wormley, W. M. (1988). *Organizational experiences and career success of black and white managers.* Paper presented at the Annual Meeting of the Academy of Management, Anaheim, CA.

Gwartney, J. D., & Long, J. E. (1978). The relative earnings of blacks and other minorities. *Industrial and Labor Relations Review, 31,* 336–346.

Hartmann, H. (1987). Internal labor markets and gender: A case study in promotion. In C. Brown & J. Peckman (Eds.), *Gender in the workplace.* Washington, DC: Brookings.

hooks, b. (1989). *Talking back: Thinking feminist—Thinking black.* London: Sheba Feminist Publishers.

Irons, E. D., & Moore, G. W. (1985). *Black managers: The case of the banking industry.* New York: Praeger.

Johnson, A. (1987). Black managers still have a dream. *Management Review, 76*(12), 20–27.

Johnston, W. B., & Pacher, A. H. (1988). *Opportunity 2000: Creative affirmative action strategies for a changing workforce.* Washington, DC: U.S. Department of Labor, Hudson Institute for Employment Standards Administration.

King, M. C. (1992). Occupational segregation by race and gender, 1940–1989. *Monthly Labor Review, 115,* 30–37.

Kolb, D. M. (1992). Women's work: Peacemaking in organizations. In D. M. Kolb & J. M. Bartune (Eds.), *Hidden conflict in organizations: Uncovering behind-the-scenes disputes.* Newbury Park, CA: Sage Publications.

Ladner, J. (1971). *Tomorrow's tomorrow: The black woman.* New York: Doubleday.

Larwood, L., & Gutek, B. (1987). *Women's career development.* Beverly Hills, CA: Sage Publications.

Larwood, L., & Wood, M. (1965). *Women in management.* Lexington, MA: D. C. Heath.

Larwood, L., & Wood, M. (1995). Training women for management: Changing priorities. *Journal of Management Development, 14*(2), 55–65.

Leana, C. R., & Feldman, D. F. (1991). Gender differences in response to unemployment. *Journal of Vocational Behavior, 31*(8), 65–77.

Leana, C. R., & Feldman, D. F. (1992). *Coping with job loss: How individuals, organizations, and communities respond to layoffs.* New York: Lexington Books/Free Press.

Lobel, S. A. (1991). Allocation of investment in work and family roles: Alternative theories and implications for research. *Academy of Management Review, 16*, 507–521.

Lyson, T. A. (1985). Race and sex segregation in the occupational structure of southern employers. *Social Science Quarterly, 66*, 281–295.

Madden, J. F. (1985). The persistence of pay differentials: The economics of sex discrimination. In L. Larwood, A. H. Stromberg, & B. A. Gutek (Eds.), *Women and work: An annual review* (Vol. 1, pp. 76–114). Beverly Hills, CA: Sage Publications.

McAdoo, H. P. (1988). *Black families* (2nd ed.). Newbury Park: Sage Publications.

McGuire, G., & Reskin, B. F. (1992). *Authority hierarchies at work: The impacts of race and sex.* Unpublished manuscript.

Morrison, A. M., & Von Glinow, M. A. (1990). Women and minorities in management. *American Psychologist, 45,* 200–208.

Moynihan, D. P. (1986). *Family and nation.* New York: Harcourt Brace Jovanovich.

Mueller, C. W., Parcel, T. L, & Tanaka, K. (1989). Particularism in authority outcomes for black and white supervisors. *Social Science Research, 18,* 1–20.

Murrell, A. J., Frieze, I. H., & Frost, J. L. (1991). Aspiring to careers in male and female dominated professions: A study of black and white college women. *Psychology of Women Quarterly, 15,* 103–126.

Nieva, V. F., & Gutek, B. A. (1981). *Women and work: A psychological perspective.* New York: Prager.

Nkomo, S. M., & Cox, T. C. (1989). Gender differences in the upward mobility of black managers: Double whammy or double advantage? *Sex Roles, 21,* 825–839.

Olson, J. E., & Frieze, I. H. (1987). Income determinants for women in business. In L. Larwood, A. H. Stromberg, & B. A. Gutek (Eds.), *Women and work: An annual review* (Vol. 2, pp. 173–206). Beverly Hills, CA: Sage Publications.

Olson, J. E., Frieze, I. H., & Good, D. C. (1987). The effects of job type and industry on the income of male and female MBAs. *Journal of Human Resources, 22,* 532–541.

Pelham, J. P., & Fretz, B. R. (1982). Racial differences and attributes of career choice unrealism. *Vocational Guidance Quarterly, 31,* 51–88.

Plowski, H. A., & Williams, J. (1983). *The Negro almanac: A reference work on the Afro-American.* New York: J. Wiley & Sons.

Powell, G. N. (1988). *Women and men in management.* Newbury Park, CA: Sage Publications.

Ramsford, E. H., & Miller, J. (1983). Race, sex, and feminist outlooks. *American Journal of Sociology, 48,* 46–59.

Reid, P. T. (1988). Racism and sexism. In D. Taylor & P. Katz, (Eds.), *Eliminating racism: Profiles in controversy* (pp. 203–219). New York: Prentice-Hall.

Reskin, B. F. (1992). *Women and work: Legacy of the last 20 years. Prospect for the year 2000.* Presentation given at the Twentieth Anniversary Lecture of the Women's Studies Program, University of Pittsburgh, September.

Reskin, B. F., & Hartmann, H. I. (1986). *Women's work, men's work: Sex segregation on the job.* Washington, DC: National Academy Press.

Rotberg, H. L., Brown, D., & Ware, W. B. (1987). Career self-efficacy expectations and perceived ranges of career options in community college students. *Journal of Counseling Psychology, 34,* 164–170.

Rytina, N. F., & Bianchi, S. M. (1984). Occupational reclassification and changes in distribution by gender. *Monthly Labor Review, 107*(3), 11–17.

Simms, M. C., & Malveaux, J. M. (1986). *Slipping through the cracks: The status of black women.* New Brunswick, NJ: Transaction Press.

Spain, D., Bianchi, S., & Bartos, R. (1988). What is a working woman? *American Demographics, 10*(7), 24–29.

Tajfel, H., & Turner, J. C. (1985). The social identity theory of intergroup behavior. In S. Worchel & W.G. Austin (Eds.), *Psychology of intergroup relations* (2nd ed., pp. 7–24). Chicago: Nelson-Hall.

Taylor, R. J. (1986). Receipt of support from family among black Americans: Demographics and familial differences. *Journal of Marriage and the Family, 48,* 67–77.

Taylor, R. J., Jackson, J. S., & Quick, A. D. (1982). The frequency of social support among black Americans. *Urban Research Review, 8*(2), 1–4.

Taylor, R. J., Chatters, L. M., Tucker, M. B., & Lewis, E. (1990). Developments in research in black families: A decade in review. *Journal of Marriage and the Family, 52,* 993–1014.

Treiman, D. J., & Hartmann, H. I. (1981). *Women, work, and wages: Equal pay for jobs of equal value.* Washington, DC: National Academy Press.

U.S. Bureau of the Census (1991). *The black population in the United States: March 1991.* Current Population Reports, Series P20–464. Washington, DC: U.S. Government Printing Office.

U.S. Bureau of the Census (1991). *Statistical abstracts of the United States: 1991* (112th ed.). Washington, DC: U.S. Government Printing Office. Table Nos. 609, 618, 622, 629, 631, 632, 635, 637, 654, 655 and 661.

Vatter, H. G., & Palm, T. (1972). *The economics of black America.* New York: Harcourt Brace Jovanovich.

Index